D1172803

We Few

We Few

The Marine Corps 400
in the War against Japan

James R. Dickenson

Naval Institute Press
Annapolis, Maryland

Naval Institute Press
291 Wood Road
Annapolis, MD 21402

Library of Congress Cataloging-in-Publication Data
Dickenson, James R., 1931–
  We few : the Marine Corps 400 in the war against Japan /
  James R. Dickenson.
    p. cm.
  Includes bibliographical references and index.
  ISBN 1-55750-168-8 (alk. paper)
    1. Iwo Jima, Battle of, 1945. 2. World War, 1939–1945—
Campaigns—Japan—Okinawa Island. 3. United States.
Marine Corps—Officers—Biography.
4. United States. Marine Corps. Special Officers Candidate
School—Biography.
D767.99.I9 D53 2001
940.54'1273'0922—dc21

                                        2001018339

Printed in the United States of America on acid-free paper ∞
08 07 06 05 04 03 02 01 9 8 7 6 5 4 3 2
First printing

To the members of the
Special Officer Candidate School
and to all the brotherhood of the
United States Marine Corps

And Crispin Crispian shall ne'er go by
From this day to the ending of the world,
But we in it shall be remembered;
We few, we happy few, we band of brothers.
For he today that sheds his blood with me
Shall be my brother.

Shakespeare, *Henry V*

Contents

Preface

In 1994, when I was working on another book, I came across an article in a back issue of the *Marine Corps Gazette,* the professional magazine of the Corps. Written by Lt. Col. George N. Mayer, USMCR (Ret.), "The Marine Corps 400" was about a unique Marine officer candidate class in World War II of which Mayer was a member. The class was unique for two reasons. It was the only Marine OCC that didn't go through the Marine Corps Schools at Quantico in World War II—the only one, in fact, since the Marine officer candidate classes were moved to Quantico from Philadelphia in 1940. The class was trained and commissioned at Camp Lejeune, North Carolina. And the class had a specialized training syllabus, one that concentrated on small-unit tactics and weapons and drew from the Marines' combat experiences in the Pacific through the battles for Saipan and Tinian. The class was convened on 17 July 1944, and of the 436 selected 372 were commissioned on 30 September 1944. Another candidate was commissioned on 19 October when he attained the minimum age of nineteen.

The Special Officers Candidate School (SOCS), as it was known, was formed because the Corps had an urgent need for platoon leader replacements after the Marianas campaign. Members of the SOCS were ticketed exclusively for the infantry. The syllabus contained little that didn't pertain directly to infantry training. The class didn't get the regular OCC curriculum, which included instruction in artillery, armor, engineering, communications, and other supporting elements. They were specifically and intensively trained to lead riflemen in combat.

For a Marine lieutenant from the Korean War and an amateur military historian, particularly of the Second World War, I found this an irresistible opportunity to write about the justly celebrated World War II generation. The editors of the *Gazette* put me in touch with Colonel Mayer, a forceful can-do type, who is a leader and spokesman of the group. He in turn put me in touch with other leaders of the organization, particularly Jack Lauck in Indianapolis, who publishes the SOCS monthly newsletter and has been instrumental in locating members of the class, and Joe Clement in Dallas, who painstakingly contacted all the members they located. Joe solicited written accounts from each of them and spent five years compiling an oral history and publishing it in book form. The book also contains maps, illustrations of equipment, vehicles, ships, airplanes, tables of organization and equipment, charts of the six Marine divisions that show the unit in which each member served, and a wealth of other information on the class and the Marine Corps in the Second World War. It is a priceless resource and I have drawn on it extensively. Other class members who were a big help in getting me started were Jack Schwartz in Petaluma, California, Bill Ditto in Greensboro, North Carolina, and the late Verle Ludwig in Twenty Nine Palms, California.

The entire class—and the Marine Corps—owes a big debt to one of its members, the late William H. Carter, who had kept a rough count of his classmates who had died or been wounded but in 1984 or 1985—the surviving members don't know exactly when—turned to the Marine Corps for a precise count. He contacted the commandant of the Marine Corps and proposed that the Marine Corps research the SOCS members who were killed on Iwo Jima and Okinawa. The commandant agreed enthusiastically. Bill Carter also suggested a plaque or other commemoration to be placed at an appropriate location of the Marine Corps's choosing, for which he would reimburse the Corps. The Corps designed a bronze plaque, which is on an outside wall of the theater at the Camp Lejeune rifle range, where the class's commissioning ceremony was held 30 September 1944.

None of the other class members knew about this until 1988 when two class members, Frederick J. Malley Jr. and Verle E. Ludwig, paid a sentimental visit to the rifle range and discovered the plaque. Malley photographed it, and a little detective work by Ludwig with the Marine Corps Historical Division turned up Carter's correspondence with the commandant. Malley and Ludwig, both of whom had been in 2nd Battalion, 7th Marines on Okinawa, passed the word on to Bill Ditto, also in 2/7, and Jack Lauck, whom Ludwig knew from Indianapolis, V-12 at Notre Dame, and the SOCS class. Ditto went to Camp Lejeune and took a number of color photos of the plaque and the theater, which subsequently were made available to the class members. This initiative led to the class's coalescing as an organization as Jack Lauck, George Mayer, Joe Clement, and others pitched in to help locate the members.

There was some concern at the beginning that some of the members wouldn't want to be bothered for this project, but that quickly proved false. As might be expected, they believe their story is worth telling, and as a long-time political journalist accustomed to dealing with less forthcoming types I can say that they have provided access that I often could only dream of. They have been cooperative and helpful above and beyond the call. This is particularly true of the ten, including Jack Lauck and Joe Clement, on whose experiences I have concentrated. The only problem I had with any of them was false modesty. Some initially demurred on the grounds that they didn't think their story was worth recounting, but with a little encouragement they overcame their reluctance. Their experiences, of course, are fascinating. In some cases there was a measure of survivor's guilt, the feeling that the book should focus on those who made the ultimate sacrifice. Some hesitated on the grounds that they weren't in combat long enough to make their stories worth retelling. This wasn't true, either, of course. Those whose combat longevity was measured in hours and days—grim and deadly hours and days—were the rule, not the exception, on Iwo and Okinawa. As they talked, moreover, it was fascinating to see long-dormant memories of events and anecdotes begin to surface. I also encountered the phenomenon, as I have in my journalism career and previous book, that some individuals' memories of details are much better than others.

About 225 SOCS members survive at the time of this telling and it has caused me considerable frustration that I couldn't deal in detail with all of them. I chose ten, somewhat at random, whom I thought were broadly representative of the group. Availability was one factor and I obviously wanted to include members of all six Marine divisions. The distribution of the class members to the divisions was by no means uniform. The largest number, more than one hundred, went to the 1st Marine Division, presumably because it had seen the most recent heavy combat, on Peleliu in September and October of 1944, and had the most re-forming to do. Between thirty-five and fifty went to each of the others, and nearly fifty went to Corps units, FMFPAC, Admiral Nimitz's Marine guard, and other miscellaneous assignments. These numbers are approximate because an exact count isn't available; Joe Clement's book lists twenty-six members whose billets are unknown to him and the other compilers.

The SOCS members believe that their class suffered the highest casualty rate and was awarded the most citations of any World War II Marine officer candidate class, but numbers for every OCC class in the war aren't readily available. Considering the battles the SOCS members fought, Iwo Jima and Okinawa, this claim is quite plausible.

The book opens with what the chosen ten were doing on that fateful day of 7 December 1941 and takes them through the V-12 program, boot camp, the SOCS course, and out to the Pacific. It ends with a brief account of their postwar lives and careers, including for many, re-call in the Korean War. I have resisted the powerful temptation to join Tom Brokaw in naming this the nation's "greatest generation." All of this country's generations have risen to the challenges they faced—the Revolutionary War and Civil War generations, for instance, who had to grapple with our first two major crises, the independence and formation of the Republic and eliminating slavery and saving the Union. Historian Arthur M. Schlesinger Jr. suggests that the generation that declared independence from Britain and wrote the Constitution may have the best claim to the title. In any event, the World War II generation also rose magnificently to their great challenge, the country's third major crisis, also a major world crisis. The SOCS members, along with the rest of their generation, laid their lives on the line to destroy a totalitarian alliance that posed one of the most profound threats ever to civilization.

Obviously, this group is not representative of the entire generation. It is, not to put too fine a point on it, an elite. To the best of the compilers' knowledge, all the SOCS members finished their bachelor's degrees and many went on for graduate and professional degrees. They represent nearly every career field that attracts educated people in this country; about a dozen made the Marine Corps their careers. They may well be an elite among the young leaders of the Second World War generation as well, as it is difficult to imagine how they can be surpassed in intelligence and breadth of vision, to say nothing of patriotism, heroism, and combat leadership. Their record in that respect, of course, speaks for itself. They are an impressive example of the citizen soldier in America's democracy—courageous and dedicated warriors when called, productive leaders in the nation's postwar growth and expansion, the embodiment of Cincinnatus returning to the plow. Getting to know them strongly underscores what we know in hindsight—that from the outset, given the quality of the Allies' people and their leadership, the Axis powers never had a chance.

Acknowledgments

All the members of the U.S. Marine Corps
Special Officer Candidate School (SOCS) that I have contacted have been
unstinting in their help on this project, above and beyond the call of duty.
First of all, my thanks to George Mayer, whose article in the *Marine
Corps Gazette* about the class first made me aware of its existence and
who has read portions of the manuscript and provided much valuable
guidance and insight. Jack Lauck, the class secretary and editor of the
newsletter, and Joe Clement, who has been tireless in helping to locate
class members and compiling an oral history, have been equally helpful
and generous. They also read portions of the manuscript. Jack Schwartz
was the first class member I met and was enormously helpful in helping
me get started after I outlined my intentions. So was Bill Ditto, both with
his memories of his experiences and his many excellent photographs.

I am particularly grateful to the other class members on whom the
book concentrates: Mark Clement, Gordon Dibble, Dan "Tim" Hurson,
Hugh "Bud" Morris, Phil Pearce, James "Red" Qualls, and Jim Ronayne.
Along with Joe Clement, Jack Lauck, and George Mayer, all sat patiently
through hours of interviews and read portions of the manuscript; without their remarkable memories and enthusiastic cooperation, the book
wouldn't have been possible. Another class member, Marius "Mo" Bressoud Jr., wrote an extensive and fascinating account of his experiences
on Okinawa, on which I drew heavily. Brig. Gen. Donald M. Schmuck
(USMC, ret.), a wounded veteran of Bougainville who was a staff officer
instrumental in setting up the class in the spring of 1944, was a great
help in recounting the circumstances under which it was created and
put together. Lois Hyndman, widow of John Hyndman, a class member
who died in 1990, collected and typed his wartime letters home and generously shared them with me.

I am grateful to Brig. Gen. Edwin H. Simmons (USMC, ret.), a veteran of World War II and Korea and an excellent historian and novelist, for his help and encouragement over the years he was director of the Marine Corps Historical Center. I also received encouragement and support from fellow Marines, including Art Buchwald, Pat Furgurson, Ed Fouhy, Dick Harwood, Nick Kotz, Jim Lehrer, Jim Perry, and Mark Russell. Finally, I want to thank Danny J. Crawford at the Marine Corps Historical Center and Charles Melson, its director, for their help in my research.

Getting to know the members of the SOCS made doing this book an unqualified pleasure. I expected on the face of it to encounter an extraordinary group of men and Marines, but my imagination didn't rise to the reality. There is nothing more fulfilling than having high expectations that are exceeded.

We Few

1 Pearl Harbor

A Date Which Will

Live in Infamy

Sunday, 7 December 1941, was a clear, sparkling day in much of the United States. From Long Island to Long Beach, Maine to Mississippi, Americans from all walks of life went about their normal Sunday activities—dinner after church, reading the Sunday sports and comics sections, going for an afternoon drive, listening to the radio.

In a room in the Old Campus's Welch Hall at Yale University, Gordon K. Dibble was suffering a touch of the Sunday blues. An eighteen-year-old freshman, he was at Yale on scholarship after graduating from high school the previous spring in Topeka, Kansas, where his parents were public school teachers. Although he had played on Topeka High's state champion football team and then, as now, was as handsome as an Arrow shirt model, he was suffering a bit of culture shock after migrating to the Ivy League and being thrown in among wealthy, seemingly better educated graduates of elite East Coast prep schools such as Groton and Phillips Exeter.

Frank K. Bosworth, another eighteen-year-old freshman at Yale, was playing bridge in his dormitory room down the hall from Dibble's. He was dummy, and he yawned and reached over to turn on the radio. He and his friends never finished the game. Bosworth and Dibble were slightly acquainted; Dibble considered Bosworth, a graduate of the Hill School in Pottstown, Pennsylvania, whose father was a banker in Great Neck, Long Island, one of those better-educated Eastern elitists who made him feel insecure. However, events were converging that would unite them for the rest of their lives.

These events would have an enormous impact on the lives of every young male of military age in the United States and would mold them into a sociological entity known as the World War II generation. Gordon Dibble and Frank Bosworth were members of this generation, but they also became part of a much smaller subset within a subset—the United States Marine Corps and their unique Marine officer candidate course, the Special Officers Candidate School (SOCS).

At 2:25 P.M., Eastern Standard Time, the first eight-word bulletin came clacking over the wire-service tickers into the nation's newsrooms: "The White House says Japs attack Pearl Harbor!" Minutes later, radio stations from one end of the country to the other interrupted their programming to relay the stunning news. In Washington, D.C., at the Washington Redskins–Philadelphia Eagles football game in Griffith Stadium, the announcer began paging generals, admirals, cabinet officers, and other high government officials to call their offices. "Admiral Bland is asked to report to his office . . ." "The resident commissioner of the Philippines is urged to report . . ." The players knew something was up but had no idea what, so they kept on playing.[1]

Responding to the primal urge for company in times of crisis, Dibble, Bosworth, and the rest of the Yale student body streamed out of their rooms and gathered in the yards and quadrangles, swapping reports, rumors, and speculation. They were the intellectual elite of their generation but no one had to be an Einstein to realize that the course of everyone's lives had just been radically altered. After milling around for a while, a group of them marched on the home of Yale's president, Charles Seymour, a rite their children would utilize and greatly expand in a considerably different context a generation later. The students spent a few minutes in the street in front of Seymour's house, then headed for downtown New Haven. Several dozen staged a sit-in on the trolley tracks in front of the Taft Hotel and the police hauled them off to jail. Some of the more rambunctious started carrying the potted plants out of the hotel lobby and into the street, but cooler heads prevailed. The plants were returned and the youthful mob returned to their dorms to begin hashing out their plans for the new and uncertain future—and to arrange bail for their incarcerated comrades.

At the time, Dibble was enrolled in the Army Artillery ROTC, but he dropped that to enlist in the Marine Corps four months after Pearl Harbor. Of the members of the bridge game, Frank Bosworth also joined the Marines and was wounded and awarded the Navy Cross for valor on Okinawa. Another was killed in a training accident as an Army Air Corps flight cadet, one became an officer on a destroyer escort that was attacked by kamikazes at Okinawa, and the fourth spent most of the war on the banks of the Hudson River as a West Point cadet.

Dibble cited a combination of reasons for joining the Marines— patriotism and the attraction of an elite unit like the Marine Corps. Like many others, he was torn between the urge to "go get 'em" and the desire to finish his degree in economics, which he would do as a Navy–Marine V-12 student at Yale. Dibble's brother John was in the Army, first with the 10th Mountain Division in Colorado (Senator Bob Dole's division in Italy), then the 82nd Airborne. "I thought I'd come back from the war alive but I wanted to finish my degree because I knew I wouldn't come back to school," Gordon Dibble recalled.

Not everyone reacted that day as the Yalies did. At Dartmouth College the student body, including freshman Hugh R. "Bud" Morris, took the news much more calmly.[2] As word spread, they gathered in small groups and began to analyze their suddenly altered futures. It took Morris a little longer to get in the Marines than it did Dibble. The son of a Washington, D.C., lawyer, Morris had attended St. Albans and Deerfield Academy and followed in his father's footsteps to Dartmouth. He went to Boston in the fall of 1942 to enlist in the Corps but was turned down because of flat feet. The doctors who gave him his physical recommended some exercises, such as picking up a pencil with his toes. When he returned to the recruiting station in May 1943, he was accepted and enrolled in the Marine V-12 program. He still doesn't know if it was the exercises or if it was the fact that Frank "Fireball Frankie" Sinkwich, an All-American halfback and 1942 Heisman Trophy winner from Georgia who also had flat feet, was accepted and commissioned by the Marine Corps. Although his mother wanted him to go in the Navy—"I think she thought I would look good in blue"—Morris chose the Marines partly because his sister was dating a young Marine officer. He went with her to visit her beau at Quantico, Virginia, and was impressed by how good everyone looked.

In Milton, Massachusetts, James Aloysius Ronayne, a freshman at Boston College, also initially shrugged off the news about Pearl Harbor. The product of a tight-knit Irish Catholic neighborhood of family, church, and Jesuit schools, he was engrossed in playing goalie on the BC hockey team after being on the freshman football team and making up the failed courses that had led to his dropping out a year before. Like many Americans, he didn't have a very clear idea of where or what Pearl Harbor was, and at first he didn't think the event would affect his life very much. He didn't entertain that conceit for long, however. On 14 February he enlisted in the Marine Corps after being recruited by a Major Hornblower, who was stationed at the nearby Boston Navy Yard and came to the BC campus in his dress blues. Boston College and Holy Cross proved to be fertile recruiting grounds for the Marines, particularly among the athletes—Ronayne estimated that 85 to 90 percent of the BC Marine recruits were from the football and hockey teams. His experience led him to the conclusion that the dedication, discipline, and teamwork of athletics and Jesuit schooling were great preparation for the Marines.

So was his upbringing by his mother, Hannah Sheehan Ronayne, who like his father was born in Ireland. Ronayne's father, John, was an easygoing man who worked as a trolley-car operator for the old Boston Elevated, now the MTA (Metropolitan Transit Authority), until he contracted tuberculosis; after he was cured he returned to the company as a security guard. Ronayne remembers the ritual of his father handing his pay envelope—in cash in those days—to his mother, who would give her husband ten cents for chewing tobacco and keep the rest for necessities. Hannah Ronayne was not easygoing, and while short on formal education she was long on drive and competence. While her husband was incapacitated she worked as a maid for Yankee families and came home one day when Jim was fifteen to announce that she had bought them a house in Milton, just across the Neponset River from their home in Dorchester, the southernmost section of Boston. The move added five miles to his forty-minute trolley-car commute to Boston College High School, a Jesuit school in downtown Boston, and he had to put up with taunts about moving to the suburbs, but Hannah Ronayne knew what she wanted. Jim still thinks that the discipline his everyday life required, including the demanding schedule of riding the trolley from high school to the football practice field (the school didn't have one of its own and played its games at the old Braves baseball stadium) and then the trolley ride home loaded down with his football gear and books, was good conditioning for the rigorous routine of the Marine Corps.

George N. Mayer, also eighteen, was a sophomore at Colgate University. He had been to a movie and heard the news while walking along Fraternity Row back to the Sigma Nu house. Born in Elizabeth, New Jersey, he had grown up in Saranac Lake, New York, where his stepfather and mother operated a tuberculosis sanitarium; four years later as a lieutenant on Guam he was picked up and given a lift in the jeep of a lung surgeon who, it turned out, had practiced at the clinic. Mayer knew where Pearl Harbor was, but like many others he had trouble assimilating the dreadful news at first. It didn't take him long, however.

Half a continent west of Boston and Colgate, and perhaps even more distant culturally, were twin brothers Joseph Frederick and Mark Anthony Clement Jr., sixteen-year-old freshmen at North Texas Agricultural College (NTAC) in Arlington; they were of such tender years because they were offered only three years of high school at that time. Joe, a tall, gangling youth, was lying on his dormitory bed waiting to go to Mass and Mark was wandering around the halls killing time when they heard the news on the radio. Like everyone else in the country, they were stunned, but not for long. NTAC (now the University of Texas at Arlington) was part of the Texas A&M system, a land-grant university with compulsory ROTC. It had a twelve- hundred-man cadet corps so they also already had some military orientation.

Joe and Mark had to wait until 20 February 1942, when they turned seventeen, to enlist. Their father, a Buick salesman in Dallas, had died of a stroke when they were three; a first sergeant in the Army engineers in World War I, he had been gassed in France and hospitalized twice with the flu that killed millions in the great epidemic of 1918, all of which his widow believed had weakened his system. They had to get permission from their mother, who had not remarried. "It was a very, very difficult decision for her but she decided we should do what we wanted," Mark Clement recalled. It was more difficult for her than for her sons, who were dazzled by the glamour of the Marine recruiters. "The Army seemed like a bunch of prunes," Joe Clement recalled a half century later. The Marine recruiters urged them to get into an officer program. "We decided to go with the best there was," Mark Clement says. "Besides, the girls liked it." Like the others, they talked about the possibility of being killed or wounded, but as with so many young men their assumption was, "They won't get me."

In Abilene, Texas, about 150 miles west of Arlington, Church of Christ services in the Abilene Christian College auditorium had ended and James Luther "Red" Qualls, a second-semester freshman from Cisco, Texas, who had graduated from high school at midterm, was walking across the campus back to his dormitory when a friend who had been listening to the radio hailed him and gave him the news. Qualls was shocked but not surprised. Like many other Americans, he had followed the news of Japanese aggression in China and other threatening moves in Asia, and he assumed that the United States ultimately would have to go to war to stop both the Japanese and the Nazis. Like most other Americans, however, he just didn't think the Japanese would "jump on America the way they did."

The day after Pearl Harbor Qualls's social studies professor turned on the radio so the class could hear President Franklin D. Roosevelt's "Day of Infamy" speech, in which he called for a declaration of war on Japan. In this class Qualls had been reading accounts of how the Japanese had been buying as much scrap iron, oil, and other industrial materials as they could from the United States and other countries. Until Roosevelt embargoed the materials, a lumber company in Qualls's hometown of Cisco, fifty miles east of Abilene, had been buying up scrap metal and shipping it to Japan, despite dark grumblings by many townspeople that the Japanese would soon be returning it by a different means of conveyance—gunpowder. Indeed, Qualls wound up carrying fragments of Japanese ammunition back to the United States from Iwo Jima in his abdomen and carries some to this day.

A scholarship end on the Abilene Christian T-formation football team, Qualls received a notice from his draft board in February that he was subject to be drafted.[3] Marine recruiters came to the campus to tell them about the V-12 program and he enlisted in November 1942, the day after the Wildcats' final game. He needed his parents' consent and told his dismayed father—his mother had died in 1940 from injuries suffered in an auto accident—that he didn't want to "be a grunt on the ground" like the Army or "be out on the water" like the Navy. In the Marines, however, he realized ruefully, "I got both." He got his induction notice shortly after he enlisted.

In the Midwest heartland Harry P. "Phil" Pearce, eighteen, a southern Illinois farm boy with a country-boy drawl and easy, take-it-as-it-comes manner, was a sophomore engineering major at Milliken University in Decatur, Illinois. He had spent the Pearl Harbor weekend at the home of a college friend and they heard the news of the attack on the car radio while driving back to school. Like most of their peers, they immediately began talking about what they were going to do with their young lives. Pearce had grown up in the outdoors, hunting and fishing on the family farm and surrounding countryside near Carmi, Illinois, just west of Evanston, Indiana. Firearms and marksmanship were part of his life, which he figured would give him an edge over the city boys in the military. He may have been right—in any event, he proved to be a superb combat leader. A few days after the Japanese attack, Pearce and several of his Sigma Alpha Epsilon brothers at Milliken drove to St. Louis to enlist in the Marine Corps. The Marines signed them up in the reserves and assigned them to the Navy–Marine Corps V-12 program to continue their studies until they were called up for officers' training. "We were ready to roll," Pearce recalled, "but we were told to wait." He chose the Marines partly because he reasoned that they would train him and his comrades "how to take care of ourselves."

In the Pacific Northwest, Daniel J. Hurson, a freshman at Seattle College, now Seattle University, was with a hiking group in the mountains east of Everett, thirty or forty miles northeast of Seattle. He was a graduate of O'Dea, an Irish Christian Brothers high school, and his father, who had migrated from Ireland in 1903, was a checker (dispatcher) with the longshoremen on the waterfront. A number of factors pointed Hurson to the Marine Corps, including several friends who enlisted, a priest who was a World War I veteran and recommended that he visit the recruiters, and, shortly after Pearl Harbor, when he went to the movies one Sunday afternoon, a platoon of Marines was performing the manual of arms in the lobby. He, too, enlisted in early 1942 and went into the V-12 program despite his reluctance to wait to go on active duty.

John H. "Jack" Lauck was an eighteen-year-old freshman at Notre Dame, home for the weekend with his parents, who owned a funeral home in Indianapolis. With his family and friends, he absorbed the fragmentary reports that gradually limned the magnitude of the disaster. Like everyone else, they were surprised by what they considered a blatant double-cross. The shock was intensified because of the prolonged negotiations between the United States and Japan, which had dragged on through the previous months. He and his family had followed the war stories from Poland and Europe for two years but the Japanese negotiations lulled them, as they did many Americans. Like his countrymen, Lauck viewed the attack as "a real stab in the back." The following day while driving the 140 miles from Indianapolis back to South Bend he listened on the car radio to Roosevelt ask Congress for a declaration of war. Lauck enlisted the following November, delayed by a shortage of openings in the V-12 program. He wasn't under any draft pressure at the time, but like so many of his contemporaries he was inspired by the stories of the Marines at Wake Island and Guadalcanal and their tradition of being "first to fight." "The reports from Guadalcanal crystallized my decision," he says.

Two and a half years after Pearl Harbor these young men would come together in the Special Officer Candidate School.

Prior to the calamitous and humiliating attack on Pearl Harbor, President Franklin Roosevelt addressed the sinister menace of the militaristic totalitarianism of Nazi Germany and Imperial Japan in his battle with the isolationists over American preparedness. Now he told the American people that they were facing "a war for the survival of democracy. We are fighting to save a great and precious form of government for ourselves and for the world. I accept the commission you have tendered me. I join with you. I am enlisted for the duration of the war."

With the attack on Pearl Harbor, the division of the American people between interventionists and isolationists instantaneously disappeared and they joined Roosevelt in enlisting for the duration. A flood of volunteers inundated the armed services recruiting offices. The entire high school football team of Lepanto, Arkansas (population two thousand), enlisted in the Navy en masse; the one member who failed his physical examination attempted suicide, later explaining, "I was afraid folks would think I was yellow because I didn't get into the service."

The World War II generation rose magnificently to the challenge, although not everyone was this heroic. Many waited for the Selective Service System to come get them, some pulled strings and wangled choice assignments, some sought draft deferments. The overwhelming majority, however, accepted without question—in many cases eagerly—the assumption that it was their duty to put themselves on the line in defense of their country. Many also had a thirst for adventure, which they came to realize was a naive desire.

Pearl Harbor pulled the Clement brothers, Dibble, Morris, Pearce, Mayer, Qualls, Ronayne, Lauck, Hurson, and about four hundred other college freshmen together in a lifelong fraternity that made the traditional brotherhood of the Marine Corps even stronger, the SOCS class. At the time of Pearl Harbor most were seventeen- and eighteen-year-old college freshmen who enlisted in the Marine reserves shortly after the Japanese attack. They came from all over the United States, from Midwest farms and Eastern cities, from New York to California, from New England to New Orleans. Postwar studies of military procurement and manpower allotment policies show that a disproportionate number of these early volunteers went into the Navy, the Marine Corps, or flight training in the Army Air Force. Those who joined the Marines generally gave the same reasons: the appeal of a glamorous, elite unit with its dress blues and globe and anchor insignia, and, not least, its swagger, plus their feeling that their chances both of being effective warriors and surviving were better in such a disciplined and professional organization.

These men were assigned to the V-12 college program, a wartime Navy/Marine Corps officer procurement plan, then put through boot camp at Parris Island, South Carolina, the traditional introduction of the civilian to the Marine Corps. Most Marine V-12s then went through the Officer Candidate Course (OCC) at the Marine Corps Schools at Quantico. The SOCS class, however, was the only class of lieutenants that didn't go through Quantico. They were trained and commissioned at Camp Lejeune, North Carolina, because the regular officer training program at Quantico was at capacity, and they wouldn't see Quantico until after the war. The Corps pushed them through as a special class because of the need for junior officers in the Pacific. After heavy casualties at Tarawa, Saipan, and Guam, and the Corps's expansion to six divisions, the Marine Corps realized with alarm that it had underestimated its infantry casualties (as had the Army in Europe) and desperately needed more platoon leaders. Upon commissioning nearly all the SOCS members were shipped out as infantry platoon leaders on Iwo Jima and Okinawa, the last and bloodiest of the land battles against Japan.

The SOCS class suffered 58 percent casualties, one of the highest rates of the war. Forty-eight were killed in action and 168 were wounded in World War II, twenty-two of them twice or more; eight others were wounded in Korea. One of the most, if not the most, highly decorated of any Marine OCC class in World War II, they won six Navy Crosses, the nation's second highest decoration for valor, sixteen Silver Stars, twenty-seven Bronze Stars, twelve Navy Commendation Medals, and a total of 245 Purple Hearts (those killed in action [KIAs] are posthumously awarded the medal). Many were recalled to duty for the Korean War and twelve of these medals, including one Navy Cross, two Silver Stars, and nine Purple Hearts were won in Korea.[4] After World War II, the class was judged by Victor Krulak, one of their senior officers in the Pacific, to have been "the finest class of second lieutenants" the proud, elite Marine Corps ever produced. Krulak knew them first-hand—he was operations officer of the 6th Marine Division on Okinawa, to which more than two dozen of the SOCS class members were posted, and retired as a lieutenant general.[5] "The Marine Corps 400" is how they refer to themselves; more than two hundred survived to see the year 2000, and they have a powerful sense of their group identity, pay dues, publish a newsletter, and hold ever more frequent reunions.

The reason for the SOCS class's high casualty and decoration rates was that it was the only Marine officer class in the war to be marked exclusively for infantry duty and it was in the Corps's two bloodiest battles. So dire was the need for platoon leaders that Gen. Alexander A. Vandegrift, the Marine Corps commandant who had commanded the 1st Marine Division on Guadalcanal, gave the SOCS commanding officer at Camp Lejeune in effect a blank check to draw on Marine Corps personnel and equipment from Quantico and other bases as needed.

As rifle platoon leaders, Phil Pearce won the Navy Cross on Okinawa, Jim Ronayne won the Silver Star, and Red Qualls got the Bronze Star and a Purple Heart on Iwo Jima. Gordon Dibble was hit in the chest by mortar shrapnel on the second day of Iwo Jima while leading his platoon in the capture of the major airstrip, the island's primary strategic value. Jack Lauck won two Purple Hearts in World War II, plus two more in Korea along with the Bronze Star and a Letter of Commendation, both with the combat V. Dan Hurson observed his twenty-second birthday on Iwo by jumping off his landing craft onto black volcanic sand beach on the morning of D-day and seeing first-hand how violently men are killed in modern warfare; Mark Clement turned twenty that day and was right behind him.

The class is epitomized by a description of one of its members, Lt. Ewing "Morg" De Mange, who was killed on Iwo by grenade fragments when his platoon in Company K, 23rd Marine Regiment, 4th Marine Division, was overrun by a night banzai attack on 7 March 1945 near a stark, murderous terrain feature known as "Turkey Knob." He was discovered by a SOCS classmate, Lt. Jack Bradford, of Company A, 23rd Marines, who found him slumped against a large rock, still at the head of "about 40 dead Marines frozen in time . . . included in the scene were some Japanese dead. I walked toward them and the first person I recognized was Tony De Mange, one of the finest men I remember from our class. He was on his knees and leaning against a rock—his body still in a firing position as if trying to carry out the mission. . . . [W]e had been apprised of the kind of leadership that would be required of our class and Lt. De Mange had not missed the point."[6]

The Yalies' exercise of their right of assembly in New Haven on Pearl Harbor Day was typical of the rest of the nation and symbolic of America's World War II experience. Large crowds thronged the streets of every city that afternoon, hoping to be told something or given something to do; bars were jammed and radios blared into the yards and streets. In Washington, D.C., anxious crowds jammed the streets in front of the White House and the State, War, and Navy Department buildings, and an enormous traffic jam immobilized the capital's streets on that evening of 7 December. In the White House one of President Roosevelt's first actions was to call his son Jimmy to help with notifications and media strategy.[7] In the late afternoon FDR worked on his "Day of Infamy" speech, and Eleanor prepared her weekly 6:30 P.M. radio broadcast on NBC. The president met from 8:30 P.M. to past midnight with the cabinet and congressional leaders.[8]

In this great undertaking, the quality of its people were America's most valuable resource. Americans have an aptitude for war that is often little-noted and underestimated; this may be in part because we are a nation of immigrants capable of taking the hard road in search of better things when necessary. European military observers of the Civil War marveled at both armies' courage and willingness to take enormous casualties. This was ironic given that the totalitarian Axis powers were convinced that "soft," decadent democracies were incapable of fighting; the Japanese, who considered themselves the superior race on the planet, were particularly contemptuous of Caucasians in general and Americans in particular.

Another American characteristic, optimism, served the nation well in the grim and demanding decades of the 1930s and 1940s. World War II, as it turned out, was a crisis made to order for Americans. It was a difficult but clear-cut problem to be solved by the American genius for organization, hard work, innovation, and its enormous economic and productive capacity; as Ronald Reagan once noted, many problems are simple, but they still are hard. Adm. Isoroku Yamamoto, Japan's chief naval strategist, studied in the United States between the wars and was one of the Japanese leaders who realized that Japan had no chance of winning a war with a nation like America; the Japanese army generals were the ardent militarists and expansionists and overrode the more moderate navy leadership. The attack on Pearl Harbor, ironically, was Yamamoto's creation, and in his mind was a desperate hope to buy time for a possible negotiated settlement.

In a thousand different ways the American people closed ranks behind their commander-in-chief, and the United States emerged from the war as the greatest economic, military, and diplomatic superpower on the globe. Those crowds on Pearl Harbor Day exemplified one factor in this development—the six years between the invasion of Poland and the bombing of Hiroshima constituted the period of greatest national unity, of pulling together in a common cause, the life-and-death war against totalitarianism, that the United States has ever known. Its two previous major crises, the Revolution and creation of the Republic, and, of course, the Civil War, had bloodily divided the country. The World War II consensus would be a stark contrast to the bitter divisions of the Vietnam War a generation later.

Although many of their fathers who had fought World War I at first expressed the traditional parent's doubt that the younger generation would be capable of emulating their example, the World War II generation quickly put this to rest. They demonstrated a constant American character trait: the capacity of ordinary citizens to surmount adversity and achieve greatness. FDR and Harry Truman, members of the preceding generation, also displayed this capability, as did their peers —Dwight Eisenhower, George Marshall, Chester Nimitz, Douglas MacArthur, Omar Bradley, George Patton, and countless others. Many of these leaders were born to ordinary circumstances but rose to greatness in crisis.

In his first inaugural address, in 1933, Roosevelt declared that "this generation of Americans has a rendezvous with destiny." In his inaugural address twenty-eight years later John F. Kennedy proclaimed his own generation's date with kismet: "The torch has been passed to a new generation of Americans, born in this century, tempered by war, disciplined by a hard and bitter peace." Kennedy, the first American president born in the twentieth century, was speaking for the World War II generation, of which to many he was the symbol. He was the first of seven consecutive presidents this extraordinary generation produced; for thirty-two years, ending with George H. W. Bush, they occupied the White House as U.S. commanders-in-chief and leaders of the free world.

Kennedy, appearing hatless and coatless on his frigid January inaugural day to dramatize his aura of youthful dash and vigor, was this generation's first hurrah in presidential politics; Bob Dole, whose right arm was maimed in Italy as an infantry platoon leader in the 10th Mountain Division less than a month before V-E Day, was its last with his unsuccessful run in 1996. They serve almost as bookends for their generation; Kennedy was the youngest man ever elected president, Dole, had he been elected, would have been the oldest.

The football team in Lepanto was by no means atypical. All during the war a large number of the males in each high school graduating class enlisted immediately after commencement exercises. Many didn't even bother waiting for that. Anxious that the war might end before they got to it, at age fifteen and sixteen they lied about their ages to compliant recruiters. There were a lot more of them in World War II than most people realize and many finished their high school diplomas on the G.I. Bill of Rights. It sometimes is difficult to apprehend how young the men, including the SOCS members, who actually fought the war were, but the burden of war has historically been borne by those in their teens and early twenties.[9]

In the eyes of their families, friends, and neighbors, the American boys who fought this war—clerks, mechanics, farm boys, college students, high school graduates—were transformed into heroic warriors as they marched off into that dark and perilous world of the 1940s. Even those who wound up as supply clerks or mechanics in the motor pool were treated as heroes. Whatever their age they were referred to as "our boys." They were the boys next door. They were portrayed on the radio as Henry Aldrich and in the comics as "Freckles and His Friends" (known to his friends as "Freck"). Their photographs generally show clean-cut kids in saddle oxfords and letter sweaters, many of whom played on the football and basketball teams, performed in the junior class play, and decorated the gym for the senior prom.

In his history/memoir, *Goodbye Darkness,* William Manchester, a Marine veteran of Okinawa, remarks on what a "tightly disciplined society" the country was and how this contributed to the implacable and victorious war his comrades "in green camouflaged helmets" waged against the Japanese, who were contemptuous of American fighting qualities.[10]

The people's trust in each other and in their society was the basis of a wartime mobilization whose speed and effectiveness was astonishing. America was the world's leading industrial nation and had the potential, which was realized during the war, for enormous productive expansion. In his *A Democracy at War,* William L. O'Neill, a historian at Rutgers University, writes that due to the success of the public school system, the nation went to war with "a relatively homogeneous, well-disciplined and well-educated work force, a huge industrial capacity, and a generation of young men who would prove to be excellent warriors." O'Neill notes that "the mighty weapon" into which the twelve million citizen-soldiers of the U.S. armed forces were forged was due in part to the fact that the country had "the best educated men of any army" in history:

> The combination of courage and quality displayed by its young fighters was America's secret weapon. . . . The contribution of public schools cannot be overestimated, not only educationally but in other ways that Americans considered equally important. Despite the Duke of Wellington's belief that Waterloo had been won on the playing fields of Eton, no country, not even Great Britain, emphasized as America did team sports and athletic competition. At much expense, and as a rite not only of passage but almost of citizenship, few school districts failed to ensure that every able-bodied young male had the chance to play football and basketball—and usually other sports also. As a result, the young Americans of that era were team players and fierce competitors, their discipline and will to win having deep community roots. Localism, the curse of effective national government, was at the same time not only intrinsic to American democracy, but a superb maker of men.[11]

The emphasis on education is important. An exhaustive study of the wartime American Army published in 1949 showed that the individual's strength of personal commitment to the nation's war effort and goals and belief in the obligation to serve in the armed forces—and effectiveness as a soldier—all were in direct proportion to educational levels.

American society at the time was much more closely knit by extended families in small towns and urban neighborhoods than it is today. There was more respect for authority and institutions and more pressure to conform. People were more openly pious and church-going; for the most part businesses were closed on Sundays. They also were more openly patriotic. By 1941 the great waves of immigrants in the late nineteenth and early twentieth centuries for the most part had been well assimilated, much more than in World War I when many in some ethnic groups, such as the Germans, still had conflicting loyalties to the homeland, or the Irish, many of whom hated the English much more than they hated the Germans.

It was a much different society than now. In 1941 only 20 percent of nonfarm Americans owned their own homes, compared to 65 percent in 1995, and the quality of housing in terms of size and amenities has improved dramatically. Only 1.4 million—1 percent of the total population, 20 percent of the high school population—were enrolled in college; in 1995 more than 20 percent of the population had bachelor's or graduate degrees and nearly 65 percent of the high school class of 1994 entered two-year or four-year colleges.

Although America in 1941 was divided by racial and other bigotries, the society was not torn by many of the problems of today. Most Americans had been united, ironically, by their mutual suffering in the Great Depression, and most shared in the increasing hope and prosperity as the economy recovered, primarily through the stimulus of the growing war effort. America was a mobile society, but less so than today and there was a much greater sense of community and neighborhood.

The greater trust in the nation's institutions, starting with government, was due in large part to the hope engendered by the New Deal; 59 percent of the voting age population turned out for the 1940 elections. The country wasn't balkanized by the demands of a myriad of special issues and ethnic groups. The fear of crime on the streets and in the neighborhoods was unknown to most Americans. Drugs were not a major problem. The idea of children carrying guns to school was unthinkable, and there was widespread support of the public school system and belief in its role in educating a democratic society.

People shared, and articulated, an unabashed pride in America and its ideals, history, and destiny. They were unembarrassed in voicing uncomplicated patriotic sentiments. In the first issue of his weekly newspaper in Kansas after Pearl Harbor, my uncle wrote, "American boys aren't robots or animals like the German and Japanese warriors who are taught to hate and kill. They have been brought up the American way with responsibility for the rights of their fellow men. But when it comes to defending what they believe in, they can, man for man, whip the living daylights out of the highly trained murderers of the bloodthirsty Axis cutthroats."

The willingness of the American people to volunteer and mobilize for the war effort not only for the armed forces but also for civil defense, scrap drives, Red Cross and health programs, paramilitary groups, and countless other endeavors outstripped the government's comprehension of it, let alone its ability to exploit it efficiently. In letters to local newspapers and national publications such as *Life* magazine, people who until then had often given assent to the proposition that

"that government is best which governs least" expressed disgust and frustration that Washington wasn't asking enough of them in the war effort. Gallup polls showed overwhelming support for rationing, a labor draft for women, and a national service program that would register all adults and assign them to war work. It was oil industry executives who sold the Navy on the idea of blacking out the East Coast to reduce the Nazi sinking of Allied tankers that were silhouetted against the bright lights at night.

In light of our subsequent experiences in Korea and Vietnam, many have come to regard the Second World War as the nation's last "good war." This is in large part because, like the Civil War, there was a profound moral dimension to World War II. World War I had nothing approaching this moral context, as disastrously destructive to Western civilization as it was. The Second World War was a life-and-death struggle against powerful totalitarians who aspired to nothing less than the destruction of Western civilization and enslavement of the world, and who committed the most monumental crime against humanity ever, the Nazi holocaust.

Jim Ronayne, Red Qualls, Phil Pearce, the Clement brothers, Bud Morris, George Mayer, Dan Hurson, Jack Lauck, Gordon Dibble, and the rest of their SOCS class were products of all this. They represented the best of America's World War II generation, which was triumphant in peace as well as war.

2 Brass Hats and Gold Bars

Warriors and Leaders

On 29 September 1944 a handful of senior admirals and generals began a three-day conference in San Francisco to resolve their differences on the penultimate strategic decision in America's war against Japan. The conferees were led by the United States's top Navy man, Fleet Adm. Ernest J. King, commander-in-chief, U.S. fleet, and chief of naval operations, and included Fleet Adm. Chester W. Nimitz, commander of the Pacific Ocean Area (POA); Adm. Raymond Spruance, commander of the 5th Fleet; Lt. Gen. Simon Bolivar Buckner of Army Ground Forces (POA); and Lt. Gen. Millard F. Harmon of the Army Air Forces (POA).

Meeting in King's luxurious suite in the elegant Saint Francis Hotel and in the more spartan Sea Frontier headquarters on nearby Treasure Island, the conferees arrived at an agreement on America's next strategic move in the Pacific following Gen. Douglas MacArthur's scheduled return to the Philippine Islands on 20 October 1944. At issue was King's support of the strategic plan for the defeat of Japan that the Joint Chiefs of Staff had worked out a year before, in August 1943, which included invasion of the island of Formosa (now Taiwan). Formosa, just off the coast of China, would then be a major staging area for the invasion of Japan. It also would be a support base for the Allied air bases in eastern China, from which the new U.S. B-29 Superfortress heavy bombers had begun attacking Japan and other targets, ranging from the Dutch East Indies to Manchuria.

The tall, humorless, short-fused King was a forbidding personality with a reputation as a bully, binge-drinker, chain-smoker, and philanderer. Franklin Roosevelt described him as being so tough "he shaved with a blowtorch," which prompted Navy Secretary Frank Knox to give him a sterling silver cigarette lighter in the form of a blowtorch as a birthday present. However, King was also the first ever to hold the combined positions of fleet commander and CNO and was a military leader of great ability. He was the Roosevelt administration's leading advocate of the war with Japan and one of its chief architects, and his top priority was to destroy it militarily primarily through a U.S. Navy campaign in the Central and Western Pacific.[1] In his focus on Formosa, however, he was by then in the minority position both within the JCS and at this meeting. Most of the Pacific commanders now favored the proposed December invasion of Luzon, the main Philippine island, to be followed by the capture of Iwo Jima and then Okinawa, which would become the forward staging base for the assault on Japan. In early July 1944 Army Chief of Staff Gen. George C. Marshall had ordered that Iwo be taken by January 1945.[2]

By September 1944 the logic of Nimitz et al. had won out with all except King, whose acquiescence obviously was necessary. The capture of Saipan, Tinian, and Guam in the Marianas gave the United States bases from which its B-29s could strike the Japanese home islands. The bases in China had become increasingly difficult to supply and defend and were under increasing pressure from the Japanese. The B-29s were 30 percent faster, had one-third more range, and could carry twice the bomb load of the fabled B-17 Flying Fortress, but there was a major obstacle to their flights from the Marianas to Japan. Iwo Jima was almost the halfway mark for the perilous and exhausting 1,500-mile flight from Tinian to Tokyo, and it lay right on the direct flight path to major targets in the home islands. Japanese aircraft from Iwo's two airfields were able to damage the U.S. bomber bases in the Marianas and destroy some B-29s on the ground; its radar station gave early warning of American raids on the home islands; and its fighters inflicted casualties on the bombers, both outbound and returning. The bombers had to dogleg around Iwo, which cost time and fuel, complicated navigation, increased stress, and reduced bomb loads. Crewmen were becoming demoralized because their exhausting, costly missions were made even more dangerous and difficult by Iwo.

Allied planners arrived at the conclusion that Formosa was too heavily defended to be attacked until the war in Europe was completed and forces there could be transferred to the Pacific. Also, Japanese offensives in China in 1944 had overrun many of the Allied air bases in eastern China, which Formosa was intended to support. In addition, the U.S. airmen much preferred the Marianas bases because they could accommodate many more aircraft and were far easier to supply than those in China.

At the end of the three-day meeting King signed off on Luzon, Iwo, and Okinawa and flew back to Washington, where the Joint Chiefs issued the official orders for the assaults on Iwo Jima and Okinawa.[3] Four and a half months later, on 19 February 1945 the U.S. Marine V Amphibious Corps, comprising three Marine divisions and more than 70,000 men—the largest Marine combat force ever—landed on Iwo Jima.

In addition to strategic considerations, another factor guaranteed that the capture of Iwo would be difficult. It is part of the Nanpo Shoto, the volcanic island chain that begins at the mouth of Tokyo Bay and stretches south for 750 miles. This area was part of the Japanese homeland, part of the Tokyo Prefecture. So are the Ryukyu Islands and Okinawa. The battles for these two islands offered a horrendous foretaste of what an invasion of the home islands would entail.

As bad as they were, the brutal, bloody battles for Saipan in June 1944 and Peleliu in September, which had sobered and dismayed the U.S. commanders, were just a taste of what was to come. In merciless, yard-by-yard, costly frontal assaults with rifles, bayonets, flamethrowers, demolitions, knives, and fists, the Americans destroyed the Japanese garrisons on Iwo and Okinawa. The underground fortifications of interlocking fields of fire and mutually supporting caves and bunkers were impervious to everything, even the battleships' great 16-inch shells, except direct assault by infantrymen.

On Iwo 6,136 Marines and sailors, mostly medical corpsmen with the infantry platoons, were killed, 18,554 were wounded, and 2,648 suffered combat fatigue, a total of 28,686—more than one-third of the entire landing force. The Japanese garrison numbered about 22,000, all but a few hundred of whom were killed, making Iwo the only battle in World War II in which the Marines' casualties were greater than the Japanese.

Okinawa claimed 4,675 U.S. soldiers and 2,938 Marines killed, with 18,099 soldiers and 18,708 Marines wounded. The Navy lost 4,907 killed and 4,824 wounded, along with 36 ships sunk and 368 damaged, mostly by kamikaze attacks, the greatest losses ever suffered by the U.S. Navy in a single operation. About 100,000 Japanese and 80,000 Okinawa civilians died and about 10,000 Japanese were taken prisoner in a battle of attrition as ghastly as any on the Western Front between 1914 and 1918. The Marine Corps suffered nearly 92,000 casualties in World War II, about 20,000 of whom were killed in action. Iwo and Okinawa accounted for nearly half of the Marine casualties.

By the end of the war the B-29s with their eleven-man crews had made about twenty-five hundred emergency landings on Iwo Jima— about twenty-five thousand airmen—and countless more had been saved by elimination of the island's radar and fighter installations and by escorts over Japan by Iwo- based P-51 fighters. By this calculation alone, the horrific Marine losses on Iwo were justified, or at least equalized.

Militarily, the United States had come a long, long way by the spring of 1945. When the Germans overran Western Europe in 1940 the U.S. Army was the eighteenth largest in the world, right behind Bulgaria; General Marshall gave Congress a rose-tinted estimation that year that he could possibly put 80,000 troops in the field, and 160 fighter aircraft in the air, a few of which were not yet obsolete. By V-E Day the U.S. Army had closed the enormous D-day gap in combat experience between it and the *Wehrmacht,* and was an awesome military juggernaut; in the Pacific the Army, Navy, and Marines went over to the offensive less than eight months after Pearl Harbor and proceeded to defeat the Japanese in detail, albeit at great cost. By V-J Day, 12 million Americans were under arms, manning the most powerful army, navy, and air force the world had ever seen, and the nation had produced three hundred thousand military aircraft, eighty-six thousand tanks, and twelve thousand ships, along with countless other arms. It was truly the "Arsenal of Democracy."

On the second day of the Nimitz-King meeting in San Francisco another convocation of American warriors was taking place three thousand miles to the east. On 30 September 1944 the Special Officers Candidate School, 372 strong, was commissioned as second lieutenants at the Marine Corps Base at Camp Lejeune, North Carolina. (Another was commissioned on 19 October when he reached the minimum age of nineteen for officers.)

These patriotic, highly motivated young men, most of whom were college freshmen when the Japanese attacked Pearl Harbor, had enrolled in the Navy V-12 College Training Program, which protected them from the draft and enabled them to continue their educations prior to becoming officers. In February 1944, the end of the fall semester of the 1943–44 academic year, about 1,600 Marine V-12s, including the 400 who ultimately made up the SOCS, were ordered from their colleges and shipped to the Marine Corps Recruit Depot at Parris Island, South Carolina. There they underwent the Marine Corps's eight-week boot camp and on graduation in early May were assembled at Camp Lejeune as "Officer Candidate Applicants" (OCAs), a holding operation where they awaited assignment to an officer candidate course at Quantico, Virginia.

Because of the pressing need for platoon leaders, the Marine Corps chose the 436 most senior academically of the OCAs at Lejeune for the SOCS. After several months of facing an indeterminate wait at Lejeune, those selected were jubilant. Their formal officer candidate school began on 17 July 1944, with their commissioning date set for 30 September, seventy-seven days later.

The featured speaker for their commissioning ceremony at the Camp Lejeune rifle range, Brig. Gen. Gerald C. Thomas, who had been operations officer (D-3) of the 1st Marine Division on Guadalcanal and subsequently would become assistant commandant of the Marine Corps, had an ominous message when he welcomed them into the Marines' officer corps. "A lot of you aren't coming back," he told the class. Not surprisingly, those words shook up some of the class members, according to George Mayer, "but most of us shrugged it off and joked about it." There was reason for concern and Thomas may not have realized how prescient he was, given the class's casualty rate and decorations.

The movies helped form our image of America's fighting men in World War II: John Wayne, Lee Marvin, Robert Ryan, Aldo Ray, big, swaggering, grown men who had seen the seamier side of the world and obviously were a match for the armed Axis thugs.

Actual photographs tell a different story. Study a photograph of the 5th Division Marines on the deck of an LST bearing them across the Pacific to their bloody rendezvous with history on Iwo Jima. They lounge artlessly on their cots with their shirts off, soaking up the sun's rays as they perform the soldier's timeless housekeeping—cleaning and recleaning their rifles and automatic rifles, sharpening and resharpening their bayonets and fighting knives preparatory to hitting the beach.[4]

Examine the picture of two of them taken a few days later, dead on Iwo's volcanic sand terraces just minutes after stepping ashore on the landing beach in the first hour of the battle. They're in full combat gear, rifles in hand, looking as though they might just be catching their breath, their bodies intact and seemingly undamaged, frozen in the position in which they died—charging straight ahead up the terrace.[5] Put a magnifying glass on the faces and marvel at how young they are. How callow and still unformed at age seventeen and eighteen, in these and in their boot-camp graduation photos as well. Ponder their smooth, still unmatured striplings' bodies in the photo on the ship, not a hairy chest in the lot, looking like a high school physical education class. No tattooed veterans of bar-room brawls and brothels from Macao and Shanghai to Norfolk and San Diego here.

Peruse the photos of their lieutenants, just three or four years older. At the age when they would normally be fraternity presidents or yearbook editors, these one-time college boys, themselves only seventeen or eighteen at the time of Pearl Harbor and many still not old enough to vote, were the leaders of the proudest, fiercest warriors on the globe, the U.S. Marines. In truth, even in the hard-bitten Marine Corps they also functioned as older brothers and counselors to those baby-faced trained killers on the boats to Iwo.

This was not a fraternity rush season or summer-camp counseling job; they were the point men in the Marines' increasingly lethal Pacific island battles. Early in the war Orville Freeman, who was elected governor of Minnesota in the 1950s, was a lieutenant in the 9th Marine Regiment, under then-Col. Lemuel C. Shepherd. Shepherd subsequently became commanding general of the 6th Marine Division, and after Freeman was seriously wounded with the 9th Marines on Bougainville in 1943, Shepherd tried to get him transferred to the 6th Division for the Okinawa campaign. Freeman's wound, however, precluded his return to combat. More than a decade later Governor Freeman met in Washington with General Shepherd, by then commandant of the Marine Corps. Freeman recalled their conversation all too well. "You know, Governor," Shepherd said, "that rifle company I had for you suffered 400 percent casualties among its officers on Okinawa. You just might not be here if you'd passed that physical."[6]

Another young Marine lieutenant, Lee Prather "Prate" Stack Jr., a Yale graduate, recalled a conversation on Peleliu in September 1944 that was enlightening in a chilling way. Stack was a tank officer with the 1st Tank Battalion in the 1st Marine Division and was in support of the 5th Marines, one of the division's infantry regiments. He was at the 5th Marines' command post when Lewis B. "Chesty" Puller, a legendary Marine hero and commander of the 1st Marines, one of the other 1st Division infantry regiments, came visiting. Stack recounted the conversation between the two regimental commanders. "'How many second lieutenants have you had killed so far?' Puller asked. He was told the number—I can't remember what it was—and he sure as hell wasn't satisfied. 'What the hell are you doing, having a Sunday School picnic?' Puller bellowed."[7]

The members of the SOCS knew nothing of this, of course, but with Thomas's words ringing in their memories, the newly minted lieutenants embarked for the Marine Corps Base at Camp Pendleton, California, where they joined the replacement drafts for the Marine divisions in the Pacific.

3 The V-12 Program

Passage into the Marine Corps

Their post–Pearl Harbor enlistments didn't immediately put the future SOCS members on a train to boot camp. They were all about the same age and the Marine Corps formed them into a cohort of the Navy college V-12 program, which for the Marines was officially designated as Marine Reserve, Class III(d), but commonly referred to as Marine V-12. The V-12 was a wartime Navy and Marine Corps officer procurement plan established to assure the two services of a predictable, controlled source of officer candidates. Even before Pearl Harbor the services were looking at their probable wartime expansion and calculating the number of ships, aircraft, and divisions they would ultimately have to man. In the summer of 1943, when the program was activated, Secretary of the Navy Frank Knox asserted that the armed forces were planning for battles that "may have to be fought in 1949." With the draft age being dropped from twenty to eighteen they knew they would have to shelter enough potential officers for the later stages of the war. The Army set up a program known as the Army Specialized Training Program (ASTP), which was more for training specialists and technicians than an officer candidate pool.

The V-12 program was established on 131 college and university campuses, forty of which had Marine detachments, and by its termination on 30 June 1946 had enrolled about 125,000 men, more than 50,000 of whom had received commissions as Navy ensigns and nearly 7,000 as Marine second lieutenants. They were scheduled to be called to active duty by age groups to provide the Navy and Marine Corps with a steady flow of officer candidates. The Navy had a number of such programs. In June 1940 it instituted one known as V-7, which was basically an OCS, or midshipman's school as the Navy preferred to call it, for recent college graduates to supplement the regular Navy OCS at Newport, Rhode Island; many of the class of 1942 at Notre Dame, for instance, entered the V-7 program there right after graduation. The Navy also had a V-5 program for potential aviators and a V-1 for college freshman and sophomores who might advance into the V-12.[1]

Many colleges and universities who foresaw financial problems as enrollments dropped with mobilization eagerly sought out the program. Considerable political clout in the form of congressmen and senators was brought to bear on the selection committee; Rep. Lyndon B. Johnson (D-Texas), a member of the Naval Affairs Committee (which after the war would be merged with the Military Affairs Committee to form the House Armed Services Committee), managed to get Southwestern University in Georgetown, Texas, included and made several unsuccessful efforts to make Baylor University and Texas A&I part of the program. The schools chosen ranged from large to small. They included all eight Ivy League universities and many of the great state universities of the South, Midwest, and Pacific Coast, and small colleges such as Milligan College in Tennessee (an all-male school whose entire student body was V-12) and Park College in Parkville, Missouri, whose very survival was at stake. The size of the detachments ranged from nearly 2,000 at Dartmouth to 68 at Webb Institute of Naval Architecture in New York City. The Navy paid the colleges for the use of buildings (4 percent of prewar book value) and instructional costs, and reimbursed them for improvements to bring shower and toilet, messing, and physical training facilities up to standard. Some had to install swimming pools or make arrangements with other institutions since swimming was a requirement for commissioning.

There was some hard bargaining in some of the contracts, but the arrangement proved beneficial to all parties. The colleges received both crucial financial support during a time of reduced enrollments and the opportunity to buy Navy surplus gear for their greatly increased postwar enrollments. The Navy acquired instructional facilities for a fraction of what it would have cost to build them; the Navy Fiscal Section determined that the program saved the Navy about eighty-one million dollars over the first two years compared to the cost of establishing its own facilities for the program. The V-12 opened higher education—and commissions—to many trainees who never dreamed of it before the war. Fifteen Marine V-12s went on to become generals, eighteen Navy V-12 ensigns rose to flag rank, and seventeen others who were appointed to Annapolis subsequently became admirals.

While most of the V-12s were college students at the time of Pearl Harbor, some were accepted out of high school based on competitive exams. Some enlisted men were assigned from the fleet and the Fleet Marine Force (FMF); the Navy's quota was 10,000 for the first year, the Marines' was 1,000, with a third to enter each term.[2] For a number of reasons, the Marine Corps initially encountered some resistance from college students. Many of the best prospects were attracted to the aviation programs and draft pressures weren't intense until late in 1942, but primary was the fact that the Marines couldn't give assurance that the students wouldn't be called to active duty before graduation.[3] Through a dint of salesmanship, the Corps managed to overcome this resistance, however, and the program eventually produced more officer candidates than it could handle at Quantico, Virginia.

Until ordered to active duty, students did not have much change in their routines. They remained in their colleges through the 1942–43 academic year, wore civilian clothes, and continued classes as they had prior to Pearl Harbor, with some adjustments. They were required to take seventeen hours plus physical training each term. Those already in college when they enlisted, known as "irregulars," were allowed to continue their majors, but they had to take some math and science courses. Those entering out of high school or from the fleet, known as "regulars," were required to follow a pre-engineering curriculum that allowed few electives, although Marine regulars were exempt from calculus in their third and fourth terms and given other requirements such as map reading. Their physical training included group sports, gymnastics, hand-to-hand combat—judo, boxing, and wrestling—and swimming. They had to swim at least half a mile with various strokes, swim twenty-five yards under water, learn lifesaving, and jump off a ten-foot platform feet first in the approved abandon-ship fashion—shielding the genitals with one hand and the throat and chin with the other.

For a while the V-12s had the best of both worlds, enjoying the cachet of the Marine Corps and the surplus of dating opportunities created as the ratio of men to women on campus declined with mobilization. Most communities welcomed their detachments and invited them into their homes and churches. Some sponsored and staffed USO centers and provided the buildings, which in some cases were American Legion and VFW halls or Elk lodges. Any trainee who attended church could count on at least one dinner invitation. The V-12s marched in their communities' Memorial Day, Fourth of July, and other parades, and the small colleges welcomed their new football stars. Some townspeople who had sons and husbands on active duty considered the trainees draft-dodgers, and resented them for it, but for the most part the respectful and well-disciplined young men were popular and fondly remembered decades after the war.

On 1 July 1943 the V-12 program was activated on schedule, and they took their next step toward the war. All the 70,000 Navy and Marine Corps V-12s nationwide, of whom 11,460 were Marines (the quota was 11,500, but a few were dropped because of low examination scores), were ordered to active duty as able seamen or privates first class (Pfc.). Those not on one of the campuses selected for the program were generally assigned to the one nearest them. They continued their classes, but with military basic training added on under the supervision of Navy and Marine officers and NCOs. To their puzzlement, the Marine V-12s were required to take some courses more related to running a ship, such as electrical engineering, physics, and mechanical drawing. For the sake of uniformity and continuity, all 131 V-12 schools were put on an academic schedule of three four-month terms.

The sailors were issued blue and white Navy bell bottoms, the Marines were fitted with khakis and greens, and all were pulled into the gravitational field of military regulations, training, and discipline. Their days now began with Reveille at 0600, in military parlance, followed by physical training, and ended every week night with lights out at 10 P.M., or 2200. In addition to regular class work they had close-order drill, inspections, and military science classes. In some units their free time was open, but in others weekend liberty began at noon Saturday and expired at 2200 on Sundays, with the detachment first sergeant posted at the entrance of their quarters to report latecomers.

The transition was less wrenching for some than others. Because

Notre Dame, Yale, Colgate, and Dartmouth were among those with V-12 programs, Jack Lauck, Gordon Dibble, George Mayer, and Bud Morris remained on their campuses until ordered to Parris Island. Phil Pearce was assigned to the V-12 unit at Miami (Ohio) University. Jim Ronayne was moved from Boston College to Dartmouth, Red Qualls from Abilene Christian to North Texas Agricultural College (NTAC), Joe and Mark Clement were sent from NTAC to Arkansas A&M in Monticello, and Dan Hurson moved across town to the University of Washington.

Like Jim Ronayne, Jack Lauck thought the transition to military discipline and hierarchy might not have been as big a change for him, a parochial-school and Catholic university student, as it was for others. "I remember the discipline, the bed checks every night at 2200, the need for a pass to stay off campus on Saturday nights, but the discipline at Notre Dame was pretty rough to begin with," he recalls. However, he had a drill instructor named Sergeant Santos who "taught us left from right in a hurry." Not that he needed it, but Santos had the added cachet of being a former prizefighter who could chill even the worst hard case with just his steely gaze.

The V-12 students brought a variety of attitudes to the program. Many grew impatient to get into the war and deliberately flunked out; when he arrived in the Pacific, Lauck encountered a couple of his V-12 friends who had done so and wound up as enlisted men manning an artillery fire-direction center because of their math courses. Others, like Lauck, Dibble, Mayer, and Qualls, loaded up their courses in an effort to get their degrees before they were ordered to active duty. Lauck, a business major, took on a five-hour physics course and had completed seven semesters when he was ordered to active duty; Mayer, a sophomore at the time of Pearl Harbor, took extra summer and night courses and finished his degree in political science at mid-term 1943–44 just before being ordered to active duty at Parris Island. Failure in one course didn't lead to expulsion but failing two did in the Navy program; the Marines forgave two failures if the student demonstrated improvement and was promising officer material. As the program progressed the screening for leadership qualities became increasingly stringent.

Joe Clement and his brother, Mark, joined the Marine detachment at NTAC on 1 July 1943. Because of mandatory participation in the ROTC program they had a few years of military training under their belts, as did several of their fellow V-12s, but that didn't necessarily prepare them for the Marine Corps. Their platoon's drill instructor (DI) was a salty little buck sergeant. On the first day when they formed up to go to evening chow he called the platoon to attention, gave them "Right-face," "Forward march," and "Column right." All went well until the DI began counting cadence. With the Marine Corps singsong of "Hey, haw, yer lep," and "Hawn, hawp, hareep, fer yer lep" (a highly individualistic rendition of the official cadence, "One, two, three, four"), he headed them toward the mess hall. The reaction was instantaneous and almost unanimous. The V-12s had never heard anything like that and snickering was followed by outright laughter. They were halted abruptly and in the next two minutes got the impression that the sergeant was nine feet tall, an image that didn't fade over the next few days. In retrospect, the Clements concluded that that may have been the biggest mistake they made in the Corps, and possibly the most valuable. In any event, their V-12 stay at NTAC was brief. They were juniors and had completed all the freshman and sophomore courses the college offered. After just a few days they were transferred with about twenty others to the Marine V-12 detachment at Arkansas A&M in Monticello, where they arrived on 4 July and registered for classes on the sixth.

Like many schools in the program, A&M had some adjustment problems. One was that in late June, just a few days before the V-12s arrived, most of the food-ration stamps allotted for the program mysteriously disappeared. An investigation showed that no Navy personnel were involved and the stamps were quickly replaced in time to avoid a serious problem.

The Clements' V-12 experience was typical. Between their arrival and first classes they were given another physical exam, assigned quarters in Harris Hall, measured for uniforms and attended a shakedown meeting with their NCOs and commanding officer, another salty Marine, 1st Lt. Jack T. Lytle, who walked with a swagger. The first sergeant was a stocky NCO about forty years old who had eighteen years in the Corps, having enlisted in 1925, the year the Clement brothers were born. The detachment also had some sergeants as drill instructors and a blond corporal who was the administrative clerk. They made an imposing impression on the college boys. As it turned out, the Clements made it overseas before Lytle did. On Saipan Joe Clement saw a roster of the 35th Replacement Draft, which left the States in late January 1945, and Lytle's name was on it. The officers from that draft joined Joe's unit, the 2nd Marine Division, but he never encountered his former CO.

They received their uniforms on Sunday, 1 August. The khaki issue included four trousers and shirts, two fore-and-aft "overseas" caps, most commonly referred to as "pisscutters" by the troops, two belts, two field scarves (ties), six skivvy shirts and shorts, six pairs of socks, and a field jacket. The wool kersey green uniform included a cap, two trousers, and a blouse (uniform coat) with a two-inch wide leather belt known as a "fair leather belt" which had a large brass buckle to polish. The issue also included two pair of very light-brown dress shoes, a non-Marine color. To remedy this they had to buy chocolate-brown leather dye and a shoeshine kit, for which their NCOs generously provided—gratis—detailed instructions on proper use. Those who failed to appreciate and heed this generosity regretted it after the surprise inspection the following morning. They also were issued the Marine field uniform, green herringbone dungarees, what the Army called fatigues, and high-top field shoes known as "boondockers." These items were to be stowed in a large olive-drab canvas seabag.

They really knew they were in the Corps when they got their first set of shots (typhoid, tetanus, and a smallpox vaccination on 12 July). This left Joe to wonder if it was their "sadistic" nurse who dreamed up the unusual technique for the tetanus shot. She had each man reach over with his left arm and grasp the point of his right shoulder and, once he was in that defenseless position, she jabbed the hypodermic needle under his left shoulder blade. It hurt worse than any shot they had ever had, before or after, and several passed out. One had a needle broken off, which had been removed from his arm by the time he came to. Mark's left arm was badly swollen from the typhoid shot. So was Joe's, but he outdid his twin by getting sick and losing his lunch. He was allowed to spend the afternoon in his rack, which left him to conclude: "Who says there aren't any good NCOs in the Corps?" This was the first—and worst—of their three inoculation sessions.

All the while their NCOs hadn't forgotten them. Up by 0600, they had calisthenics, marched to morning chow (and the other two meals as well), then went to classes. There was physical training (PT) every afternoon they weren't in class and in between the NCOs frequently put them through close-order drill. No rifles were issued, however, and most V-12s learned the manual of arms in boot camp. The temperature reached 105 degrees, with high humidity, in Monticello in July and August when they first arrived, and they were ordered to take two salt tablets three times a day because their PT NCO wasn't going to let the weather dictate *his* schedule. Some took three or four showers a day and lounged around the large communal shower/washrooms with towels around their waists in an effort to keep cool. There was no air conditioning in those days and an electric fan was a luxury. Much of the time they were bathed in sweat even in the classroom with all the windows wide open. They began getting lessons in leadership—Lieutenant Lytle and the NCOs shared their miserable conditions and in Joe's opinion set a high standard.

On 1 September the NCOs put them to the test with the two-mile run—a run, not a trot—and most surprised themselves by not having to stop and take a moment's rest. Lest they get overconfident, however, the PT NCO ran them through the obstacle course again afterwards. The first obstacle was a nine-foot wall, which they scaled by running at it, jumping to grab the top, and pulling themselves over. Next was a three-foot barrier they had to dive over, then came a barbed wire entanglement under which they crawled on their backs, pushing themselves forward while lying on their backs. There were several more obstacles, the final one another nine-foot wall. By that time they were exhausted, but they all made it. The course was run as fast as they could move, and if one slowed for any reason he was pulled out of line and sent back to the start. They also ran what they thought were astronomical distances around a small airfield adjacent to the course, and the Tail-end Charlies were rewarded by being forced to run an extra lap.

There was a POW camp near the school, which the V-12s could see while doing PT. The prisoners were moved in on the second Sunday of August, a month after the V-12s had arrived, and the camp was closed to the Marines, who had been attending Mass there. All the prisoners were young Italians who had been captured in North Africa. The V-12s never did get an opportunity to talk to any of them but were able to watch them through the fence for several minutes one day. A small group of the prisoners waved at the Marines in a friendly manner and the V-12s returned their greeting.

The V-12s found weapons training much more congenial. They were introduced to the Thompson (Tommy) submachine gun and learned to disassemble and reassemble it. Joe found it an easy weapon to master and it pumped his adrenaline when he got his hands on one. Several months later he found one while on patrol on Saipan and carried it the rest of his time overseas. The Clements and other ROTC students enjoyed some advantages over many of their classmates. Their ROTC training at NTAC included disassembling weapons, military procedures, and marching.

They also had experience in commanding their own units at NTAC, where Mark had been a cadet major and Joe a cadet captain. Except for the physical training, college life as a V-12 was quite similar to that of former ROTC students like the Clements, who thought that some of their freshman hazing at NTAC was more punishing than their V-12 workouts.

In addition to the more demanding Marine Corps training, the V-12 offered some of them another benefit. Joe's roommates at Arkansas A&M, Willie and Moe, were four or five years older than he and veterans of Guadalcanal who frequently would tell him sea stories of their time on the 'Canal. Much of it was blarney but often they were serious and would advise him on how to react under certain situations, what to do and not to do. They were looking out for their "Chick," as they called him. They were together seven months but he never saw them after he left for boot camp.

Some of the Clements' letters suggest that they suffered from a problem common to college students and servicemen—the quality of food. Nearly every letter contained requests for cakes and crackers and jam and peanut butter. They knew there was no shortage of food in the chow hall, however, because every few weeks they reported that they had gained another pound or so. They each gained more than fifteen pounds during their five-month tour at Arkansas A&M, with Mark coming out weighing 176 pounds and Joe 184.

The physical exertion stood Joe in good stead the Saturday night in late October when he missed the liberty bus. His buddies on board waved at him, laughing at his misfortune. His only recourse was to run the three miles, every inch of the way. As he pulled up on the steps to Harris Hall, the bells in the tower started chiming 2200 hours, the end of liberty. At the top of the steps was the first sergeant, who looked at Clement and said, "You're AWOL, Clement. You're on report. See the skipper in the morning at 0800." Clement almost panicked at the dimming of his chances for a commission and didn't sleep well that night.

The next morning the first sergeant ushered him into Lytle's office and remained standing behind him. Lytle sat reading something on his desk for what seemed like ages and finally looked up at Clement with a flat, stern face. "What's the matter, Clement?" he asked. "The first sergeant tells me you were late getting back from liberty last night."

His heart in his throat, Clement croaked, "No, sir, I was not late."

Lytle sat toying with his pencil, a technique Clement remembered and used himself in his military career. "Why do you say you weren't late?" he asked.

"Sir, I would have been at the check-in desk near the top of the steps before the tower bells stopped ringing if the first sergeant hadn't stopped me," Clement responded.

"Well, how did you get back from town?" Lytle asked.

Clement's answer was simple and direct. "Sir, I ran like hell."

Lytle appeared to suppress a laugh and responded, "Get your butt out of here and don't let me see you here again."

Clement concluded that Lytle was pleased that someone in his command could, and would, run all the way from town to avoid being late from liberty.

Two weeks after the V-12s reported in, they realized their first reward for becoming Marines—their first payday in the Corps. To them, the twenty-five dollars cash—the V-12s were paid fifty dollars a month—seemed an astronomical amount. Some thought they'd never had it so good. There were other benefits to their service, however, one of which was the girls registered at the college. The women may have been outnumbered by the Marine and Navy V-12s and the hundred or so male civilian students, but there were enough to make life interesting. All the servicemen were restricted to campus except on weekends, when many of the Marines headed in the direction of Pine Bluff, fifty-five miles north of Monticello and the second largest city in the state. One incentive for leaving Monticello was that there was some local resentment of the V-12s. While the V-12s were still in school, and had some freedom and comfort, many of the area's young men had been called up in the National Guard and were serving in the frigid Aleutians; many V-12s encountered this hostility.

Pine Bluff was the closest town of any size and a nearby munitions factory had hired a number of women in their late teens and early twenties. Their jobs paid very well for that time in that part of the country and they were very understanding people. Some occasionally picked up the tab for an evening when the Marines were strapped for cash before payday, and on occasion several of them visited the Marines in Monticello. One group had bought an old convertible touring car and were able to accumulate enough gasoline rationing stamps to make the trip in a car that only got about ten miles per gallon.

The Marines became well known in Pine Bluff during the last half of 1943—and not always for the best of reasons. Only one place in town was ever put off-limits to the V-12s, a restaurant called the Oasis, which was a monstrous barn-like structure that featured a bar and a huge dance floor, complete with band. It was one of the nicer places in town, as it served meals in one section at individual tables. There had been several "misunderstandings" among the clientele that winter and Joe was present at the final one, on an evening he was having dinner with an Army first lieutenant and his wife. The lieutenant was in his late twenties and they had developed a nice friendship.

Eight Marines from the V-12 unit were drinking at a table on the opposite side of the dance hall and appeared to become increasingly relaxed as the evening wore on. At the table behind them were four husky civilians in their mid-twenties, loggers from the nearby pine forests, and their dates. At one point the girls went to the powder room and the four men went to the men's room. The women returned before the men did and, apparently, one was irritated with her date because he wouldn't dance with her. She sat for a couple of minutes, then turned to the table of Marines and asked the one nearest if he would dance with her. Nicknamed "Tinker," he was from Oklahoma and in his socially lubricated state considered himself the perfect Southern gentleman. He rose both to his feet and to the occasion, bowed slightly, and responded, "It would be my pleasure, ma'am." He could navigate well enough to dance and they were on the floor for several minutes. Meanwhile, the four loggers returned and the one with the missing date spied her dancing with Tinker. He sat and stewed while his buddies heckled him. Finishing their dance, Tinker returned the young woman to her table, seated her, and thanked her with another half bow. His stance, with his chin jutting out, was more than the ego-injured date could stand and with one swing he laid Tinker out on the floor.

Almost instantaneously, the other Marines at Tinker's table were on their feet. The PT instructor took control. Before anyone could move further, he yelled, "Hold it. We have to be fair about this. There are four of them, and there should be four of us. That means me, you, you, and you." The contestants established, the battle lines were drawn. Tables and chairs were pulled back in a circle and the combatants moved to opposite sides of the ring with Marines two or three deep around its circumference. Surveying his opponents, the sergeant said, "Okay, follow me," and clobbered the logger closest to him.

The only entrance had two heavy, full-length swinging doors, each with a U-shaped brass handle in the center where they adjoined. Two Army MPs were stationed outside, and two Marines quickly moved to the doors where one of them stuck his left arm through the handles and shouted, "No one goes in or out until this is finished." The Marines were in their winter green uniforms, which had the two-inch "fair leather" belt with its heavy, square brass buckle worn on the outside of the blouse. With the belt removed and the strap partly looped back through the buckle, it became a formidable weapon when grasped by the loop, similar to a medieval chain and mace, and the door guards brandished theirs to discourage any attempts to open the doors from the inside.

The MPs yelled and beat on the doors but were kept shut out. The fight didn't last more than a couple of minutes, which was time enough for the Marines to win. The tables and chairs were quickly put back in order and the sixty or so Marines returned to their tables and dates. The young Marine guard at the doors withdrew his arm, retreated to his table, and the MPs charged in. The Marines thought it was a very brief, neat, and nondestructive encounter, but the management didn't agree. No one was thrown in the brig that night, but the Oasis got no more Marine business during the V-12ers' tour at Monticello.

Different people responded to the scholastic grind in different ways. Some turned out to be uninterested and washed out, going into the Corps as enlisted men, but most strove to make good grades and not endanger their eligibility for commissions. Most carried a fifteen- to seventeen-hour semester load. Mark Clement exercised an initiative in his Engineering Surveying class that paid some substantial secondary benefits. The only professor available to teach the course was confined to a wheelchair and couldn't go into the field with the class. Clement was in his seventh semester of engineering by then and had taken surveying at NTAC. He struck a deal—the disabled professor would do the classroom teaching while Clement supervised the field course, thereby getting credit for an advanced surveying course. Clement selected only surveying routes that ran along the most direct route on the three miles from the campus to town. The class members were the only Marines allowed off campus during the week and they surveyed the location of nearly every building in town, aided by as many coeds as they could entice. It was the best duty they had enjoyed to that date and Clement just regretted that there wasn't any way to work it more than one day a week.

On one occasion, Joe Clement yielded to a temptation that imperiled a grade. The class had ten days leave for Christmas of 1943, but a test in analytical geometry was scheduled for Friday. For about a dozen in the class, it was the only exam scheduled after Tuesday. They asked the professor to excuse them from the test or give them a makeup. They told him they were sure they would be overseas within a year and that some weren't going to make it through the war, which, of course, was true. They felt that the extra three days leave was more important than their grade, but they didn't want to risk an *F* and washing out. The professor was understanding and promised to help in any way he could, but said he couldn't commit to any specific grade. He seemed so sympathetic, however, that they decided to take a chance and left for home that Tuesday. Joe had a *B* at the time, but the professor gave each of them a *D* regardless of the grade they were carrying. They greatly appreciated his not flunking them, however, and thanked him profusely. Another member of the SOCS in this group, Ken McCreary had an *A* average but he didn't complain, either. He became a rifle platoon leader with the 3rd Marine Division and was killed on Iwo Jima. He was awarded the Silver Star posthumously for his action against a Japanese defensive stronghold known as "Cushman's Pocket," named for Lt. Col. Robert Cushman, McCreary's battalion commander and a future Marine Corps commandant. When the dean's honor roll came out in early November, Joe wasn't on it, but Mark, McCreary, and another SOCS member, Curtis Myers, were.

At least the Clement brothers were well dressed for their holiday leave. Their grandmother's concept of a Marine was one uniformed in the familiar dress blues, which unfortunately were not part of their issue. She gave them each a set as an early Christmas present, however, and while on leave in Dallas in the summer of 1943 they were measured for the uniforms. They arrived in the mail at Monticello on 2 August and the twins were as impressed as all their buddies. The dress blue uniform in those days cost $64.30 complete with belt, blouse, trousers, cap, shoes, alterations, and postage. The only opportunity they had to wear them was while home on Christmas leave, when they had their pictures taken in uniform.

The brothers have another vivid memory of that Christmas leave. They went to a local dance hall with two V-12ers from Dallas. Shortly before midnight, the four went to a nearby café and took seats in a high-backed booth. After they had ordered food, they became aware that someone was singing the Marine Hymn, but something was wrong. It was being sung to the tune of "My Darling Clementine." Four Army men, or "dogfaces" as the Marines call them, who had a few beers, appeared to be in the mood to take on the entire Corps, or at least its four eighteen- and nineteen-year-old representatives in the café. Joe was seated on the outside of the booth facing them and all he could see was their olive-drab trousers and blouses. Each soldier was a few years older and at least twenty pounds heavier than the Marines were, but the four Marines couldn't just sit there and have their honor impugned. They knew if they tried to shut the soldiers up, they were likely to get their

Mark Anthony Clement Jr.
and Joseph Frederick
Clement, Christmas 1943.
MARK AND JOE CLEMENT

rear ends kicked, and they were pretty sure that the soldiers wouldn't let them leave without following them outside. Just when they started to unbuckle their "fair leather" belts with the big brass buckles, Joe felt a tap on his right shoulder. Turning his head, he saw a big, husky sailor with two hash marks on his sleeve (service stripes representing four years of service each), a petty officer's (NCO) rank above them, and a wide smile on his face. Behind him were three other sailors, each as big and salty as the first and also grinning. The first announced in a voice loud enough for everyone to hear, "Mates, we just want you to know that if there are any problems with which the Navy can help you, just feel free to call on us." The strains of "Clementine" no longer drifted through the café.

"The term 'Mate' has always had a special meaning to me after hearing it that night," Joe recalls. It was his first exposure to the special relationship that exists between Marines and sailors—particularly the medical corpsmen who accompany the infantry platoons—the Seabees, and the landing boat coxswains and LST skippers who risked their lives putting the Marines on the beach and then, as at Iwo, bringing an unending stream of supplies and equipment ashore to the embattled troops.

While the Clement brothers were transferred to Arkansas A&M

from NTAC, Red Qualls was sent *to* NTAC from Abilene Christian for his V-12 training. His only explanation for this apparent anomaly was football. Football turned out to be a big part of the V-12 program, even though the officer in charge of the Physical Training Section, Cdr. James Joseph "Gene" Tunney, the former heavyweight boxing champion, adamantly opposed intercollegiate athletics. He was a favorite of President Roosevelt, but Tunney lost on this issue and as a reward was assigned to make a study of physical training opportunities in Australia.

The V-12s were a major factor on the college football teams of 1943 and 1944 and the coaches transacted considerable business among themselves at first. Under V-12 Bulletin No. 5 V-12 commanding officers could transfer up to 5 percent of their trainees for "valid academic reasons." But early in the first term (July–October 1943) Navy Lt. Raymond Howes, the second-ranking officer in the V-12 College Training Section, was visiting Northwestern's head football coach, the legendary Lynn "Pappy" Waldorf, when a huge sailor knocked and announced himself to Waldorf: "I am the new guard from Wisconsin, traded for a halfback," and then, noticing Lieutenant Howes, added, "I am a V-12 transfer, sir, for valid academic reasons." Howes saw to it that this practice ended immediately, but Waldorf's 1943 team was 6–2, ranked ninth in the nation, and beat the Great Lakes Naval Training Center, a powerhouse that dealt number one Notre Dame its only defeat of the season. It was no coincidence that the schools with Marine detachments were among those with the leading football teams in 1943—Notre Dame, led by Marine V-12 Heisman Trophy winner Angelo Bertelli, Michigan, Purdue, Northwestern, College of the Pacific, Southern California, Washington, Duke, Georgia Tech, plus some previously obscure colleges like Arkansas A&M, Southwestern Louisiana Institute, Western Michigan, Southwestern University, and Colorado College. Of the twenty-five players named to the various All-American teams in 1943, thirteen were Marine V-12s. The football players won two Navy Crosses, seven Silver Stars, three Bronze Stars, and various other awards including the Purple Heart on Iwo and Okinawa.

The Arkansas A&M football team was a particular Cinderella story. The school dropped football after many of its players were called to active duty in the National Guard after Pearl Harbor. Its equipment was stolen by a semi-professional team that had been allowed to play under its aegis in 1942, but a number of V-12s who had been stars in the Southwestern Conference raised the matter in the summer of 1943 with the A&M detachment athletic officer, Navy Lt. (jg) Homer Cole, who had been a trainer for the Chicago Bears. Cole arranged an early practice game with the University of Arkansas at Fayetteville, which lent uniforms and equipment to the Aggies, who expressed their gratitude by beating the Razorbacks, 20–12. Shortly after that, the football program at the Naval Air Technical Training Command in Memphis was disbanded and its equipment given to Arkansas A&M. The team posted a 7–1–1 record, including victory over a powerful team from Keesler Field, an Army Air Force base near Biloxi, Mississippi.

Jim Ronayne was a second-string tailback at Dartmouth on a team with a number of college stars. One was his SOCS classmate Jim Landrigan, who was a star lineman at Holy Cross in 1942—an honorable mention All-American—and starred with the Baltimore Colts for two years after the war.[4] Running the Notre Dame box formation, Dartmouth beat Cornell, Brown, Princeton, and the Coast Guard Academy, among others, while losing to Penn and its All-American tailback, Howie O'Dell.

Red Qualls had been a high-scoring, touchdown pass–catching star end in high school in Cisco, Texas. He made the Abilene Christian varsity as a 170-pound freshman, won a scholarship as a walk-on, and dreamed of playing professionally until the war intervened. Although he heard rumors that he might be sent to Millsaps College or Northeast Louisiana or Southwest Louisiana on 1 July 1943 for his V-12 program, he and several other teammates from Abilene Christian were assigned to NTAC, which with all its servicemen transfers had a pretty good wartime season. They routed Texas Tech, 34–14, beat Southern Methodist and two teams from Army bases at Waco and Tyler, and tied Texas A&M. They narrowly lost their last game of the season, 20–13, to a powerful Army Air Force team from Randolph Field, Texas, whose star was halfback Glenn Dobbs, an All-American from Tulsa University. When Qualls says he loved football he can be taken at face value; he left the sickbay, where he was recovering from food poisoning, to play in the game and his illness didn't seem to slow him much. "I dumped him [Dobbs] on his can a few times," he recalls. Randolph Field played Texas in the Cotton Bowl and the NTAC players, to Qualls's disappointment, voted against accepting a Sun Bowl bid. One of Qualls's teammates, guard Joe Aikins, was activated from the V-12 program and sent to Parris Island in midseason, at the end of October, the end of the V-12ers' first term. Aikins was commissioned at Quantico, but Qualls beat him overseas; they met at Pearl Harbor, where Aikins was with a support unit, when Qualls was in the naval hospital there after being wounded on Iwo; Aikins was killed with the Army at Pusan in Korea.

Front row, third from left: *Pvt. James L. "Red" Qualls, Platoon 99, at Parris Island boot camp, March 1944.* RED QUALLS

The V-12 program wasn't all football for Qualls. NTAC built a block of quarters for the Marines, small apartments of three rooms and a bath for six men; Qualls's roommate was a young Mormon straight out of high school in Salt Lake City. They drilled every Wednesday, and in addition to the Navy's technical courses the Marines got a good dose of map reading and topography, which put them in good stead later on. NTAC beefed up its curriculum for the V-12 program enough that Qualls was able to complete all the requirements for his degree in business administration except for a three-hour business course. "I wanted to be a rancher but they only had one course in animal husbandry," he recalls. "So I took business administration, some classes taught by the coach, but they ran out of courses in that, too." When he and his V-12 group were ordered to Parris Island in February 1944, Qualls arranged with Abilene Christian to get the credits by correspondence course, which he completed in a short time. He hadn't heard from Abilene Christian by the summer of 1944, so when he was at Camp Lejeune he contacted the college, which sent him a telegram informing him that with the payment of a fifteen-dollar fee he would be a full-fledged Bachelor of Science. Qualls's father was presented the degree by the president of Abilene Christian in Red's stead.

Although the requirements and routine were basically the same for all, V-12 was somewhat simpler for Bud Morris and Gordon Dibble because Dartmouth and Yale were V-12 schools and the only move they had to make was to a new dorm. This may have been a mixed blessing for Morris and his comrades—the Dartmouth campus at Hanover, New Hampshire, is a self-contained and relatively isolated community so the opportunities to miss curfews and get into other trouble were limited. The Marine V-12 cadre at Dartmouth had 622 men and, like the others, they were issued uniforms and began a military regimen on 1 July 1943. With the other Marines Morris moved from his quarters in Wheeler Hall to Topliff Hall. Their commanding officer was Maj. John Howland, a wounded veteran of Guadalcanal and an Old Corps officer who sported a Navy boat cloak with his uniform. For a brief period Howland was commanding officer of the entire program at Dartmouth, the only Marine officer to hold that position. The first CO, Cdr. William Bullis (USN, ret.), was relieved because of complaints that he ran the program like his private academy, Bullis School, a prep school for the Naval Academy, treated the V-12s like prep-school students, and that academic performance and morale suffered as a result. A Navy captain, Damon B. Cummings, commanded it for the rest of the war and Howland returned to his post as officer-in-charge of the Marine detachment.[5]

A geology major, Morris received college credit for working the summer of 1942 for the U.S. Geological Survey. He was part of a team that searched abandoned mines and other sites in the mountains of northern New Hampshire for deposits of two minerals that had strategic wartime value, mica and beryl, which are essential elements in forming beryllium, a strong, hard alloy used in manufacturing vehicle springs. With these and summer-school credits in 1943 Morris completed his degree in February 1944, just before he and his cohort were ordered to Parris Island.

The highlight of his V-12 experience was the night the movie theater, the Nugget, a local institution, burned down. Three or four V-12s shared a room in the dormitories and when they heard the alarm Morris and his roomies got dressed and went out to help fight the fire. They spent several hours helping the firemen with the hoses and other tasks and when they returned to the dorm they were read the riot act by their barracks NCO, a Sergeant Bernardi, for unauthorized absence from quarters and getting their uniforms soaked and filthy. However, they were vindicated a week later at a college convocation when Major Howland commended them for their action, and the Marine Corps awarded them official Letters of Commendation, which went into their personnel jackets. Howland consistently backed his Marines. Three Navy V-12s who had been drinking visited two Marines in their room one night, and when the Navy men became obnoxious, the Marines threw them out the second-story window into a deep snowbank. Fortunately, no one was hurt but the Marines were run up to the CO for disciplinary action. Howland asked that they be remanded to him; when they recounted the event, he broke into laughter, said the sailors got what they deserved, and ordered the offenders to serve as his aides for the following week as punishment.

Most of the time, however, passed in a blur of classes, physical training, close-order drill, marching to chow, and studying. The Marines got a lot of strenuous physical workouts and were encouraged to participate in athletics, varsity, intramural, and informal, but for the most part the college classroom routine prevailed. Morris was a lacrosse player and skier and sang in the college glee club. He formed a quartet of two Marines and two Navy V-12s called "The Leatherjackets"; when the sailors were transferred they were replaced by two Marines and the name was changed to "The Leatherneckers." Morris also had a girlfriend at Colby-Sawyer College in nearby New London and caught a break when a faculty member there proposed that he help teach a geology class. For a while, Morris commuted to the job, and to his girlfriend, on an old Indian motorcycle he picked up for twenty-five dollars. He subsequently bought a 1925 Ford sedan for fifty dollars and faced the common problem of getting enough gasoline ration coupons to keep it running.

At the University of Washington, Dan Hurson recalls his NCOs as "drill instructors from San Diego," site of the Corps's West Coast boot camp. "We went through boot camp there," he says of V-12. An equally strong memory, however, was of his detachment's commanding officer, Capt. Paul Moore Jr., who won the Navy Cross, Silver Star, and Purple Heart on Guadalcanal as a platoon leader in Company F, 2nd Battalion, 5th Marines. Moore went on to become the Episcopal Bishop of New York and a prominent spokesman for peace and other liberal causes in the decades after the war.

Returning from Christmas leave, everything seemed to change a bit and the pace quickened. On their campuses from coast to coast the V-12s knew they were to leave for Parris Island soon. Their NCOs had worked hard on them and, while they weren't veterans, they had developed a comradeship and strong esprit. To the final day, the Marine staff bore down in emphasizing that the tough part was still ahead and that they couldn't slacken their efforts. No one mentioned commissions—just the importance of being good Marines.

One reason was that it was by no means certain who and how many would be ordered to active duty. In one way the V-12 program gave the Marine Corps an embarrassment of riches, in that it had more prospective officers than it could process through Quantico. It had another embarrassment, however, because it was projecting a shortage of second lieutenants needed for its six infantry divisions in the meat-grinder operations in the Pacific. The pipeline to the Marine Corps Schools at Quantico was jammed to capacity because the schools could commission only 300 new second lieutenants a month and prospective officer candidates were backing up at Camp Lejeune. So the Corps had to delay the activation of more than 2,000 V-12s in October 1943 and February 1944, which wreaked havoc with morale. It wound up offering the opportunity to go to Navy OCS instead, which more than 600 Marine V-12s accepted. All this had an adverse impact on the Marines' academic performance in the program's first two terms, which subsequently improved as the course smoothed out.

The V-12s were on something of a yo-yo. Because of the heavy officer casualties in the Pacific in 1944, the Marine Corps increased the number of activations from the program in July 1944 from 1,600 to 1,900 and on 1 November 1944 from 1,800 to 2,125. But since the Corps planned to add relatively few trainees to the program after that, it closed down twenty-six of its V-12 programs in 1944, sending their members to other schools, mostly near Parris Island; it finished the war with twelve units.

In the second week of January 1944, however, lists of people to be sent to Parris Island on the first of March were posted at the various V-12 schools. Red Qualls, Jim Ronayne, George Mayer, Phil Pearce, Bud Morris, Jack Lauck, Dan Hurson, and the Clement brothers were on them. They attended classes. They studied. They marched. They waited. The graduation ceremony for Morris and the other Marine V-12s at Dartmouth who had earned enough credits for a degree entailed having a beer with the college president in his office. And in the last week in February, after the midyear break, they all said goodbye to their campuses and entrained for South Carolina.

They weren't the only ones who said goodbye. Because of attrition and the large number of V-12s ordered to active duty that month, the Marines began consolidating their V-12 program by combining detachments. NTAC and five other colleges said farewell to their Marine detachments that February, and Arkansas A&M was one of twenty more that closed their Marine programs the following October.

About seventy from Arkansas A&M, including the Clement brothers, boarded the train to boot camp. They embarked at McGhee, Arkansas, and went through Little Rock on the way to Parris Island. People at the different towns where the train stopped along the way gathered at the stations to express their support and give them food and drink, and the Marines, in turn, were grateful for the demonstrations of appreciation. More than fifty years later, Joe Clement would note with regret that he didn't see that kind of support for the troops again until Operation Desert Storm, the brief confrontation with Iraq in 1991.

Their trip ended the way it has for hundreds of thousands of Marines over the years. The train backed into the station near Beaufort, South Carolina, and the V-12s were greeted by the Marine Corps Recruit Depot NCOs. After they entered the base their ears rang with the traditional taunts from the recruits who had preceded them there: "You'll be *sorr-eee!*" They were at the fabled Parris Island boot camp and the gates of mercy closed behind them.

4 Parris Island

All Hope Abandon,

Ye Who Enter Here

These words from *The Divine Comedy* aren't chiseled over the gates at Marine Corps Recruit Depot, Parris Island, South Carolina, but all the Marines who have passed through them could sardonically argue that they should be—Marine Corps boot camp is not divine, and it certainly is no comedy. Just a week's seniority in boot camp makes a recruit consider himself an "old salt" to those coming along behind him. The SOCS members remember their greeting very clearly—"You'll be *sorr-eee!*"—and concluded that it was quite apropos that the arriving trains backed into the siding at the nearby town of Yamasee.

Parris Island, commonly referred to as "P.I." or "the Island," is probably the Corps's most storied base. The training syllabus at the West Coast Recruit Depot in San Diego is identical, but Parris Island has the mystique. This is partly because of its somewhat exotic name, partly because it's located on an island, which increases the recruits' sense of isolation, and partly because of its justifiably infamous bad weather. When it isn't semitropical hot and humid, it is beset by rains from Atlantic Ocean storms, often borne on raw, chilling winds, and always there seems to be blowing sand—and sand fleas. Ironically, Parris Island is only about ten miles across Port Royal Sound from the luxury resorts on Hilton Head Island. There have been countless arguments and fistfights in Marine squad bays between P.I. and "Dago" graduates on their arrival at their units in the Fleet Marine Force over which boot camp is toughest. The Island alumni contemptuously dismiss their San Diego comrades as "Hollywood Marines," and the West Coasters return the favor with the alliterative "Parris Island Pussies."[1]

Entering the gate of either recruit depot as a boot is a chilling experience of being completely cut off from previous life and delivered over to people trained in violence who give every evidence of slavering to commit it on interlopers who presume to aspire to the drill instructors' beloved Corps: "Did you enlist and come here to fuck up *my* Marine Corps?" was a frequent DI's question, posed actually as an accusation. The term "boot camp" is taken from the Navy, whose recruits are distinguishable by white canvas leggings into which they tuck their bell-bottom trouser legs. Some graduates have compared Marine Corps boot camp to Southern road gangs as a lifestyle, an obvious exaggeration born of pride in having undergone it, but in fact it is unmatched in its severity by any other U.S. armed service basic training. Until recent years it has included both the threat and the infliction of physical violence on the laggard and unwilling, which on occasion has gotten out of hand. This was the case in World War II, although none of the SOCS members admit to experiencing or witnessing it. The enormous wartime expansion put great pressures on every area of the military, including recruit training, in which many relatively young and inexperienced NCOs were made drill instructors and given enormous authority over their charges. They were under great pressure to turn a flood of civilians into Marines in a very short time, in contrast to the more relaxed prewar training schedule run by more experienced senior NCOs.

Boot camp features sixteen-hour days of arduous physical training and an even more grueling mental and emotional harassment. The stated theory is to obliterate civilian individuality, replace it with the Marine Corps identity,[2] and create a warrior. The first priority is discipline and instant obedience and the only acceptable response to a command is to leap to attention and scream, "*Sir, yes sir!*" Few errors or failings escape notice or punishment.

Over the years, boot camp has changed along with societal changes, but not much; it still is a hazing initiation into a life-long brotherhood of warriors. From the time he enters boot camp until he possibly dies assaulting an enemy bunker, the Marine is constantly reminded that he is the best fighting man on Earth and he had better never, ever, do anything to disprove that. He undergoes constant indoctrination in what the Corps considers to be the moral superiority of a warrior culture—and the Corps's preeminence in that culture. One of the major changes in boot camp came in the 1990s when the Corps responded to what it perceived as the coarsening of society and prohibited any profanity, not even "hell" and "damn," by the drill instructors, let alone the physical maltreatment that unfortunately had sometimes been inflicted on past recruits. Correction of errors and discipline remained as rigorous and uncompromising as ever, enforced by push-ups and other forms of physical training. The goal is to posit a society and brotherhood of integrity—to oneself, to one's comrades in arms, and to society in general. In previous generations the Corps and the other branches of the service assumed a relatively genteel civilian society whose young men had to be indoctrinated into the coarse and violent military life.[3] The V-12s, no doubt because they were known to be potential officers, weren't subjected to physical maltreatment as were some of the unfortunate regular recruits.

At the beginning of March 1944 nearly sixteen hundred Marine V-12 trainees descended on Parris Island from colleges and universities all over the country. When their trains backed into the station they were greeted with shouted orders, threats, and constant abjurations by their drill instructors. The time-honored tactic is for the DIs to have the recruits fall in on yellow lines painted on the cement deck after debarkment from trucks or "cattle cars," fix them with threatening glares, slap the side of a leg or the open hand menacingly with their swagger sticks, then immediately get into the recruits' faces, screaming orders and threats. In the process the DIs gang up on the largest and toughest-looking newcomer to harass, threaten, and break him down, to send a message to the rest as to who is supreme in that society. There is no ambiguity in that message.[4]

After de-training—on the double—the V-12s were trucked to the recruit area where they were formed into seventy-two-man platoons under three DIs—the senior DI, generally a staff or gunnery sergeant, an assistant DI, and a junior DI, generally buck sergeants or corporals. Most were quartered in quonset huts, some in eleven-man tents. The first thing they did was draw their "bucket issue" of soap, shaving cream, razor, toothpaste and brush, pencils, notepaper, and other personal items along with a galvanized bucket, which had a variety of uses. One, of course, was the traditional function of holding water, but it could also be filled with sand to be carried for punishment purposes or worn as an impromptu helmet while the DIs rapped on it with their swagger sticks, another punishment and "educational" technique. Then came the infamous boot-camp haircut, which took about twenty seconds and resulted in a shaved head, for which the only comfort was that everyone could laugh at each other. Next was the issue of "782 Gear"—field equipment such as bayonets, packs, canteens, web belts, so called for the Department of Defense (then the Navy and War Departments) Form 782 that the recruit signed on receipt.

Then began the grueling training schedule of close-order drill, physical conditioning, weapons instruction, other classes in military subjects, and countless inspections—rifle inspections, personal inspections, barracks inspections, locker box (foot locker) inspections, "junk on the bunk" inspections (all clothing and gear laid out on the recruit's bunk or "rack" in prescribed fashion), field equipment inspections with prescribed pack contents spread out on the poncho on the "grinder" or parade ground. For the rest of their time on the Island, the recruits were constantly serenaded with the "Song of the Island," the sing-song cadence counted by the DIs as they marched their platoons—"Hey, haw, threep, fer lep," a drawling, slurred, almost musical version of the official naval establishment cadence of "One, two, three, four" that reflected the influence of Southern NCOs over the years. And they marched everywhere they went, often at double-time.

Early in boot camp Joe and Mark Clement and their platoon experienced what they at first considered a classic case of mindless harassment. Rain one night left puddles in low spots in the street and while marching to morning chow their DI gave them a "Right oblique—march" command, which took them to the other side of the street where he deliberately marched them through a puddle about a hundred feet long. Then "Left oblique" back to the other side of the street, where they marched through the puddles there. They marched through every puddle of water they encountered that day and every day afterward. By the time the platoon made its first all-day hike with full pack, about a month into boot camp, however, they came to appreciate the method in this madness. There is nothing better for breaking in new boots and shoes than soaking them thoroughly and the V-12s had been issued brand-new "boondockers," as the Marine field shoe was known. This brown high-top shoe has a cord rubber sole and heel and the rough side of the leather on the outside, like a very shaggy suede.

Under the constant reminder that "the Marine's best friend is his rifle," they stripped down their M-1s to oil and clean them several times a day until they could take them apart and reassemble them blindfolded. They quickly learned that a Marine's cardinal sin is to drop his rifle; the punishment for that was severe. One was to sleep with it that night. Another was to "dry shave" with just the razor, no water or lather; a diabolic embellishment of this for the truly hopeless was to have one recruit dry shave the culprit while both double-timed down the grinder. Yet another was to hold the nine-pound weapon out on the backs of the hands, arms fully extended, until it was dropped through fatigue, which led to another round of punishment. The penalty for swatting sand fleas while marching was "port pushes," holding the rifle at port arms, pushing it out to arms' length, then bringing it back into the chest, and repeating this drill unto exhaustion.

Sand is an educational tool at both boot camps. Recruits who have trouble getting "right face" and "left face" commands straight are aided by having the right trouser pocket filled with sand to help them remember which side is which. After a day of marching this leaves an abrasion as a continuing reminder of right and wrong. One of the future SOCS members, a football player from Penn named George G. "Bernie" Gallagher, hiked the drill field with a pack full of sand as reward for the sin of seeing something humorous about one of the day's proceedings.

The toothbrush was another teaching aid. Gordon Dibble and his buddy, Rawle de Land, both of whom received the Purple Heart on Iwo, were caught laughing at something while in formation and their DI ordered them to clean the "head"—latrine—until it was spotless. He gave each of them all the cleaning equipment they would need—a toothbrush. A lot of the V-12s scrubbed the heads and the decks of their huts during their sojourn on Parris Island. "Field days," carrying all the racks and lockers outside and scrubbing the huts fore and aft with swabs and brushes, were regular events. Every day began with sweeping and swabbing the hut, then calisthenics, followed by a half-mile run that was extended to a mile.

It's an understatement to say that boot camp is a culture shock to everyone who enters it. "The military was all new to a farm boy like me," Phil Pearce recalls. "I just tried to stay out of trouble." It was less so for some like Jim Ronayne who had grown up in a strict Catholic home

Wash day on the racks in front of the Quonset huts at Parris Island boot camp.
BILL DITTO

and attended Jesuit schools. He saw a close parallel between the Church and the Marine Corps, two strict, hierarchical institutions. "The DIs were the equivalents of the nuns who taught us," he recalls. "The sisters were tough. They carried rulers and if you were out of line or didn't know what you were supposed to they'd whack you on the back of the hand." His first-generation Irish mother may have been the toughest, however. "I told her after I got home, 'Ma, you were the perfect drill instructor.'"[5]

As a result, Ronayne didn't encounter much grief in boot camp— "I was a mouse," he says—but he did dodge one potentially serious bullet. "The strict schedule—it was like parochial school—kept you going without stop and you'd just fall down at the end of the day with exhaustion." He had a two-hour fire watch—one recruit is always awake and patrolling his platoon area with rifle and cartridge belt at night. In the predawn hours while checking the head one night, he sat down on one of the stools at the far end of the quonset hut and fell asleep. He was awakened by the sound of somebody opening the door and jumped to his feet just in time. It was the corporal of the guard, checking the posts. With the adrenalin up he had no trouble remembering his general orders—and how close he had come to blowing his chance to put up lieutenant's bars.[6]

At the end of their first month they stowed their gear into their

"Snapping in." Mastering the positions required for firing for record at Parris Island boot camp. BILL DITTO

packs and seabags and hiked the three miles to the rifle range, where they were quartered in large wooden barracks. The two weeks at the range is a high point of boot camp. The mental harassment is cut down and the emphasis is on marksmanship. The first step in the training is "snapping in," learning to aim and steady the rifle in the four basic shooting positions—standing, prone, sitting, and kneeling. After five days of instruction they fired their first live rounds—six to establish a shot group so the sights could be adjusted to hit the bull's-eye, and to learn not to pull or jerk the trigger but to squeeze it along with the stock. If it is done right, the percussion surprises the shooter. They fired several familiarization rounds with .22-caliber rifles, then fired a qualifying course of fifty rounds on the thousand-inch range from various stances.

This was followed by "snap firing" the M-1 to practice proper breathing and trigger squeeze. This is a two-man drill because no ammunition is involved and the M-1 is semiautomatic. The expanding gas from the powder of a live round drives the operating rod to the rear. This, in turn, drives the bolt back, which extracts the empty cartridge case and then recoils forward to chamber a new round and cock the hammer and firing pin. In snap firing the shooter aims from the various positions and squeezes the trigger; his partner sits or stands to his right and after the trigger squeeze hits the operating rod handle with the palm of his right hand to push it to the rear and cock the hammer for the next shot, as the gas from a live round would. The process requires practice because the operating rod has to be hit hard enough to cock the hammer but not so hard that the bolt locks open. The exercise also is hard on the hand and the second man needs a glove or pad to protect his palm. The recruits also underwent familiarization firing with other weapons such as the Thompson submachine gun (the famous "Tommy gun") and the M-1 carbine, which would be issued to them as officers.

The main event was qualification with the M-1 rifle. Joe and Mark Clement had adjacent positions on the firing line and their coaches had a bet on which would get the highest score. Joe's coach noticed that he occasionally would pull one shot out of a normally tight group. Joe told him the problem was that his right forefinger, the normal trigger finger, was a half-inch shorter than the other after he had broken it seven years before. Joe said he was more comfortable with the middle finger on the trigger and his forefinger wrapped around the front of the trigger guard. He and his coach got permission from their range officer to try it that way for a day and see how it worked. It worked. On record day Joe's score was 309 out of the possible 340, which qualified him as Expert, the highest category of marksman.

The Marine Corps rifle course in World War II was sixty-eight rounds fired from various distances and positions, with five points for a bull's-eye; the targets also have four-point, three-point, and two-point circles. The minimum score for Expert was 306, and Mark missed it by one point because of a mistake that is not uncommon on the rifle range. He fired a bull's-eye on an adjacent target and instead of getting five points for that round he got zero. This is signaled by the fabled and humiliating "Maggie's Drawers," the red flag the men in the butts who pull and mark the targets wave across the front of the target to signal a complete miss. If Mark had put the errant round on his own bull's-eye he would have beaten his brother by a point. He qualified as Sharpshooter (the lowest of the three qualifying categories is Marksman). This mistake also cost him money—Experts were rewarded with an extra five dollars pay per month, Sharpshooters with three dollars.

Mark drew a lesson from his error, however. "I just let up in my concentration. That little lack of attention . . . was good experience, though. It taught me the importance of always paying attention to details. Never think you have it down so pat that you can let up and coast."

Joe wasn't the only one who fired the range at a disadvantage. Gordon Dibble is left-handed and the M-1 is a right-hand weapon—the bolt is on the right and it's driven sharply to the rear with every round that's fired. It could put the eye out of anyone who tries to fire it left-handed. Even so, Dibble managed to qualify—barely—as Marksman.

It was the first time many of the V-12s, city boys like Jim Ronayne, ever fired a rifle and some had never shot anything larger than a .22-caliber. "I was very pessimistic about it," he recalls. "At first I didn't think I could do it. I was scared on the thousand-inch range." He managed to qualify as Marksman, however. In the end it may not have mattered, however. Ronayne never had occasion to fire his M-1 carbine in combat on Iwo; his job was to direct the movement and fire of his platoon.

The range itself wasn't a particularly new experience for Phil Pearce, the southern Illinois farm boy. Weapons and the physical aspects of military training were familiar friends to him. "A lot of people had no experience at what I'd done, hunting and fishing," he recalls. "The M-1 was the first time many of them had ever had a rifle in their hands. The DI harassed us about the same as everyone, but a lot of the others [the regular recruit platoons] weren't in as good shape as we were. I looked at them and wondered how they'd do." Pearce himself did fine. He and two others fired 322 out of the possible 340, the highest score of the nearly sixteen hundred V-12 contingent.

Red Qualls didn't go to the rifle range with his platoon. He was plagued with high blood pressure, which the doctors detected just as the platoon was scheduled to go to the range, and there was some talk that he might be medically disqualified. He spent two weeks working in the sickbay to get his blood pressure down and got to the range with another platoon. His blood pressure had been a question when he enlisted in the Corps. It plagued him again in the SOCS at Camp Lejeune, where a platoon sergeant advised him not to eat breakfast before the precommissioning physical, and came up yet again at Camp Pendleton, just before he was sent out to the Pacific.

Because of their intelligence, previous training, physical maturity, and conditioning, the SOCS members generally fared better in boot camp than the regular recruits, often much better. They were marked as officer candidates, which caused trouble for a few who had envious and resentful DIs; a handful initially made trouble for themselves by arriving with a "salty," know-it-all attitude, a serious error of judgment in boot camp. Most, however, were eager to do well and not jeopardize their chances for a commission. Many had appreciative NCOs who recognized their qualities and pushed them ahead of the training syllabus. They were so good that one group of V-12s got an inside look at the DIs' views of them and learned that the DIs privately were almost in awe of them.

Through some wartime snafu the twenty-seven men in the North-western University Marine unit, for reasons they still don't know, were summarily pulled out of their classes midway through their second V-12 term in November 1943 and sent to Parris Island about three months early. No one at the recruit depot had been informed of their arrival before they showed up, wearing their forest-green winter uniforms and looking to be trained. After a hurried conference with Headquarters Marine Corps, the Parris Island commanding officer concluded that the only sensible thing was to assign them to a new recruit platoon and get on with it.

The "Northwestern 27" went through boot camp as part of a regular platoon and after their graduation ceremony, which included a parade and pass-in-review, the graduates were lined up and given their orders to their duty stations. On receipt of their orders each group marched off to their quarters to pack for departure. All except the Northwestern V-12s, for whom there were no orders. They stood fast in formation. The base commanding officer approached them and asked who they were and why they were still there. One of them, James E. Denebeim, who ulti-mately wound up with the 2nd Marine Division, recalls the exchange: "'Who are you and why are you remaining here?' the CO asked. 'Sir, we are the Northwestern V-12ers,' one replied. 'What are you doing here? The next group of V-12ers are not supposed to arrive for another couple of weeks,' the CO said. 'I'll have to call Washington to find out what to do with you. Meanwhile, you men return to your quarters and stand by.'"

They stood by for nearly two weeks, eating, sleeping, and becoming increasingly bored. Finally, about 1000 one morning the captain in charge of recruit training and an NCO were inspecting the area where the incoming V-12s were to be quartered and noticed that the door on one of the quonset huts had no padlock. The sergeant entered, turned on the light, and found the Northwestern 27 in their racks peacefully "cop-ping a few Zs," which in the Marine Corps is as unheard of as praising the Army. He loudly and profanely rousted them and fell them into for-mation outside the hut where the captain, like the base CO before him, demanded, "who they were and what the hell they were doing there?" It was clear that the Marine Corps had completely forgotten them again. The solution was to assign them as junior DIs for the incoming V-12s. Although the Northwestern 27 had been reduced to the rank of private for boot training, their V-12 rank of private first class had been restored when they graduated.[7] This was when they learned that the regular DIs had developed a high regard for their V-12 trainees. They were older, better educated, and more highly motivated than the regular recruits, already had the rudiments of drill and other basic military skills, and were in better physical condition—many were college athletes.

"They had nothing but praise for the V-12ers," Denebeim recalls. "It seems that the various V-12 groups broke every record which existed at the time they started their boot training. The DIs had never seen a group like them. They were the answer to a DI's prayer. They were shocked by how good they were. This was a time when some recruits had to be taught to read and write by the military." Denebeim found that the V-12s, partly because they had been exposed to NCOs in their V-12 units, caught on to the DI "head games" and "got salty," that is, savvy, pretty fast. The DIs realized this and quickly gave up trying to play games with them.

Because the V-12s had learned close-order drill in college, Denebeim conducted an experiment with his platoon. One of the members had been in his college marching band and Denebeim pulled him aside one day and marked off a thirty-inch length on the sidewalk. He had the man practice taking a thirty-inch pace for a while, then reminded him that the marching pace was 120 steps per minute. "Can you count that off in your head?" he asked. Affirmative. So, whenever Denebeim marched the platoon he put the musician in the platoon guide's position at the front and had him set the pace. The man kept time perfectly and Denebeim took increasing pleasure at having the only recruit platoon that marched silently around the Island without cadence. This occasioned some incredulous looks from other DIs and one asked him: "Who are these guys? What kind of platoon is this?"

His experience also gave Denebeim some insight into the Southerners' impact on the DI corps. "The Southern drill instructors treated recruits like blacks, lower than blacks," he recalls. "They set the tone, the standard. We Yankees [he's a native of Kansas City, Missouri] felt that we had to adopt a Southern accent in order to match their command presence. I tried to be as tough as the regular DIs but the guys got salty pretty fast." When the V-12 platoons completed boot camp, the Northwestern 27 were sent to Camp Lejeune along with the rest of them. "We did catch some hell from some of them in the platoons we had been training," he recalled. But nothing serious.

As good as they were, the V-12ers made their share of errors and were rewarded with the usual punishments. "It could be pretty bad. It was a shock," one SOCS member, Jack Lauck, recalls with a smile. But time has mellowed his memory of "the Island": "It was difficult, but we had a lot of talent in our platoons. My platoon had two Golden Gloves fighters who won all their matches in the recruit boxing tournament and we had many who fired Expert and Sharpshooter on the rifle range. The whole platoon, including the DI, gloried in this competition and achievement."

For many, boot camp was succinctly summed up by one SOCS member: "Surviving boot camp was the single overriding goal." But they all realized that there was worse to come down the road, the prospect of death or maiming in the increasingly bloody Pacific war. As Phil Pearce put it: "At Parris Island you realized you were getting closer. And that it would be even faster if you were an officer."

5   The SOCS 400

A Lot of You

Are Not Coming Back

On 5 May 1944 the V-12s, newly graduated from boot camp, rode the train from Parris Island up to Camp Lejeune, the Marine Corps's major East Coast tactical and amphibious training base—the Fleet Marine Force (FMF) Training Command. About sixteen-hundred strong, they were designated as Officer Candidate Applicants (OCA), formed into platoons and companies, and immediately assigned an arduous training regimen while they waited to be transferred to the Officer Candidate Courses (OCC) at Quantico. For two and a half months the OCAs were intensively drilled in small-unit tactics for fire teams, squads, and platoons.[1] They made innumerable training and conditioning marches with full field-transport packs, underwent infantry weapons training and classroom instruction, and spent hours in physical conditioning and running obstacle courses. Many of their marches, small-unit tactics, and map and compass exercises were at night and some field problems lasted three or four days.

They ran a sixteen-hour-day, six-day-a-week schedule, with Sundays clear for checking out the skimpy liberty opportunities in the over-crowded nearby towns or staying on base writing letters, squaring away gear, and recovering from Saturday night liberty, such as it was. They were at Hadnot Point, the mainside base, which after the tents and quonset huts of Parris Island struck them as a lovely installation of large red-brick and white-concrete buildings set in spacious green lawns and many trees.

Most of their instructors in OCA and then in the SOCS were officers and NCOs who had been wounded on Guadalcanal, Bougainville, or Cape Gloucester; many had been decorated, many were haggard, with haunted eyes, and skin yellowed by the quinine and Atabrine they had taken for malaria. Gen. Alexander A. Vandegrift, the commandant of the Marine Corps and the Commanding General (CG) of the 1st Marine Division on Guadalcanal, where he was awarded the Medal of Honor, ordered a number of wounded veterans back to the States to lend their combat experience to the training. It was only a temporary respite, how-ever, as several of the V-12s' boot camp, OCA, and SOCS instructors sub-sequently returned to the Pacific. Some were killed or wounded on Iwo or Okinawa; one of their OCA company commanders, Capt. Carl Con-ron, who won the Navy Cross on Cape Gloucester, was killed on Oki-nawa as a major with 3rd Battalion, 4th Marines.

The class was organized into six platoons and the tone for SOCS member Vilas Young's unit was established early on. Initially, officers were in short supply, and Young's platoon temporarily had a gunnery sergeant as platoon leader. "Gunny Stocks made the 6th platoon what it was," Young recalls. "He was a little, short, stocky fellow with a slight bay window and slightly bald head. He was about 45 years old and had been in the Corps for a long time. His voice resembled a foghorn more closely than any I have ever heard—and he used it constantly."

In the first week Gunny Stocks took the platoon on a night condi-tioning hike with rifles and full packs. They started by running the obstacle course, climbing walls, jumping holes, crossing creeks on logs, climbing ropes, negotiating barbed wire and tunnels, and other obsta-cles. The hike was ten miles, part of which they ran. On the road into camp Gunny Stocks formed them up and began counting cadence as they marched back. "We were all tired but proud that none had given up," Young recalls. "I got a great thrill when the platoon straightened out and began hitting the pavement with our heels. I think the gunny did, too, because he was much warmer toward us from that time on. The

Left to right: *Dan Hurson, John Hyndman, unknown, Lester Hutchcroft, SOCS program, Camp Lejeune, c. August 1944.* DAN HURSON

'spirit' of the 6th platoon was born that night and that spirit was never broken." In addition to his foghorn voice and gung-ho spirit, Gunny Stocks also understood that loyalty runs both ways. "John Terry, a true son of Texas with a nice drawl and an abundance of tall stories with which he entertained us constantly, was about the friendliest guy in the outfit, but was always getting into trouble," Young recalls. "John had to go before the major twice and each time the gunny went with him and saved him from dismissal from the class."

Joe Clement has warm memories of a machine-gun instructor, a 1st Lieutenant Drucker, a Guadalcanal veteran who had been a history teacher in civilian life. "He was the only officer who was trying continuously to raise our spirits," Clement recalls. "His favorite comment was: 'Don't let the bastards get you down.' It helped . . . during our periodic trials with physical and mental exhaustion." On one exercise, Clement's squad was moving through an area of trees and underbrush pocked with potholes filled with brackish water and came to a shallow stream about ten feet wide, which most waded across. One OCA spotted a log that had fallen across it and was tightrope-walking across it when one of the platoon NCOs, who was standing in the stream, reached out and pushed him off. The man floundered in the water for a few seconds and Drucker called the sergeant to one side and quietly reminded him that their mission was to train the troops, not kill them; there were plenty of Japanese waiting to do that.

The intensive infantry training of the prospective officers and gentlemen included a large-scale landing exercise with elements of the 29th Marine Regiment, two battalions of which were being formed up and trained at Lejeune, and became part of the 6th Marine Division on Okinawa. The landing exercise was marked by a number of altercations with the some of the troopers of the 29th Marines, who served as hostiles, or "aggressors" for the OCAs' landing. One of these enlisted men was the journalist and historian William Manchester, a student at Massachusetts State College (now the University of Massachusetts) when the war broke out, who deliberately washed out of Marine OCC at Quantico and wound up on Okinawa with the S-2 section of 3rd Battalion, 29th Marines.

"Hostile was the right word and college boys were not the 29th's idea of prospective officers," George Mayer, a member and chronicler of the class, later wrote in the *Marine Corps Gazette,* the Marine Corps's professional magazine. "The dunes erupted into numerous altercations between the opposing forces. This exercise was probably the turning point that made us warriors." And a good thing, too. There was some irony in these altercations. Most of the SOCS class wound up as infantry platoon leaders on Iwo and Okinawa and several were in the 29th Marines in command of their former "adversaries" in this exercise.

Liberty at Camp Lejeune was (and is) something of a problem. "Lejeune was a flea-bitten place that looked like something the Army had rejected," Gordon Dibble says. Jacksonville, North Carolina, the nearest town, is a drearily typical military-base town dominated by beer joints, pawn shops, and tattoo parlors, and, of course, overrun by servicemen. Liberty call began noon Saturday and many of the candidates would head for the nearby towns. "There was a nice hotel in New Bern and we tried to find girls, but with no luck," Dibble recalls. Wilmington, a town of about forty thousand, was about sixty miles down the coast from Lejeune and was also overcrowded, but some had better luck there and found support from an unexpected and welcome source. "We'd pull liberty at the Cape Fear Hotel in Wilmington and load up the rooms," Mayer recalls. "We partied with women Marines [from Lejeune and the Marine Corps air station at Cherry Point]."

The liberty situation was not helped by the fact that North Carolina, a strongly Baptist state, was generally "dry" at the time. Except for 3.2-beer joints, the bars had to be private clubs. Lejeune itself had relatively nice facilities with several movie theaters, post exchanges, and "slop chutes," outdoor beer gardens for enlisted men old enough to legally drink or able to fake their way to being served.

As a result, some of the class discovered one unintended benefit of their OCA status. They were issued shiny brass OCA pins to wear on the left side of their overseas "fore and aft" caps opposite the globe and anchor emblem. On a hunch, Jim Denebeim hitchhiked to Myrtle Beach, South Carolina, now a major resort area, to check it out as a liberty town and found it to be a big improvement over Jacksonville and Wilmington. Myrtle Beach, however, was about seventy miles south of Wilmington and off-limits to Marines, but on their next liberty Denebeim and five others hitchhiked there anyway. They were headed for the Ocean Forest Hotel that evening and were stopped by Army Air Force MPs who began to question them. When a streetlight reflected off one of their OCA pins, the MPs said, "Sorry, sir, we didn't know you were officers," saluted, and drove off in their jeep. "You can bet that sigh of relief was heard all the way back to Lejeune!" Denebeim recalls. He and his buddies learned their lesson well from that scare—whenever they returned to Myrtle Beach they borrowed more OCA pins and put them on their collars as well.

The OCAs also constituted a cheap labor force between training exercises. They were turned out for three days to fight a forest fire, which on the last night almost proved fatal to the inexperienced Marines. The fire jumped a broad, paved road and a wall of roaring flame almost cut off Joe Clement and several others who were trying to stem it with shovels and axes. At the last moment they were told to evacuate the area and they barely made it; they found several abandoned trucks and bulldozers charred and gutted when they returned the next day. Many also pulled several weeks mess duty. While scrubbing pots and pans in the scullery, Joe, a Texan, was drafted as a butcher by the mess sergeant.[2] "Any of you idiots know anything about being a butcher?" the bandy-legged little sergeant demanded one day. "My grandfather was a butcher and he taught me how to carve and bone meat, sir," Joe responded. "Bone" was the magic word and Joe spent the rest of his mess duty rescued from the scullery and with free access to the sergeant's ice-cream supply in the food freezer.

After nearly two and a half months, the OCAs were assembled on 12 July and informed that because of heavy casualties and expansion of the Corps 430 of them were to be formed into a Special Officer Candidate School (SOCS), which would be convened the following Monday,

17 July, at Camp Lejeune. They were told that the Corps had lost about 450 officers, mostly lieutenants, in the Marianas that summer. Actually, the losses were greater than that. The 2nd and 4th Marine Divisions lost 169 officers KIA and 596 wounded on Saipan and Tinian in June, and the 3rd Division lost nearly 200 officers killed and wounded on Guam in July. The 1st Division would run up a similar butcher's bill on Peleliu in September and October.[3]

Nevertheless, most who were chosen for the SOCS were "overjoyed," in Joe Clement's words—no more waiting to go to Quantico and get into the war. "I think a great part of our exuberance was that we thought we had won the 'game of OCA'—we were the ones selected for this unique SOCS out of the couple of thousand people available. It strengthened the pride and camaraderie between us." Vilas Young recalls, "We went wild! We wouldn't have to go to Quantico! We would get our commissions in September instead of three or four months later. . . . [T]he lucky men were assigned to the SOCS."

They also heard shortly after that every NCO at Lejeune who had any college background was offered the chance to go to OCC at Quantico. In retrospect, some wondered if they would have been so eager if they had stopped to ponder the reason for all this apparent generosity. At the time, however, they were delighted to get going.

Although the demand for second lieutenant platoon leaders increased steadily as the war progressed, the Corps's need for them fluctuated substantially with the fortunes of war. An anticipated shortage of platoon leaders in 1943 didn't materialize so the length of training at Marine Corps Schools (MCS), Quantico, was lengthened, for a while.[4] The Corps's practice of sending its officer candidates through boot camp at Parris Island, then giving them infantry training at Lejeune while they were waiting to go to Quantico, was a way to get their basic training out of the way before they got to Quantico and relieved the pressure on MCS.

On 17 November 1943 the Corps adopted a plan to send 3,600 candidates a year through Quantico in officer candidate classes to be convened every three weeks. In addition to the eight weeks of boot camp and eight weeks of pre–OCC training, they would go through a twelve-week OCC course, be commissioned, then undergo a twelve-week Reserve Officers Course (ROC), a basic infantry officer's course, after commissioning. Candidates selected from the enlisted ranks would go to Quantico for pre-OCC courses; there also were overseas battlefield commissions of Marines who demonstrated leadership in combat. On 22 July 1944, however, the Corps reduced the OCC and ROC courses to ten weeks each to speed up production after the losses in the Marianas. In 1945 the separate OCC and ROC courses were combined into a single sixteen-week Platoon Commanders Course (PCC) at the end of which the candidates were commissioned and sent to the FMF; this was because of the increasing number of lieutenants who had to be decommissioned at the end of ROC because of lack of military aptitude and leadership qualities, a high of 16 percent one month in 1944. Between Pearl Harbor and V-J Day 16,084 candidates were commissioned in the officer training program and the Corps had about 37,000 officers on active duty at war's end.[5]

In addition to casualties, the Corps had to replace second lieutenants who were promoted to captain and major and to man its expansion to six divisions and four air wings. The four and a half months the SOCS class spent at Parris Island and as OCAs gave the Corps time to plan and organize the SOCS program. Early in 1944 General Vandegrift convened a meeting with his top staff in Washington to discuss officer procurement, specifically, second-lieutenant platoon leaders; there were plenty of captains and majors. They quickly determined that training space was the critical need and that Camp Lejeune had plenty of room and facilities to train a class of 400-plus.

Among those at the meeting were Col. Edward W. Snedeker, assistant G-3 for Plans and Policies at Headquarters Marine Corps, Lt. Col. William K. Enright, representing Marine Corps Schools, and Maj. Donald M. Schmuck, the head of Snedeker's Infantry Section.[6] They devoted a great deal of thought to the SOCS curriculum in their many meetings that spring and determined that it would be based on the past two years' combat experience and would focus primarily on infantry tactics. The training in artillery, engineering, communications, naval law, mess management, and other supporting services that were given to the regular classes would not be needed. "We pretty much dispensed with the classrooms after about the first two weeks and spent all the rest of the time in the field," George Mayer recalls. Enright played a crucial role in this because the curriculum at Quantico was being revised to "better root out the fanatical Japanese defenders and reduce the soaring casualty rate" in Mayer's words. Schmuck believes that Enright was the single most important individual in forming the curriculum.

The candidates were given insight into Japanese doctrine. For instance, the Japanese didn't traverse their artillery fire from side to side, they walked it straight ahead back and forth. This observation would save Mayer and about fifteen members of his mortar section on Okinawa when he moved his troops laterally after they came under barrage. Another Japanese practice was placing snipers in trees, a major factor in the early jungle campaigns in the South Pacific. Some forgot that, to their regret, on Okinawa because they weren't thinking in terms of jungle warfare. They also were constantly hectored to put out security quickly after capturing an objective because of the Japanese propensity for prompt counterattacks.

"This training was the single most important contribution to the success of the SOCS," says Mayer. "When executed by the combat personnel under Colonel Fawcett's direction at Camp Lejeune it capped off the all-out effort of everyone involved." Lt. Col. Marion A. Fawcett was commanding officer of the SOCS, which was run by the Schools Regiment, FMF Training Command at Camp Lejeune.[7] Vandegrift ordered that whatever personnel and equipment needed be supplied on a priority basis, which was guaranteed when Schmuck suggested that he put this in the form of a directive. This made it clear that the program was being closely watched by the commandant and headed off any attempts at delay or empire building or to grab individual members of the class, such as football players for the Camp Lejeune team; Mayer had played at Colgate and was approached by a Lejeune coach. They all went to the Pacific. Mayer credits Schmuck with being "the catalyst in the success of our program."[8]

Schmuck hit on the idea of searching for the right place and the instructors to train them while they were in boot camp at Parris Island. The veterans of the early Pacific campaigns were obvious choices as instructors. The members of the class chosen from the pool of OCAs had completed most of the required course work for their degrees, seniors along with a few graduate students.[9]

The Marine Corps had good material to work with. Most of the SOCS members' General Classification Test (GCT) scores were well above the minimum of 120 (roughly equivalent to IQ test scores), with many above 145 and some as high as 170. They were also in superb physical condition after their months of rigorous training. Joe Clement was assigned as clerk in the duty room one day, an easy day off, and overheard two instructors, who were captains, talking about the class. "You know, these people are in better shape than any damn group I have ever seen," one said to the other. At the time, Joe was 6 feet 2 and weighed 175 pounds; when he returned from overseas in 1946 he weighed 205 as a result of his less physically demanding occupation duties.

There was a downside to this rigorous schedule of sixteen-hour days and six hours of sleep in a course that wound up with a fifty-mile continuous march, however. "When the doctors gave us our commissioning physicals, they said we were the most rundown guys physically they'd seen," Mayer says. "The Marine Corps put us through a crucible before we got to the one in the Pacific." In retrospect, some had questions as to whether their training in the traditional small-unit fire and maneuver tactics really prepared them for what they encountered with the interconnecting bunkers, caves, and tunnels on Iwo and Okinawa.

Marius L. "Mo" Bressoud Jr. received the Purple Heart as a platoon leader with Company I, 3rd Battalion, 7th Marines on Okinawa. For a brief few days in early June of 1945 there was maneuver and movement as the Japanese retreated from Shuri Castle to their final defense line. "On the road to Itoman (a town south of Shuri) we fought my kind of war," he wrote. "At least it was the war for which I had been trained at Camp Lejeune. . . . The Japanese cooperated in ensuring the similarity by scattering snipers and light machine gun units in precisely the same kinds of locations that our SOCS instructors placed the Marines who played 'enemy' as we advanced . . . through North Carolina's coastal piney woods." Of course, the Japanese didn't fire blanks, and the brutal war of attrition started up again on that last defensive line.

That was in the unknown future, however. Monday, 17 July 1944, was the first day of the SOCS and the class was welcomed with what Joe Clement considered an "inspirational" speech by Maj. Gen. John Marston, Commanding General of the Training Command, who had been CG of the 2nd Marine Division in 1942 and 1943. They spent their first three weeks in the SOCS at Hadnot Point, then moved into brick barracks at the rifle range twenty-five miles away, where they stayed the rest of their time at Lejeune, undergoing their field training in the mosquito- and poison ivy-infested pine forests and swamps. They had mosquito nets and repellent but the insects speared them through their dungarees. "I have no doubt that every man in the class gave more blood to the mosquitoes than any civilian did to the Red Cross," Vilas Young recalls ruefully. The rifle-range barracks looked fine at first glance, but inside they looked like they had been "commandeered from some hog farmer," according to Joe Clement. "However, the Corps had brought in its experts at cleaning up that type of situation," he noted. They certainly were—they had gotten lots of experience with "field days" in their squad bays at Parris Island.

They also were introduced to the unpredictability of warfare. One group led by Craig "Tuffy" Leman, who won the Silver Star and Purple

Heart on Iwo, got a particularly graphic lesson in this on a field problem. "My platoon was going up against an ambush set up by overseas returnees (instructors) near the waterfront," Leman recalls. "I was the fire team leader of the point unit and we were fired upon. The point man hit the deck and I saw a low concrete wall a few yards to our right and waved Paul Koppitz and Jack Lowry to take cover behind it, as that was the only cover in sight." Koppitz and Lowry leaped the wall and there was a splashing noise, followed by groans and imprecations. They stood up floundering and covered to the waist with brown slime. They had jumped into a sewage lagoon.

"Sergeant Buckins, a large and good-natured instructor whom we called 'Bubbles,' came over to help and grabbed Lowry by the arm, but dropped him as soon as he got a whiff and realized what had happened," Leman recalls. Fortunately they were near the water. The two unfortunates went to the bay and washed off, but Lowry had dropped his rifle and had to go back to fish for it—unsuccessfully. Lowry received the Purple Heart on Iwo with the 5th Marine Division, Koppitz was wounded on Okinawa with the 1st Division.

There was no interruption for mess duty and other work details as when they were OCAs, but the training day ran from 0730 to 2045. "Stream crossings at night were routine; 50 miles of continuous marching and assaulting fortified positions with live ammunition were also commonplace," Mayer recounts. "Assault, dig in, put out security, read maps, compass marches at night, live mortar fire, and machine-gun fire on our front, too close for comfort many times. We got to know the mortar thump, the crack of rifle fire, and much more about fatigue. The complete absence of parades and rifle inspections was a surprise to all of us."

"Almost every day, rain or shine, found us out in the boondocks creeping and crawling, slipping and sliding, sweating and cussing," Young recalls. "Every day except Sundays we ran, walked, and crawled over the hills and swamps of North Carolina. I got tired, my buddies got tired, our instructors got tired—we were all tired, but we had to keep going. They kept pounding into our heads, 'You've got to be in physical condition to lead men. . . . You are a leader. You must be able to lead.'"

The class was drilled in offensive and defensive tactics, scouting and patrolling, combat intelligence, map reading, stream crossing, field fortifications, and "technique of rifle fire." They fired the Browning .30-caliber machine gun, the 60-mm mortar, the Browning automatic rifle, and the 2.36-inch rocket launcher, an antitank weapon popularly known as the "bazooka," which they were to employ primarily against caves and bunker apertures.[10] Joe Clement hit a rusted old tank frame on the live firing range from about a hundred yards with his first two rounds. They were surprised at how accurate the machine gun could be and impressed by its fire power. After familiarization with about 400 rounds each on the thousand-inch range, each got to fire half a belt, 125 rounds, across the firing range toward a copse of small pines about a hundred yards away. Some quickly cut the six-inch trees in half, which prompted an order: "Stop desecrating the forests!"

In all their exercises they rotated as fire-team, squad, and platoon leaders and their leadership was graded with written chits. "It was always quite disconcerting while acting in a position of responsibility to see an instructor looking directly at you and writing in his chit book," says Young. "We learned later that most of the chits we saw written were only bluffs to spur us on."

In addition to their exhaustive physical, tactical, and weapons training, the prospective lieutenants had the importance of leadership constantly drilled into them. As Mayer wrote:

> The special OCS instructors made it clear that the troops were our responsibility *at all times.* . . . it was made clear to us that the troops expected second lieutenants to lead. "Follow me" was the order of the day. . . . When we hit the lines we were in charge of our platoon or section. We were getting paid to lead! . . . The essence of this class was its honorable observance of duty as front-line platoon and section leaders on Okinawa and Iwo Jima. We had been apprised of the kind of leadership that would be required of our class. . . . One of the most remarkable things about this class was the large number of men who carried out their responsibilities as "warriors" with quiet determination. . . . We were told that we had to assume leadership on the lines from Day One. It was expected of us. It was accomplished. . . . "Follow me" was a way of life. . . . Lead! Lead!! That's what you are paid for. . . . T]he troops are your responsibility; know them and know their problems; take care of them and they will take care of you.[11]

Mayer contends that a majority of the class members who were killed were victims in part of the sketchy training many of the later replacement troops received due to the pressure of mounting casualties. "Many were killed by snipers, maybe as many as 65 percent, because they were standing (and exposing themselves to fire) while directing their troops." This wasn't as necessary with the better trained men originally in the ranks.

Pfc. Eugene Sledge, known affectionately to his comrades as "Sledgehammer," developed a somewhat different view of second-lieutenant platoon leaders. Sledge's detailed and perceptive memoir, *With the Old Breed: At Peleliu and Okinawa,* is one of the best ground-level accounts of infantry combat ever written. A V-12 who dropped out of the program at Georgia Tech in order to get to the war (and went on to get a Ph.D. in biology after the war), Sledge wound up as a 60-mm mortar man with Company K, 5th Marines on Peleliu and Okinawa. Sledge became an astute and knowledgeable observer of the murderous nature of the war in the Pacific as the Japanese dug in for a war of attrition. Sledge described his company commander on Okinawa giving his lieutenants their orders for an attack in early May:

> The senior NCOs and the veteran officers stood by with serious, sometimes worried expressions as they listened. Those of us in the ranks watched their familiar faces carefully for signs of what was in store for us. The faces of the replacement lieutenants reflected a different mood. They showed enthusiastic, animated expressions with eyebrows raised in eager anticipation of seeing the thing through. . . . They were very conscientious and determined to do their best or die in the effort. . . . During the course of the long fighting on Okinawa, unlike at Peleliu, we got numerous replacement lieutenants. They were wounded or killed with such regularity that we rarely knew anything about them other than a code name and saw them on their feet only once or twice. We expected heavy losses of enlisted men in combat, but our officers got hit so soon and so often that it seemed to me the position of second lieutenant in a rifle company had been made obsolete by modern warfare.[12]

Sledge was talking about the SOCS. Six class members were platoon leaders in Sledge's company. One, Duncan M. Crane, was killed and four were wounded. Mayer suggests that the tactics of attrition, particularly on Okinawa, were what was obsolete.

As grueling as the training was, the "harassment and chickenshit level," as one class member put it, was low and the candidates knew why: they had already been culled by the V-12 program and boot camp and the Marines needed them as cannon fodder in the Pacific. "There was a good atmosphere at Lejeune because they wanted as many good officers as possible," according to Mayer. As a result, he added, some of the class had something of "a blow it out your ass attitude" during the final weeks of the course. Others, like Young, however, recall that seeing the seemingly distant and elusive prize of gold bars appear within reach induced anxiety. "Hidden under a show of bravado, each of us was deathly afraid we might do something to endanger our chance of graduating," he wrote. "This was the last lap. As far as we were concerned the

Break time on a field problem, Camp Lejeune, summer 1944. Left to right: *Gordon Dibble, Rawle Deland, Melvin Dacus, and Scott Day.* BILL DITTO

world began with our commissioning, just as surely as it would end if we failed." But many, probably most, like Mark Clement, drew strength and reassurance from their rigorous screening and training: "It was there that I got to find out if the Marine Corps thought I was capable of leading company level Marines in combat."

There were a number of dropouts, and 372 were commissioned on 30 September, with one more, J. D. Eppright, commissioned nearly three weeks later on 19 October when he turned nineteen, the minimum age for an officer; he wound up with the 1st Marine Division on occupation duty in northern China. The training schedule for the week of 14 August shows 426 under instruction. Most of the nearly sixty left behind were for medical reasons, illnesses such as pneumonia, and injuries, and most later went on to Quantico and a regular OCC. One of the most bizarre of the injuries was suffered by a candidate whose patella was slashed and shredded on the sharp end of a sapling that had been cut off with a machete and was under the swampy water when he and his squad were making a crossing. Surgeons had to remove half the damaged patella.

On 28 September the survivors picked up their new officers' uniforms from the tailors and were promoted to the permanent rank of platoon sergeant, with much being made at the ceremony of the honor and duty inherent in that rank. "At the time I thought these points were primarily rhetorical," said Mo Bressoud. "Later in combat, they were confirmed—and escalated." Two days later, on Saturday, 30 September 1944, after eight months of rigorous training at Parris Island and Lejeune, the 372 survivors of the sorting-out process were commissioned as second lieutenants. It was a bright, clear day and the class marched to the rifle-range theater in their newly tailored summer officers' uniforms, carrying their officers' barracks caps and gold bars. One after the other they mounted the stage to receive their commissions and a congratulatory handshake from the featured speaker, Brig. Gen. Gerald C. Thomas, the Marine Corps G-3, who had been operations officer (D-3) of the 1st Marine Division on Guadalcanal (and a future assistant commandant of the Marine Corps). The lucky ones whose families and sweethearts lived close enough to make the trip had their bars pinned on by mothers or girlfriends; the others pinned them on each other. Then they went out into the street to encounter a waiting crowd of enlisted men, each prepared to carry out the Corps tradition of paying a dollar to the one who tendered him his first salute.

Most spent some time calling their families and girlfriends. Some went to celebrate at the Camp Lejeune officers' club, which was crowded. Some went into Jacksonville, others made it down to Wilmington, and all found slim pickings. One group in Jacksonville was turned away from the USO because they were no longer enlisted men and wound up at one of the state liquor stores where everything was labeled: "Private Stock. This whiskey is less than one year old. It is colored and flavored with wood chips." Nevertheless, they drank it and spent the night in a rooming house in Jacksonville, counting it a blessing that the only damage the rotgut inflicted was hangovers of varying severity.

Wherever they went, they struggled back to their barracks on Sunday morning to be greeted by the word that the Sabbath was not to be a day of rest and recuperation. They'd already been told that half of them would undergo a three-week Reserve Officers Course (ROC) at Camp Pendleton, California. The other half would take their ROC course at Lejeune, then go out to Pendleton, where they would be formed into replacement drafts for the Pacific. Those ticketed for Pendleton were informed that their troop movement was to be at 1800 that day. They spent the day frantically packing uniforms and other personal gear, standing in line to draw field gear including M-1 carbines, and get the requisite forms and papers signed in preparation for boarding the train to the West Coast.

As a sobering counterpoint to the celebration of their hard-won goal—commissions in the Marine Corps—General Thomas welcomed them into the officer corps with an ominous note: "A lot of you aren't coming back." Not surprisingly, this shook up some of the new lieutenants, but most handled it in typical fashion—they kidded about it.

6 To Westward

For Duty Beyond the Seas

With Thomas's cheery words in their ears, 186 of the new lieutenants, half the graduating class of 372, were loaded aboard a train a little more than twenty-four hours after their commissioning ceremony. They were bound for Camp Pendleton, California, the Marines' major West Coast base, where they would stage to the Pacific. The other half of the class stayed at Lejeune where they were given the Reserve Officer Course (ROC) for new second lieutenants and went to Pendleton later in smaller groups.

Their cross-country treks were classic wartime troop-train movements, lasting five to seven days depending on how often they were sidetracked for higher priority traffic. The trip gave most of the new officers their first real look at the huge, enormously diverse nation they were putting their lives on the line for. Their routes took them through Georgia, Alabama, Louisiana, Texas, New Mexico, and Arizona, on to Los Angeles or San Diego, and finally to Pendleton, a huge, sprawling base on the Pacific coast whose southern end is just thirty miles north of San Diego. Melvin O. "Mo" Dacus, who wound up with Weapons Company, 23rd Marines on Iwo, had the bad luck to have demonstrated leadership qualities that led Colonel Fawcett to pick him as the train detachment commander. "Mo should have gotten the Navy Cross—*at least*—for getting all the group to our new (duty) station in one piece—it wasn't exactly a dry trip," Joe Clement remarked later.

Although they knew their destination, details of the route apparently were classified as a military secret. On the first day they rolled through the red-dirt cotton and tobacco fields of the Carolinas and Georgia into Alabama where Vulcan, the God of Steel, gazed down on them from the hills south of Birmingham. The next morning they had breakfast while crossing Lake Pontchartrain just north of New Orleans; hopes of a liberty call in the Crescent City were unrealized and they had to settle for a thirty-minute stop on the far outskirts of the city. They proceeded up the east bank of the Mississippi to Baton Rouge, running between the river levee and vast stretches of flat cane fields and swamps. They had lunch while crossing the river on a ferry. Vilas Young, a farm boy from Ridgeway, Missouri, which is northeast of St. Joseph near the Iowa line, recalls his feeling about the big river: "I looked at that muddy water with almost a feeling of reverence. Some of that (an infinitesimal amount, to be sure) might have fallen on, and run off, the farm up in Missouri."

They crossed the terraced rice fields (the first terraced flat fields Young had ever seen) of western Louisiana, which were dotted with shocks of harvested rice and towns with French names. They crossed the Sabine River into Texas that evening, which evoked a rousing cheer from the Lone Star contingent. They passed through Houston during the night and awoke the next morning near Temple, 125 miles south of Dallas, headed northwest toward the Texas Panhandle. "I'll never argue with anyone about the size of that state," says Young. "It is big and with a great variety. We passed through cotton country, wheat country, cattle country. . . . That afternoon we started running into the wide open spaces for which the West is famous—long miles without seeing anything but scrubby brush and a few cattle here and there."

The train entered New Mexico at Clovis during the night. The next day Young began to understand the hold the great Southwest has on the people who live there. The train rolled through vast stretches of sagebrush and mesquite and along dry arroyos, winding around high, flat-topped mesas sculpted out of a vast plain by millennia of wind and water erosion of the sandy, arid soil. "To a boy from the Midwest those mesas looked like mountains," Young recalls. "You get the feeling that this kind of vastness could go on forever. . . . You no more than get past the corner of one mesa until another, or many more just like it, moves into view. You look through the gaps between the mesas and see fifty or a hundred miles." Young found the nights, if anything, even more impressive. "Those stars, brighter than they ever looked at home, looked as though they were just out of reach—some of them so low they were cut off from view by the huge, now shapeless, mesas and hills. . . . [R]arely did I find myself sufficiently bored to turn away from the indescribable views and lose myself in a book or magazine."

There were a few signs of humans. There were occasional clusters of ranch buildings and a corral in the shade of trees next to a stream. Once in a while a horseman riding through the sagebrush would wave his hat at them. There were Indians and Mexicans in the small towns and on the railroad section gangs; the Marines would open the windows and shout greetings at the workers, sometimes in Spanish—*"buenas dias"* and *"buenas tardes."* "Those workers were as tough looking as any crew I ever hope to meet, but when we passed, their dark, homely faces, above dirty red neckerchiefs and nondescript clothing, would break into wide grins," Young recalls. Some of the lieutenants, detraining in Albuquerque, were surprised to learn that the local populace didn't recognize their Marine uniforms—they were asked if they were Canadians.

They weren't supposed to leave the train, a proscription that was observed with about the same fidelity as the Volstead Act and in the same context. By the end of their first day on the train they had organized themselves into committees to get ice, mix, liquor, beer, and food. At each stop some debarked to "refuel" at nearby liquor stores, buy food, and flirt with the local girls. They frequently shared their supplies with soldiers on Army troop trains that were stopped in the same marshaling yards; at one stop outside New Orleans Joe Clement was seen pouring into the soldiers' paper cups from a gallon jug of bourbon. This was a significant contribution to interservice harmony and the grateful "doggies" concluded that the "jar-head lieutenants" sure were "regular guys." Occasionally some laggards had close calls with missing the train when it pulled out but somehow always managed to catch up with it. At a number of stops some of the contingent returned to the train with pretty Southern belles who hung on their arms and gave them lingering farewell kisses, to the amazement and envy of their fellows who marveled at what fast workers these Southerners were. They didn't learn until later that the charmers in question were girlfriends who were following the train.

Military police and other authorities along the way occasionally managed to confiscate their liquor supplies but most efforts failed primarily because the Marines paid the porters to hide the booze in their personal lockers; whenever the MPs boarded the train they were told that they could search anywhere but the porters' private quarters and lockers. In a restaurant at a meal stop near Flagstaff, Arizona, an Army MP determined that some of the lieutenants were somewhat under the influence and called ahead to Kingman. The contraband was safely stowed by the porters, but the precaution was for naught. "The train just roared on through Kingman at about 70 miles per hour and didn't stop," recalls Joe Clement. "The only casualty was an unopened bottle of Golden Wedding bourbon I had purchased during our short stop earlier in New Orleans. It was broken." The MPs in Kingman apparently learned from the experience, however, and some later groups lost supplies to the searches.

They awoke the next morning, the final day of their trek, with the train crawling down the coast south from Los Angeles in the dark fog typical of Southern California at that time of year. By 9 A.M., when they arrived at the small station at San Onofre at the north end of Camp Pendleton, the sun had burned the fog off. The sparkling blue Pacific was on their right, Pendleton's hills, some brown with grass from the dry summer and fall seasons, some blackened by brushfires, were on their left. The hills were marked by what appeared to be broad roads leading to their peaks but actually were firebreaks. After a long delay, trucks arrived to take them to Camp San Onofre, a primitive facility informally known as "Tent Camp 2," where they would undergo their ROC.[1]

The rest of the class followed generally the same routes and had the same experiences. Hugh "Bud" Morris was one of those. At the end of October he was named troop train commander of a contingent of about five hundred Marines leaving Wilmington, North Carolina, for Pendleton. The kitchen car didn't work and although railroad officials assured him that the troops somehow would be fed he made his first command decision. He stationed half the group in front of the train and half behind it so it couldn't move. The kitchen was fixed in about two hours and the train rolled south and west through the Texas Panhandle to San Diego. These later detachments were in smaller groups assigned to two or three cars that hooked onto westbound trains, most of which also had civilian passengers. Because of delays in making connections their trips

generally took a day or two longer than the first group's. One detachment had a long-enough stopover in Memphis to enable them to call the
registrar of Southeastern College and arrange to take forty-two coeds
out to dinner. Some were subsequently told that their connections
delayed them long enough to miss drafts for Iwo and that they were
assigned to the Okinawa divisions instead.

A few were lucky enough to meet women bound for Los Angeles
whom they looked up after they settled into Pendleton. "Several of us
were wandering through the train seeing who was in the regular Pull-
man cars ahead of us," recalls Bill Ditto, who wound up as an 81-mm
mortar officer in 2nd Battalion, 7th Marines. "Bob DeLong (Company
A, 1st Marines) and I happened to sit down and strike up a conversation
with a lady by the name of Thelma Carr. Thelma was in her late thirties,
but was very friendly and told us all about the West Coast. At a quick
stop, we managed to run out and get some sandwiches and bring them
back to her and this started a long friendship. Later, Thelma would let
us come to her apartment, which was located right in the middle of Hollywood, and use her facilities for staying there while we went out on the
town. She introduced us to some very nice people."

Camp Pendleton is named for Maj. Gen. Joseph H. Pendleton, a
World War I officer who between the world wars became known as the
father of the Marine Corps's activities on the West Coast. Originally a
Spanish land grant, Camp Pendleton was known as the Rancho Santa
Margarita y Flores when the Marine Corps acquired its 130,000 acres in
1942 as its major West Coast training and staging base; the original
Spanish-style ranch house serves as the hospitality and reception center. It is bounded on the west by the Pacific Ocean. Stretching eighteen
miles south to north from Oceanside to San Onofre and about fifteen
miles east to west at its widest, it has a seemingly infinite number of hills
to climb, plus ample room for maneuvering and live firing ranges for
artillery, tanks, mortars, and rockets. It is ideal for training because it
features a varied topography—beaches, steep-sided canyons running
into the high cliffs above the beaches, rolling hills, mountains, broad
valleys, and wooded areas with swampy stream beds and undergrowth.
Mainside is at the southern end of the camp, near Oceanside, with tent
camps for training regiments and battalions scattered to the north.

Most of the new lieutenants detrained at San Onofre and were
trucked the three or four miles to their dusty, wind-swept tent camp,
where they endured primitive living quarters including outdoor cold-
water showers. Even for men who hadn't exactly lolled in the lap of lux-

ury over the past couple of years, the little dustbowl known as Tent
Camp 2 was something of a comedown. The trucks that picked up the
large first group wound slowly up into the hills, through a large truck
farm and gladiolus field the Marine Corps had leased to civilian farmers,
before depositing their cargo, still in brand-new officers' greens and
low-cut dress shoes, at their new home, which was still in the process of
being erected and by no means an appropriate venue for such attire. A
warrant officer met them and led them past row after row of quonset
huts to a group of newly erected tents perched precariously on a hillside. "These will be your home for the next few weeks," he informed
them.

So much for being officers and gentlemen. "One hundred and eighty-
six pairs of eyes gaped in awe at the sight," Vilas Young recalls. "Where
were those beautiful BOQs [bachelor officers' quarters] we had expected?
. . . Perhaps this was to so thoroughly disgust us with stateside duty that
we would not pine for it later. The tents were barely standing. They had
no decks or lights. Dust from the camp was already coloring the canvas."
In Southern California's semi-arid Mediterranean climate, dust is a constant mess-mate.

With a minimum of order and maximum of confusion, in Young's
words, the officers and gentlemen were organized into platoons and
assigned tents. Then they were ordered to grab their mess kits and
march to noon chow. For three weeks they marched half a mile three
times a day to stand in line and dine in an open tent just as they had in
boot camp and SOCS—the only difference was that as officers they now
had to pay for their meals. Cold was another companion; the days are
generally warm year-round in Southern California, but in winter the
tropical current that warms the ocean shifts away from the coastline and
the water is too cold for swimming; the on-shore breezes that blow up at
night are raw and penetrating. They produce impenetrable fogs when
they hit the warm land and make a comfortable night's sleep in tents
problematic. The camp water supply was a wooden tank on a hill and its
only warming was from the sun's rays. Like English schoolboys, they
became inured to, if not accepting of, showering and shaving in ice-cold
water.[2]

The three-week Reserve Officer Courses at Pendleton and Lejeune were abbreviated versions of the ten-week course the OCC classes
at Quantico went through after commissioning. They emphasized platoon and squad-sized assaults on bunkers, pillboxes, and other fortifications, supporting arms, particularly machine guns and mortars, and

conditioning marches. The lieutenants sometimes found it hard to take the ROC seriously, for several reasons—they had already undergone a great deal of such training, they were considerably disgruntled by their living conditions, and many of their instructors were themselves brand-new second lieutenants fresh from Quantico.

Nevertheless, the time when they would assume responsibility for rifle platoons worked to greatly concentrate their minds, as did such incidents as a class on demolitions—TNT blocks, primacord, and grenades—they would use in combat. The lieutenant conducting the class was demonstrating how to disassemble a grenade and change its fuse delay time from five seconds to three, to prevent the Japanese from throwing it back at them. When there wasn't time to do this, he demonstrated pulling the pin, releasing the spoon, holding the grenade for two seconds, then throwing it. Unfortunately in demonstrating this, he lost track of which grenades were which and picked one whose fuse he had cut to three seconds. He held it for two seconds and threw it. Fortunately, it didn't ignite the supply of explosives stacked in front of him, which probably would have ended the war for him and most of the class right there. But it was a dramatic and valuable lesson to keeping one's mind focused at all times, particularly around explosives. Keep track of them and take nothing for granted, including the assumption that all grenades have five-second fuse trains.

After the ROC course, many of the SOCS members—both those in the first group and the others arriving after the ROC at Lejeune—were assigned to the infantry training regiment at Camp San Onofre and given platoons of replacement troops fresh out of boot camp in San Diego. "We had a good group of boys in the company, most of them being fresh from boot camp," recalls Young. "The NCOs were experienced men and helped immeasurably." The new lieutenants conducted rifle and equipment layout ("junk on the bunk") inspections, the first time they had been on the giving end of these rituals. In some cases they were inspecting staff NCOs, many of whom were combat veterans. But they quickly picked up the knack.

They also found that the new Marines had only had lectures about infantry tactics and were eager to put their knowledge into practice. "I talked to the company about combat and night patrol for about an hour and then let them practice what I had told them," Young recalls. "That was when I really appreciated those NCOs. They probably all knew more about patrols than I, and they really ran the boys ragged. But they liked it! . . . This was their first chance to try out what they had only heard about. When I promised to try to get some blank ammo for them to practice with they cheered."

Some of their trainees were Navajo, who were used extensively on Iwo and Okinawa as "code-talkers" on the field radios and telephones. The Navajo language was one code the Japanese couldn't hope to break, and the code-talkers devised code words of their own for important items to further mask crucial information. When five of them didn't get back from weekend liberty until Monday afternoon, Bill Ditto, who commanded their training company, had to decide how to discipline them. He didn't believe their leader's story—although he was a son of a chief—that they walked back from Los Angeles, but could see nothing to be gained by putting them in the brig, so he restricted them to base for the balance of their training and returned them to duty.[3]

Other class members were sent down to mainside to await orders for overseas and were reintroduced to running water and flush toilets in their BOQs; the fact that those hastily constructed wartime frame buildings seemed luxurious spoke volumes about Tent Camp 2. Every day runners would arrive at the tents in Tent Camp 2 or the wooden buildings at mainside with orders for various of them to report to replacement drafts. That meant a stand-by to rise at 0230 and make ready to board trucks to San Diego at 0630.

In the meantime, at the end of the workday, they changed into their greens and walked or hitchhiked to catch the train at San Onofre, or bummed rides with the few who had cars to nearby San Clemente, Laguna Beach, or Los Angeles, where they sought out the abundant single women. Even on weeknights, they often would rent a hotel room in San Clemente or Laguna Beach, where they could shave and shower and then kick the gong around in the local bars and restaurants till the wee hours before returning to the tent camp for two or three hours sleep. "I think the instructors were bored, too, because they never complained about the amount of sleeping in class," says Young.

Red Qualls and Bill Peterson, who would be together on Iwo in the 9th Marines, bought a 1940 De Soto in Los Angeles, chipping in to make a four-hundred-dollar down payment. Red concluded that they paid too much for it and heard later that their dealer had been charged with cheating servicemen. "You couldn't get over the hills at Camp Pendleton in it without shifting into low gear," he recalls. "A tire blew out and he never did give us the radio he promised." Although he only recalls making a couple of runs to Los Angeles in it—"We didn't use all the gas rationing coupons my dad gave me"—the car was in constant use.

Someone borrowed it every night. Milt Raphael, another classmate who was with Red in the 9th Marines (and also with him in the 1st Tank Battalion in Korea in 1951 and 1952), borrowed it for his wedding. When they shipped out to the Pacific, Red turned the car over to his sister, who sold it back to the dealer and sent him and Bill Peterson each a check for about a hundred dollars, which arrived while they were on Guam staging for Iwo.

Jack Lauck and three or four buddies would walk, or hitchhike if they were lucky, to catch the train or bus at San Onofre for Los Angeles after they'd secured for the weekend on noon Saturday. Their hotel in Los Angeles was the Clark, which was downtown near the bus terminal and one of the big famous-name hotels. It also had the virtue of always being available. "We'd go into the lobby, get on a pay phone, and call the desk to make a reservation," Lauck recalls. "We'd wait a few minutes, then go to the desk and get the room. We'd look around town, have din-

2nd Lts. William Peterson and James "Red" Qualls in Los Angeles before shipping out to Guam and Iwo Jima, October 1944. RED QUALLS

ner and spend the night, then after lunch on Sunday the bus from L.A. to San Diego would drop us off at San Onofre. We'd generally walk, we were never lucky enough to catch a ride, to Tent Camp 2, and would be back in plenty of time to get squared away for Monday morning."

Many were married and had their wives in San Diego, Los Angeles, or the small coastal towns such as Oceanside and San Clemente in between. Some got married in the base chapel at Pendleton, often one right after another, using the same chaplain, flowers, and organist. One of them, Jim Banta of Grand Rapids, Michigan, recalls one event: "Sonny [Horace Johnson, who got the Purple Heart on Iwo and the Navy Cross in Korea] and Kitty were married at the same time as Jan and I in the chapel at Camp Pendleton on October 21, 1944. Bill Baker, who was KIA on Iwo, was also married at the same time. We all used the same flowers and decorations. They had been arranged for by a woman Marine stationed at Pendleton who had been a high school classmate of mine. Jan and I still remember a great weekend spent with Sonny and Kitty in L.A. just before we shipped out." Another class member, Richard P. Berry, who was waiting his turn was victimized by friends who jokingly told him that the bridal overture being played was for his ceremony. When Berry, who was awarded the Purple Heart on Okinawa with 1st Battalion, 7th Marines, stepped into the room next to the altar he was astonished to see a strange woman at the rear of the chapel ready to begin her march down the aisle. Two class members, Bob Euler and John Ware, both of whom won the Purple Heart with the 4th Division on Iwo, had buddies cover for them at roll call one day while they were in Laguna Beach getting married.

Joe and Mark Clement's mother visited them in California before their departure. She said goodbye to her sons at Camp Pendleton in a driving rainstorm and took a taxi back to Los Angeles. In the lobby of the Biltmore Hotel, just before she left to catch a flight back to Dallas, she encountered a group of Marine lieutenants. One, Darrell Clemmer, was Mark's roommate at Pendleton and Mrs. Clement gave him a letter to hand-deliver to Mark and Joe. Clemmer subsequently was severely wounded in the upper right arm on Iwo, which ended a promising baseball career.

Gordon Dibble also took his ROC training at Pendleton. His father made it out to California from Topeka to see him before he went overseas. Mr. Dibble got a flight as far as Las Vegas, then went on to San Diego where he stayed with a niece. Her husband worked for Convair, the big aircraft manufacturer that built the B-24 Liberator.

Those pleasant memories were fleeting.

Their replacement drafts to the divisions in the Pacific were soon formed up, and after shipping their officers' winter green and summer worsted uniforms home, they stowed their dungarees, khakis, and field gear in their seabags and val-packs and boarded ship in San Diego harbor "for duty beyond the seas," as their orders read. In November and December, one ship after another, including Navy personnel transports, known as Assault Personnel Auxiliary (APA), Liberty ships, and converted civilian ocean liners, weighed anchor. The ships slipped away from their piers at the main Navy base, circled north around North Island Naval Air Station, followed the channel south to the mouth of the harbor, circled the end of Point Loma, which forms the harbor, and breasted the Pacific's long, rolling tide, heading west to the war. About 175 went to the 1st, 2nd, and 6th Divisions for the Okinawa campaign, about 125 went to the three divisions on Iwo Jima, the 3rd, 4th, and 5th. The others were assigned to billets with FMFPAC, Admiral Nimitz's headquarters on Guam, V Amphibious Corps units, MP and engineer battalions, or were delayed and joined their divisions after the battles for Iwo and Okinawa were over.

Left to right: *Clarence J. "Lou" Louviere and John H. "Jack" Lauck, at a nightclub in Los Angeles, October 1944.* JACK LAUCK

Most were given command of platoons in their replacement drafts. Some made detours to San Francisco, some stopped in Hawaii and the Marshalls or the Marianas en route to their destinations. They underwent the traditional initiation ceremony for "Pollywogs" at the hands of the "Shellbacks" of "King Neptune" and his court when they made their first crossing of the International Date Line, the 180th meridian, about fifteen-hundred nautical miles west of the Hawaiian Islands. This rite consists primarily of old salts who have made the crossing playing Neptune and his consort and court, dressed in outlandish costumes and headgear and carrying tridents, wands, swords, and other accouterments. They presided while the greenhorns had their heads shaved while sitting in a hinged chair and then were dumped, fully clothed, into a huge tub of cold seawater. This entitled them to a certificate signed by the ship's captain certifying that they were now officially Shellbacks.

The ships followed a zigzag course across the Pacific, but the only actual peril was that perpetual bête noire of amphibious troops, seasickness. Most of the vessels carried three thousand men or more, few of whom were seasoned sailors, and those who ran into storms had periods of something close to horror in their hot, airless, densely packed troop holds, where they lay on canvas bunks five and six tiers high with little more than two feet clearance between them. The only virtue of the storms is that most were short-lived and many of the drafts didn't encounter them.

Jack Lauck had a somewhat circuitous path to the 5th Marine Division. He was assigned to the 5th Division's 27th Replacement Draft but, due to a shortage of berthing on the converted French liner *Rochambeau,* he was shipped to Hawaii, along with about three dozen others, with a 4th Division draft aboard an APA, the *General McClellan.* After a detour to San Francisco, the group arrived at the 4th Division's base on Maui on Thanksgiving Day and spent about ten days there with the 24th Marines, who badly wanted them as replacements after Saipan and Tinian. The Marine Corps, however, had ticketed Lauck and his companions for the 5th Division and others for the 4th Division. "We would have liked to stay with the 4th Division because we'd gotten to know the guys in the draft, but Headquarters Marine Corps informed them that the drafts had been allocated to the divisions and that was that," Lauck says. What HQMC wants, HQMC gets. "It was kind of uncomfortable because we ate in the Headquarters Battalion officers mess, as did General Cates [Clifton B. Cates, the division CG] and Colonel Pollock [Edwin A. Pollock, the division D-3, or operations officer]. They'd been hit hard on

Saipan and when they saw two or three dozen warm new bodies they wanted to keep us."

Finally, Lauck and the others got an overnight passage on a pineapple boat to the big island of Hawaii and the 5th Division. "The crew was a rough lot who tried to entice us into poker games," Lauck recalls, but what he most vividly remembers about the trip was sleeping on the deck topside under the stars of a beautiful Pacific night, and the boat's unusual head, a wooden plank on a two-by-four frame attached to the railing on the starboard side near the fantail. "You made sure you kept a good grip on the ship's metal railing," Lauck recalls. "If you thought the Parris Island heads were a blast with the gushing water running through a trough underneath you, imagine the sensation with a beautiful blue Pacific rushing by your backside some 30 feet below you, your feet on a two-by-four bracing hanging over the side of the ship." It was a relief to finally arrive at Hilo, where they were billeted at the Naval Air Station. Because the 5th Division's units were up to strength Lauck and his fellow replacements weren't assigned to rifle companies but were given replacement platoons that helped combat-load the ships' vehicles and other cargo. Command of a rifle platoon came later on Iwo. They got in on some field exercises but ship loading took priority.

While loading APA 119, the USS *Highland,* Lauck became acquainted with his future battalion commander, Maj. John W. Antonelli, CO of 2nd Battalion, 27th Marines, who would come to the port at the end of each day to see how the loading was going; Lauck wondered later if this had anything to do with his winding up in 2/27. After it embarked, the 5th Division made a practice landing on Maui, proceeded to Saipan, and then to Eniwetok, where it had another practice landing before going on to Iwo Jima. Of the thirty-eight SOCS in Lauck's 27th Replacement Draft, eleven were KIA and seventeen wounded, a casualty rate of 73 percent.

Dan Hurson also was in the 27th Replacement Draft for the 5th Division, but unlike Lauck he was assigned immediately to a unit, Company C, 1st Battalion, 27th Marines. He thinks it might have had something to do with the fact that the first night he was on Hawaii, he and four or five others from the draft were throwing their K-Bar combat knifes at a piece of paper they'd posted as an improvised target on the wall of one of the buildings. A sergeant major inside came out to see what the banging was about and invited the three young lieutenants in to see a lieutenant colonel, who gave them a chewing out and assigned them to companies in the division.

Two other SOCS members, Robert D. Holmes and Dunbar Jones,

were assigned to 1st Battalion, 27th Marines with Hurson; both were killed on Iwo. Hurson was highly impressed by his battalion commander, Lt. Col. John A. Butler, who won the Navy Cross and was killed on Iwo. "He was a Naval Academy graduate and a fine man," Hurson recalls. "I guess we hadn't been taught the fine points of military courtesy at Lejeune and at one point in our conversation I responded by saying, 'Yes,' and he said, 'Yes, who?' I corrected myself quickly, but he made me feel at home, as did my company commander, and my platoon sergeant." Hurson's platoon sergeant was none other than Gunnery Sergeant John Basilone, a legendary Marine Corps hero by this time. Hurson was assigned as the Charlie Company machine-gun platoon leader and Basilone was an expert machine gunner. He was known throughout the Corps as "Manila John" because he'd done a prewar hitch in the Philippines, where he'd been a light-heavyweight Golden Gloves boxing champion with the Army prior to joining the Marines. He also was the first enlisted Marine to win the Medal of Honor in World War II, as a machine gunner with the 1st Marine Division on Guadalcanal.[4] At the time Hurson didn't know any of this about Manila John. "He was a good old sergeant and he made me feel right at home. It seemed like everyone knew him, though. I ran into a guy at Pendleton in 1950 when I was recalled for Korea and he knew all about John Basilone—he was a machine gunner, too." Basilone was killed on D-day on Iwo and was awarded the Navy Cross.

Basilone put the platoon through its training paces and ran a tight, efficient ship, as the Navy would say. "I ordered a gun inspection one time and he turned them to the night before," Hurson recalled. "When I showed up in the morning the guns and all the gear were laid out in precise rows on shelter halves. I inspected one and it was spotless, immaculate. I asked him if the others were like that, too, and he said, 'Yes, sir.' I ended the inspection right there. The whole thing didn't take more than five minutes. I wasn't going to insult him by even looking at the other ones."

Because the machine guns were generally assigned to the rifle platoons and were under the control of their leaders, Hurson had some time on his hands. "We did live firing, gun drills, and platoon and company assaults, and maneuvers on imaginary bunkers and pillboxes. Basilone taught them and ran the drills. There wasn't much for me to do so I spent most of my time watching the rifle platoons because I figured that's what I'd wind up doing." He was right.

On the ship to Iwo, Hurson and the others were finally told their destination and briefed on their mission, although he didn't get an idea of how hard it might be. "They had a mock-up on the deck and told us where we were going to go, what we were going to do, and how to do it. What we were going to do was to cross the southern edge of the airport (Motoyama No. 1, the main airfield), turn right and head north."

Gordon Dibble left with the 24th Replacement Draft on the USS *General McClellan* in early November (the same ship that Jack Lauck was sailing on, but they didn't yet know each other), to join the 4th Marine Division on Maui, where he landed on Thanksgiving Day. Along with SOCS classmate Ewing "Morg" De Mange, Dibble was assigned to Company K, 3rd Battalion, 23rd Marines, 4th Marine Division. They were the only officers in the company without combat experience, so Dibble was assigned as the machine-gun platoon leader and De Mange was given the mortar section.[5] Dibble recalls that "to a naive, inexperienced young lieutenant it looked like a great outfit, which it was." Along with the 2nd Marine Division, the 4th Division had suffered heavy losses in the bloody battle for Saipan and had the same dubious honor on Iwo; it had one of the highest casualty counts of any Marine division for the war, 17,722 killed and wounded, 21.6 percent of its total committed strength.[6]

On the Liberty ship to Iwo, the troops increasingly got the feeling that the battle was going to be a tough one. A number of junior officers who were veterans of Saipan and Tinian, the division's two previous battles, spent a great deal of time playing poker, and as they neared Iwo Dibble noted that the stakes steadily increased. The losses on Saipan and Tinian resonated with Dibble and the other SOCS members because it brought into focus their understanding that the steep officer casualty rate on those islands was a major factor in the creation of their class.

On 12 November 1944, six weeks after they were commissioned, Jim Ronayne and Red Qualls shipped out of San Diego on the *Rochambeau* to Guam where they joined the 3rd Marine Division. They were part of a draft of three thousand Marines, all ticketed for Iwo Jima. The two new lieutenants were given command of replacement platoons, which they trained on Guam and then led into combat on Iwo. They arrived on Guam forty-seven days later, three days after Christmas, with a stopover at Eniwetok, where they were allowed to go swimming in the harbor. For six weeks on Guam they pulled work details for the division Pioneer battalion, primarily loading the ships for Iwo and training for the landing. The training included practice assaults on fortified bunkers and caves and long, full-pack marches around the island. The climax was an amphibious landing exercise at Guam's Taloforo Bay, hitting the beach in DUKWs, the first time they had seen the amphibious trucks known as "Ducks," that would prove so valuable in hauling supplies ashore on Iwo. Qualls, however, remembers his introduction to the vehicles primarily as the only time he came close to getting seasick.

V Amphibious Corps landed on Iwo less than five months after Ronayne and Qualls were commissioned. En route to Iwo, they didn't know what their objective was—there was talk of Chichi Jima, another island (for which there was no battle) in the Volcano Islands chain, before they heard Iwo mentioned. Once they neared the objective, however, the secrecy was lifted. They repeatedly went over the terrain, the Japanese fortifications, and their objectives on the maps and sand tables that the intelligence and operations sections provided, and speculated on how difficult the battle would be. Some, including Qualls, got the idea that the operation might be quick and easy, a cakewalk, and that the 3rd Division probably wouldn't even land on the island. This turned out to be a pipe-dream if ever there was one.

Bud Morris had a cousin who had been a naval aviator in World War I and was recalled to active duty in the Second World War. He was stationed at the Naval Air Station at Miramar, just north of San Diego, and each morning he drove Morris up to Tent Camp 3. Since Morris had undergone ROC at Lejeune before coming to Pendleton, he spent most of November with nothing to do but await orders. Finally, after Thanksgiving, he was ordered aboard the APA *Seabass* and departed San Diego. Morris was first told that he was going to the Russell Islands to join the 1st Division, but on board ship he learned that his destination was Guadalcanal and the 6th Division. After a placid voyage and Christmas aboard ship, he arrived in the Solomon Islands in January.

Morris and another lieutenant were assigned to the division intelligence section for an experiment in expediting the flow of combat intelligence to division headquarters. The division's senior officers, from Maj. Gen. Lemuel C. Shepherd on down, were dissatisfied with the time it took for battlefield information to filter up through the command levels. The two lieutenants were each given a six-man observation post team equipped with an SCR-610 back pack, line-of-sight FM company-level radio. They were to go up with the frontline units and radio intelligence directly to the division command post. The concept worked fine in exercises under optimum conditions on the 'Canal, but the teams experienced insurmountable difficulties with radio transmissions on Okinawa's rugged terrain.

Morris had time to explore Guadalcanal a bit and, while the natives were very friendly to Americans, he found them somewhat disconcerting at first blush—they had learned from their Anglo-American allies how to bleach their hair an eye-catching blond. They were friendly for the most basic of reasons—there was a lot of work on the island, which had become a major rear-area base, and whereas the British had paid them ten cents an hour, the American wage was one dollar. This made them tolerant of the efforts by Morris and others to teach them baseball using thick sticks and coconuts.

On 1 March the Okinawa invasion fleet began assembling and Morris was back on the *Seabass.* The fleet spent several days at Ulithi Atoll, which had been taken without a fight in the summer of 1944, and was an ideal fleet staging area with its huge lagoon. The troops were given liberty on the recreation island, Mog Mog, which featured softball and beer, of which Morris partook liberally. He caught the last landing craft back to the fleet, but when the coxswain asked him which ship was his in that enormous armada he hadn't a clue. The boat pulled alongside the first APA they encountered and Morris, not totally sober, made high adventure out of getting aboard. A swell was running in the harbor and he mistimed his jump to the landing net on the ship's side and fell into the water between the boat and the ship. The boat crew fished him out with a boat hook. "The mighty lieutenant," he recalls wryly. "Like a drowned rat."

The ship was moored next to the scorched and battered aircraft carrier, the USS *Franklin,* which had been hit and nearly sunk a few days before by kamikazes who turned her into an inferno of exploding aircraft ordnance and gasoline, with 724 killed and 265 wounded. Two Marine fighter squadrons were deployed on her at the time, one of which was VMF-214, Maj. Gregory ("Pappy") Boyington's famous "Black Sheep" squadron. (Boyington, who shot down twenty-four Japanese and won the Medal of Honor, was a POW after being shot down on 3 January 1944.) The next day Morris was transferred to another ship and then finally made it back to his own.

Mark Clement's replacement draft left San Diego in mid-November and after a detour to San Francisco arrived Thanksgiving Day at Maui, where he joined the 4th Marine Division. The forty members of the SOCS were tabbed as replacements in the 24th Marines. All but six went to the line companies, one of whom was Clement. The first week they were there, the adjutant for the 4th Pioneer Battalion came by the replacement draft to see if there were any officers who had engineering experience. Two—Clement and Charles "Breck" Breckenridge, another class member—were the only two listed as having pursued engineering in college. Breckenridge went to A Company, Clement to B Company as assistant platoon commanders. Breckenridge would be wounded and evacuated on D-day.

Clement and Breckenridge were fortunate in having about a month to get to know their platoons and familiarize themselves with the battalion's bulldozers, cranes, and other heavy equipment. "Your ability and efficiency are increased tremendously when you have an opportunity to learn the capabilities and assignments of the rolling stock you have at your disposal," Clement says. "I could already survey and calculate stress on a bridge design. That's not what I needed. I concentrated on learning the names of my NCOs and developed a fair recall of the names of most of the platoon and others in the company. Even a month makes a lot of difference in the comfort level you can develop with many of your troops' abilities and it would serve me well."

Just before Baker Company was to ship out of Maui, 1st Lt. John Marsh, Clement's platoon commander, told him that he was going on the APA with the bulk of the platoon and that Clement was to take thirteen men with the armored assault bulldozers and cranes aboard a landing ship medium (LSM) on which he would make the full two-month trip to Iwo Jima. The 4th Division embarked just before Christmas and the LSM group followed a few days later. Clement's voyage to Iwo took eight weeks on LSM-60, "206 feet of flat-bottomed, rolling bronco which rode (in lieu of sailed) the ocean from Maui to Iwo," as he described it. The slow, eleven-knot LSM couldn't keep up with the main convoys so it joined a group of landing ship tanks (LST), destroyers, and destroyer escorts that formed their own convoy to Tinian and then Iwo.

The division made a practice landing at Tinian but the Pioneers just watched because all the heavy equipment had been cleaned and they didn't want to expose it to beach sand and saltwater at that point. They had problems enough with bad weather. "Whoa, Nellie, how that ship could roll!" Clement recalls. There was serious danger that the bulldozers and cranes would break loose from their chain shackles on the well deck and inflict devastating damage. The Marines double-checked everything before the storm and increased the tension and number of chains for each of the big rigs. Fortunately, nothing broke loose.

At evening mess, about the fourth day after leaving Maui, the LSM captain, a Navy lieutenant, asked Clement to take his meals in the wardroom with him and invited the other Marine lieutenant as well because he liked to meet all the officers on board his ship. Clement developed a credibility problem when he informed the skipper that he was the only Marine officer on board, there was no other. The crew was alerted to be on the lookout for another Marine officer who, of course, they never found. "It wasn't until years later at one of my company reunions that I learned that one of my Pfcs had 'borrowed' my fore-and-aft cap and emblems for a couple of days and was having a ball touring the ship in the shank of the evening. I was always wearing my utility cap so I didn't miss the other. My comedian did replace it, but only after my Marines had their fun and games with the Navy crew."

The Marines and sailors became friends on the voyage. One of Clement's heavy equipment mechanics, an Italian American named Gentile, was expert at making pizza. Shortly after embarking he had met the cooks who invited him to join them in the galley. As a result, the crewmen standing watches and all the Marines were treated to hot pizza at night. The days were spent primarily exercising and checking the vehicles, starting the engines and performing preventative maintenance. At times the Marines took target practice off the fantail, firing at objects in the water. The cooks put the garbage in weighted perforated bags which were heaved over the side and would always attract something, mostly sharks, who made prime targets of opportunity. The crew also had antiaircraft drills with planes towing target sleeves on long passes alongside the flotilla. "We got a little concerned about the towing aircraft pilots when, by some fluke, a 20-mm shell cut the target sleeve towline. That stopped the exercise but not the whooping and hollering. Everyone was excited. You would have thought we had sunk the entire Japanese Navy."

The convoy pulled into Eniwetok for a day and while Clement didn't get ashore he could swim off the ship in the lagoon, whose waters were so clear he could identify anything on the lagoon floor as clearly as though it were at the surface. Then came Tinian and the landing rehearsal. "My twin brother, Joe, was with the 2nd Division on the adjacent island of Saipan. I did get ashore on Tinian, but try as I might, I just couldn't find a sure way to get over to Saipan without being left by the ship, so I missed seeing him and we then went back to sea heading for Iwo Jima."

On 14 December Joe Clement departed San Diego aboard the APA *General Langfitt* for the 2nd Marine Division on Saipan. The twins had gone all through grade school, high school, college, V-12, Parris Island, Lejeune, and Pendleton together, practically as bunkmates. This was the first time in their lives they had been separated; the first time as Joe put it, "we'd been more than three feet apart."

Joe's draft landed on Saipan on 7 December 1944, a historic anniversary. He was assigned to the Company C, 1st Battalion, 2nd Marines, 2nd Marine Division, and given the 60-mm mortar section. The 2nd Division was designated as III Amphibious Corps reserve for the Okinawa landing and on "L-day" (L for landing) made a feint amphibious landing on the southeast coast of the island, near the Chinen Peninsula. The only regiment of the division to see combat on Okinawa was the 8th Marines, which relieved the 7th Marines in the final week of the battle. However, Company I, 3rd Battalion, 2nd Marines suffered the most casualties of the mostly unopposed L-day landings when its LST was hit by a kamikaze Zero fighter, whose engine plunged into the tank deck and set the amphibious tractors afire. Eight Marines sleeping in them were burned to death, and the survivors had to abandon the burning ship. Another kamikaze, a single-engine Val dive-bomber, also hit the APA USS *Hinsdale,* carrying the 3rd Battalion's headquarters group. Most of the casualties there were Navy crewmen, many of whom were in the engine room.

The 2nd Division naturally assumed that it was headed for combat again and, along with his fellow officers, Joe Clement turned to the job of training his section—and vice versa. He and his section sergeant, John McInnis, a twenty-one-year-old veteran of Tarawa, Saipan, and Tinian, were putting the section through gun drill one day and one of the three squad leaders, a corporal, was training a new replacement as a gunner. The kid was doing everything wrong and Clement got fidgety because he didn't see any indication that his squad leader was going to correct him. McInnis noticed Clement's concern and when Clement suggested that they were going to have to intervene McInnis suggested that they wait. When the drill was over the squad leader profanely reamed the rookie for being a dummy and a menace to the rest of the section, then calmly listed all his mistakes. The man's second time through the drill was nearly perfect and Clement learned a valuable lesson about trusting his NCOs. McInnis turned down Clement and the battalion commander's recommendation for OCC and retired from the Marine Corps as a sergeant major.

All the new lieutenants who were fortunate enough to join their units before landing on Iwo or Okinawa got the benefit of such experience and education. The little details were endless—don't fasten the chin strap on your helmet because the concussion of a near-miss by an artillery or mortar shell could break your neck, put toilet paper between your helmet and the plastic liner to keep it dry, use condoms to keep small things dry and to keep water and dirt out of the muzzle of your rifle, carry extra socks and lighter fluid. A mosquito net that fit on your helmet was highly prized, tuck articles like field glasses, which signaled that you were an officer, inside your dungaree jacket, and if you carried a pistol, put it in a shoulder holster under your jacket.

Those who were assigned to companies before they went into combat were considered lucky because they got the benefit of this sort of training and familiarization with their troops, NCOs, and fellow officers. Rifle platoons form a powerful bond for the obvious reason—their shared, intense combat experience. One of the toughest parts of being a brand-new officer, particularly a brand-new second lieutenant, is the realization that while the unit has bonded, the lieutenant isn't part of it yet, and that all the troops are watching closely with some apprehension to see if their new officer is the type that might get them killed. Is he competent? Or is he the chickenshit martinet type? This obviously was just as hard, if not harder, for those who joined their platoons as combat replacements, but the testing process was far shorter.

Because of the B-29s Saipan was a target for night Japanese bombing attacks from Iwo. The Marines would watch from their foxholes, cheering when the antiaircraft hit an attacker and booing when one dropped its stick of bombs. Part of Joe Clement's duties—and training—included search patrols for Japanese troops who were still hiding in the hills, and one of his patrols ambushed and killed one of them. There was a celebrated instance one night at a movie in a large open-air theater that was in a sort of bowl formed by low hills near an Army Air Force bomber field. When the lights came on at the end the Marines saw several hundred Japanese sitting at the top of the hills, also taking in the movie. The Marines weren't armed and the Japanese quickly disappeared. Several thousand finally surrendered when the war ended in August.

Like the other junior officers, Clement performed the normal bivouac duties of censoring mail and counseling the troops on marital and other problems—mostly they needed a sympathetic ear and encouragement to do the obvious, common-sense thing. One of Clement's men came to him for counseling. The man's parents, presumably trying to be helpful, had written that they thought his wife (they had two young children) was fooling around and accepting favors such as the loan of a couple of thousand dollars from her boss to replace her "totaled" car. His wife's sister, however, wrote that nothing was wrong. What should he do? the man asked. Clement, still a month away from his twentieth birthday, was temporarily dumbfounded, but after looking as sage as he could for a minute or so, he recommended that the man consult the chaplain and have the Red Cross check his family situation. He advised the man that since he was getting contradictory reports he should trust his wife and take her word until he had evidence to the contrary. A couple of months later, the man informed him that everything was fine and had turned out just as Clement had said it would. "God's twenty-year-old gift to the lovelorn? I felt as lucky as I was relieved," Clement recalls.

7 Iwo Jima

Red Blood and Black Sand

D-day for Iwo Jima, 19 February 1945, is a historic, almost hallowed, date for the Marine Corps. Iwo was the largest and most storied of the Corps's many battles and claims a special niche in its history. V Amphibious Corps, which comprised the 3rd, 4th, and 5th Marine Divisions, was the largest force the Corps ever deployed, and Iwo was not only the biggest but also the bloodiest of the Corps's battles—5,931 Marines were killed, 17,913 were wounded, 46 were missing in action, and 2,648 suffered combat fatigue in the thirty-six-day struggle for the tiny, isolated volcanic island in the North Pacific.[1] Nearly 10 percent of the casualties, an estimated 550 killed and 1,775 wounded, were incurred on 19 February alone, making it the costliest D-day of the Pacific war.

The men in the landing force received varying intelligence estimates of the difficulty of the battle for Iwo, which is part of the Volcanic Islands chain and whose name translates as "Sulfur Island" in Japanese.

While some were told that they would make short work of the island, and others were told that it was going to be a desperate struggle, no one foresaw how long and hard it would actually be. Intelligence officers seriously underestimated the number of defenders at about thirteen thousand—the actual number was nearly twice that. This mistake occurred for a variety of reasons: the defenders were mostly dug in underground, and the intelligence staff had tried to estimate their water supply by counting the fresh-water cisterns and calculating the average rainfall.

The battle seemed to drag on forever—thirty-six days of such murderous combat can seem like an eternity. Some briefing officers were sure that after the seventy-two-day aerial pounding by Air Force and Navy bombers, plus a great naval bombardment just before the landing, little opposition would be left, but the Marines had heard that song before. They remembered that when Navy officers had boasted how they would pulverize Tarawa, Maj. Gen. Julian Smith, then commanding the 2nd Marine Division, retorted: "When the Marines land and meet the enemy at bayonet point, the only armor a Marine will have is his khaki shirt." The Marines wanted ten days of naval bombardment, but the Navy said it had to conserve ammunition for the upcoming Okinawa operation. Adm. Raymond Spruance's Fifth Fleet also was conducting major carrier air strikes on the Japanese home islands, and the Navy judged that it could only give Iwo a three-day preparation. As it turned out, the Marines didn't even get that. Because of bad weather and the competition for the sea and air resources, they estimated that they only got about thirteen hours. Marine commanders suspected that the Navy really was in competition with the Air Force because most of Spruance's targets were aircraft factories the B-29s had missed a few days before.[2]

Lt. Gen. Holland M. "Howlin' Mad" Smith, commander of the ground forces, and the other senior Marine officers suspected that three days of bombardment would be grossly inadequate because aerial reconnaissance showed that most of the Japanese fortifications were securely underground and they became increasingly pessimistic about the operation. A last-minute preinvasion bombardment concentrated on the positions near the landing beaches, prompted by the Navy's concern about the large number of untouched targets, did damage or destroy many of them, but it didn't have much impact on the underground fortifications on Mount Suribachi and the high ground in the center and north of the island. In those areas, two Japanese defenders noted, the bombardment's chief accomplishment was to rearrange the sand.[3] Even so, the most pessimistic Marines didn't realize how bad Iwo would be, that it would be nearly a month later, on 16 March, D+25, before the island in military argot would be pronounced "secured." Even then, bloody mop-up operations lasted another ten days.[4] The inadequate bombardment and the system of feeding often inadequately trained replacements into the units piecemeal, plus Holland Smith's decision not to land the 3rd Regiment, are matters of controversy to this day.

The battle was a major event, *the* major event for many, in the lives of the Marines who fought it. This included about 125 members of the SOCS. D-day also happened to be the birthday of two members of the class: Dan Hurson, in C Company, 1st Battalion, 27th Marines, turned twenty-two when he hit Iwo's dark and bloody beaches that morning, and Mark Clement, a platoon leader in Company B, 4th Pioneer Battalion, turned twenty that day. Mark's twin brother, Joe, was on Saipan with the 2nd Marine Division, training for the invasion of Okinawa. Hurson and Mark Clement, however, had their minds on far more spectacular fireworks than birthday candles that day. Hurson went in with the third wave. The first wave comprised sixty-eight armored amphibian tractors ("amtracs"), each armed with a short-barreled 75-mm howitzer and deployed as mobile artillery. The second and third were the first troop waves.

The assault battalions of the 4th and 5th Divisions had been transferred from their APAs to LSTs at Saipan, and off the Iwo beaches they were fed the traditional predawn "blitz breakfast" of steak and eggs. They also were given a flash-retardant cream to smear on their faces because the planners feared a possible fire barrier along the beach fed by underground fuel lines. From their LSTs, Hurson and the third wave of nearly fourteen hundred men were loaded into amtracs, which made their headlong dive down the LST's front ramp into the water, and spent a couple of hours circling and bobbing in the ocean swell waiting to make the final H-hour run to their landing beaches. The first wave landed as scheduled at 0900 and the second and third waves came plowing in just a couple of minutes later; Hurson thinks that he and Bob Holmes, in Company A, 1st Battalion, were the first SOCS members to land on Iwo.[5]

V Amphibious Corps landed on Iwo's east beaches. Two regiments of the 5th Division, the 27th and 28th, landed in column on the left, or southern, flank in the shadow of Mount Suribachi, with two regiments of the 4th Division abreast on the right, and the 3rd Division in reserve.

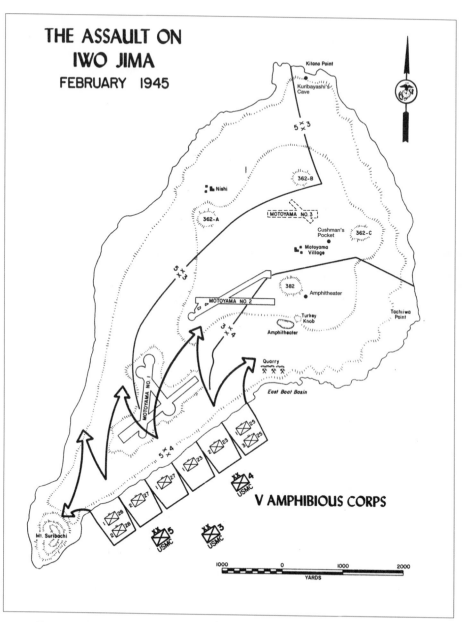

The assault on Iwo Jima, February 1945. From Bernard C. Nalty and Danny J. Crawford, The United States Marines on Iwo Jima: The Battle and the Flag Raisings. HISTORY AND MUSEUMS DIVISION, HEADQUARTERS, U.S. MARINE CORPS (HQMC), WASHINGTON, D.C.

The 4th Division landed under the guns of the cliffs and rock quarry overlooking the East Boat Basin and drove northwest toward the main airfield, Motoyama No. 1, the primary reason for taking the island. The 27th and 28th Marines quickly pushed across the narrow neck of the island at the foot of Suribachi, a 556-foot-high dormant volcano, the island's dominant terrain feature; the 28th Marines then were assigned to capture Suribachi. Hurson's machine-gun sections were supporting the Charlie Company rifle platoons as they assaulted the pillboxes and bunkers on their front. Shortly after 1000, about an hour after the first wave landed, the Marines' landing beaches erupted into an inferno of artillery and mortar fire when the Japanese commander, Lt. Gen. Tadamichi Kuribayashi, pulled the lanyard on his ambush of V Amphibious Corps. With more than six thousand Marines packed into a two-mile stretch, Kuribayashi's hundreds of artillery pieces and thousands of small arms turned the area into a frightful killing ground. The first hour was probably the worst bombardment the Marines have ever experienced. Nevertheless, Kuribayashi waited too long—too many Marines were ashore to be dislodged. They also were superbly trained in small-unit, combined arms tactics against the sort of dug-in fortifications they encountered.

Hurson's battalion was on the northern flank of the 5th Division sector, tied in with the 4th Marine Division on its right. In its drive toward the western beaches, the battalion pushed across the southern end of Motoyama No. 1 and, after crossing it, pivoted to the right and began driving north along the west side of its landing strips. One of Charlie Company's rifle platoons encountered a blockhouse that had a heavy machine gun on top, and Gunnery Sergeant "Manila John" Basilone crawled around to the back of it and disabled it with hand grenades. He and four others were killed by a mortar round a few minutes later as they were leading a tank to the approaches to the airfield. Basilone, who had won the Medal of Honor on Guadalcanal, was awarded the Navy Cross for this action.

The Marines took heavy casualties from the devastating fire from Suribachi on their left and the high ground above the airstrips to their right. The lieutenant leading Charlie Company's lead platoon was severely wounded and evacuated early in the afternoon of D-day. Hurson was ordered to replace him. This was what he had anticipated from the day he joined the division. "During training on Hawaii I spent a lot of time watching the rifle platoons in maneuvers on bunkers and other positions because I knew that's what I'd soon be doing," he recalls. He and the rest of the 27th Marines moved across the island under Kurib-ayashi's withering bombardment, dodging from shell hole to shell hole, past knocked-out bunkers and other fortifications. The main thing he remembers was dead Marines and a constant rain of artillery and mortar fire.

"I told God that if he gave me just another ten years, I'd settle for it," Hurson recalled. God allotted him much more time than that, but it wasn't free. In the afternoon of D+1 Hurson jumped into a shell hole and was hit in the back by shrapnel. A corpsman bandaged him up and told him to go back to the battalion aid station, but Hurson refused. "When we met with the company commander that night he looked at me all splattered with blood and asked, 'What happened to you?'"

As they moved north the Marines ran into a thicket of concrete and steel-reinforced bunkers, blockhouses, and caves around the two air-fields, as well as dummy emplacements and tanks that had absorbed much of the bombardment. At least 135 heavy gun emplacements and pillboxes, plus an estimated fifteen hundred caves ringed Motoyama No. 1, which the Marines had taken by the end of D+1, and a belt of fortifications a mile and a half deep extended completely across the island between Motoyama Nos. 1 and 2.

By early afternoon on D+2, when the 27th Marines had penetrated about a thousand yards into this stronghold, mortar and artillery fire became so intense that all movement, including tanks, was halted. The 4th Division on the right had advanced one hundred to two hundred yards and a gap between the two divisions had opened. Hurson's battalion was shifted four hundred yards to the right to close it. In the rain of Japanese fire, Hurson was hit by another mortar fragment just an inch from his first wound, but much worse. It was bad enough to force his evacuation. The corpsman insisted that he go back to the aid station this time and the doctors there ordered him off the island. He was able to walk to the beach, however, where a boat took him out to an APA that had been converted into a hospital ship. After treatment in hospitals on Saipan and Tinian, Hurson rejoined Charlie Company at Camp Tarawa on the big island of Hawaii, the only officer casualty in the company to do so. He saw a lot of dead Japanese but never saw a live Japanese soldier or a firefight of the kind that platoons and squads had in Vietnam and Korea. "It was a different war. The Japanese were all underground."

Bob Holmes, in Able Company, was wounded twice before he was killed. Late in the afternoon of D-day his company was moving across the runways of Motoyama No. 1, which were swept by 47-mm cannon, machine-gun, mortar, and sniper fire. Holmes had taken a bullet in one calf and the corpsman who bandaged it asked if he could walk back to the battalion aid station. Holmes looked at him as though he were out of his mind and responded, "I can't fool around with that stuff, I've got a platoon up there." He crawled out of the shell hole and moved on forward. The corpsman could see Holmes's platoon a hundred yards forward and knew that "they were really catching it." Half an hour later Holmes was brought in again. A mortar round had landed next to his shell hole and he was nicked by fragments, but he seemed to be suffering more from concussion. "His nose and mouth were bleeding and he seemed to have trouble breathing," the corpsman recalled. "He had some shrapnel nicks in his tail, too. I fixed him up as best I could and told him to lie quiet until we could get a stretcher party that wasn't busy already. He didn't say anything, but half an hour later, he just took off after telling me, 'Three strikes and you're out.' He returned to the front line and his platoon—lugging his Tommy gun."[6] Three hours later, after Able Company had crossed the airstrip, Holmes was killed instantly when a shell landed next to him. "That guy deserves a Navy Cross," the corpsman contended. "He could have been alive . . . if he'd wanted to quit the first time they got him. He's the fightin'est man I ever saw."[7]

Dan's best friend and SOCS classmate, Lester E. Hutchcroft, was also killed on Iwo. Hutchcroft spent the first two weeks on Iwo commanding a shore-party platoon and on 9 March was assigned to Company B, 1st Battalion, 28th Marines, and given command of 1st Platoon. On 11 March, first and second platoons, both severely depleted, were merged under his command and he was killed that same day. Baker Company proved to be a particularly lethal assignment for company officers. It had six different company commanders, three of whom were wounded and evacuated. First platoon had seven leaders, two of whom were killed, three wounded, including two sergeants and one private first class; second platoon had eleven leaders, one twice, with three killed and three wounded, including a gunnery sergeant, a sergeant, two corporals, a private first-class, and Pvt. Dale O. Cassell Jr., who was killed his second time around leading the platoon. Five SOCS members were in B-28 and all were casualties—Hutchcroft, John Hyndman (WIA), Daniel Ginsburg (KIA), Clark King (WIA), and Franklin Fouch (WIA). Hutchcroft succeeded Hyndman in first platoon and Ginsburg with the second.

Gordon Dibble also landed on D-day. Dibble had the machine-gun platoon of Company H, 3rd Battalion, 23rd Marines, 4th Marine Division. His battalion was in reserve and they were eager to get off the ship and get on with it. They could see the bombardment of Suribachi, but their immediate concern was seasickness on the little LCVP landing boats. Along with 2nd Battalion, 24th Marines, which was also in reserve, Dibble's battalion was landed in the afternoon of D-day to relieve 1st Battalion, 23rd Marines (1/23), which had suffered heavy casualties in its frontal assault on Motoyama No. 1.

Loaded down with his combat gear—M-1 carbine, full field transport pack, extra ammunition, grenades, canteen, steel helmet with the Marines' distinctive camouflage cloth cover—and wearing high-top "boondocker" field shoes and canvas leggings, Dibble gingerly led his men down the landing nets draped along the side of the ship. At the bottom, they timed their jump off the nets to the pitch and roll of the little landing boats bobbing vigorously in the ocean swells, which were increasingly choppy as a storm front approached. All were intensely aware that anyone who mistimed the jump would sink to the bottom like an anchor. Some, pulled backwards by the weight of their packs, did fall ten or fifteen feet into the boats on their unfortunate comrades.[8]

Like the rest of the landing force, Dibble and his machine-gun platoon made their way through the Japanese artillery and mortar fire and terrible chaos on the beach. They struggled up the steep terraces of the landing beaches, which had been formed by storms in 1943, sinking to their ankles in the volcanic ash, "a terrible climb" as he recalls. They passed through 1/23 about 1800 and moved up to the airfield. Dibble fired a few rounds from his M-1 carbine at Japanese defenders who briefly showed their heads above ground but he had no way of knowing if he hit any.[9]

The Marines established a night defensive perimeter on the edge of the airfield, about five hundred yards inland, with Dibble positioning his machine guns to provide interlocking fire across the company front. They assumed that the Japanese would counterattack during the night and try to drive them off the island. Dibble discovered that he had a short supply of hand grenades, a prime night defensive weapon because there is no muzzle flash to betray the defender's position. His company commander gave him permission to take a half dozen men to the beach to get grenades, but he encountered some initial reluctance from the Seabees who operated the supply dump. He pointed out that a collapse of the defense perimeter could result in the Japanese descending on them in the dark, a prospect that greatly concentrated the Seabees' minds as Dibble hoped it might. He and his men humped several cases of grenades back up the terraces, an even more arduous climb with their heavy loads, and settled in to await the expected onslaught.

They were awake all night but were pleasantly surprised that there was no major infantry assault, and they were comforted somewhat by illumination rounds fired by the destroyers offshore. Even so, the night was far from easy. The temperature in the North Pacific drops to 60 degrees at night at that time of year and it seemed much colder to Marines accustomed to the South and Central Pacific. Many had unwisely dropped their packs and blanket rolls during the day and shivered through the night. And the Japanese poured heavy artillery and mortar fire onto the beachhead all night and made many infiltration probes. Some were by three- and four-man "wolfpack" teams whose targets were fuel and ammunition dumps on the beach; they got one 4th Division dump that had two boatloads of ammunition and fuel, which went up with a roar and a sheet of fire that could be seen miles out at sea. The Japanese didn't make a major attack because they had concluded that their banzai attacks were wasteful and generally ineffective and they concentrated on infiltration and raiding supply sources.

In his brief time on Iwo, Dibble learned a lot that wasn't in the stateside training syllabus. He was struck by how young his men were, how many were from the South, and how patriotic they were. "My runner was only about five feet two," he recalls. "He was built to run through fire between the sections." He described his platoon sergeant, who had been decorated on Saipan, as a "tiger," whose citation was for climbing on top of a tank and pointing out targets to the crew; on Iwo he was wounded doing the same thing.[10]

The next morning, D+1, the 23rd Marines, supported by tanks and a battalion of the 24th Marines, took Motoyama No. 1 against fierce resistance. The regiment moved its lines ahead about a thousand yards but Dibble wasn't part of it. Along with the other platoon leaders he had gone to the company command post first thing in the morning to get their orders for the assault—his gun sections were to move out in support of the rifle platoons. About ten minutes before his battalion jumped off in the assault, he was sitting in a mortar shell crater with one of his section leaders when a mortar round dropped in. Dibble was hit in the right side of the chest by shrapnel. When the section leader rushed over to check on him, the only words Dibble could get out were, "I'll see you on the high ground." He meant that he intended to return to lead the platoon against the ridges and hills ahead of them.

Dibble slipped in and out of consciousness as some of his troops put him on a poncho and dragged him down to a landing craft, which took him out to a troop transport that had been converted into a hospital ship. One of the harried surgeons, who were swamped by the flood of casualties and not knowing that Dibble had briefly regained consciousness, remarked to a colleague that "I don't think this one's going to make it."

The section leader in the shell crater had also been wounded and was evacuated. Several weeks later he was shocked when Dibble looked him up in a hospital on Oahu. Seeing the seriousness of Dibble's wounds, the sergeant had interpreted Dibble's words about the "high ground" differently—he thought Dibble was referring to Heaven.[11]

The hospital ship, still anchored off-shore when the flag was raised on Suribachi, a day or so later hauled anchor for Saipan, which had become a major rear-echelon base. From the hospital there, Dibble went to a Navy hospital in Hawaii. He had a lot of company on the casualty list. Many from his platoon and company wound up in the same area of the hospital in Honolulu, which made it possible for him to track what had happened to everyone. He heard that his drill instructor at Parris Island was killed on Iwo as were two of his instructors at Lejeune, an NCO and a first lieutenant, both veterans of Guadalcanal, who had given encouragement to the SOCS members when they needed it. Six months later, after stints in the naval hospitals in Saipan, Oahu, San Francisco, and San Diego, Dibble was returned to duty, assigned to a guard unit at Camp Pendleton.

The Iwo Jima invasion fleet, bringing the 3rd Division from Guam and the 4th and 5th Divisions from Hawaii, rendezvoused at the Marianas for a rehearsal landing on Tinian a week before D-day. This afforded the men a view of the major purpose of their mission as they watched the heavily loaded silver B-29s take off for Japan in a constant, deadly stream. As impressive and intimidating as the Superforts were, however, the Marines had no way of knowing how much the difficulty of their missions, made even worse by Iwo, depressed the morale of their crewmen. However, Iwo was the rare battle in which every rifleman, tanker, and truck driver clearly understood its purpose and relevance to the overall picture, including the bombing campaign, while they were still fighting it. The first damaged B-29 made an emergency landing midway through the operation, on 4 March, in full sight of nearly every man on the island and was a morale booster much as raising the flag on Mount Suribachi had been. The bomb tonnage dropped on Japan increased by more than ten times in March. By V-J Day, 2,251 B-29s with 24,761 crewmen had made emergency landings on the island, which was about equal to the Marines' causalities.[12]

The battles for Iwo Jima, and Okinawa after it, were even more intense than their predecessors. They were part of the Japanese homeland. Iwo is only 660 miles from Tokyo. The Japanese annexed Okinawa, which is just 375 miles south of Kyushu, the southernmost home island, from China in 1879. Second, with the fall of the Marianas, the Japanese realized that their only hope was to ratchet up the war's cost so high that they could bargain for peace terms. After Tarawa the Japanese became increasingly convinced that the Americans wouldn't accept such horrendous losses on every island they had to take. Tactically, the Japanese also had come to understand that their banzai charges, often fueled by sake and marked by bad planning and blundering execution, were romantic, suicidal gestures based on the disastrous doctrinal assumption that the élan of their troops would overcome the Americans' disciplined firepower. In reality, the banzais' primary accomplishment was to feed brave, hapless men into the meatgrinder of modern industrial warfare. There was one exception on Iwo, on the night of 8 March, when one of Kuribayashi's subordinates became so frustrated that he ordered a counterattack by eight hundred of his surviving troops, who were cut down to a man out in the open.

The small size of the two islands enabled the Japanese commanders, Kuribayashi on Iwo and Lt. Gen. Mitsuru Ushijima on Okinawa, to construct mutually supporting Maginot Line–like defensive positions across the islands. Iwo is about eight square miles, five miles long, and two and a half miles at its widest. Okinawa is about sixty miles long but the fighting was concentrated in the southern quarter of the island, an area about fifteen miles long north to south and about six miles wide at the main Shuri Ridge defensive line from Yonabaru to Naha.

Although not continuous like the trenches of World War I, these defenses had mutually supporting fields of fire and were not often susceptible to fire and maneuver and flanking attacks. They could only be reduced by direct fire and frontal assaults by the infantry, which Lt. Gen. Simon Bolivar Buckner, commander of Tenth Army on Okinawa, characterized as "blowtorch and corkscrew"—*blowtorch* referring to flamethrowers, *corkscrew* to demolition charges, both of which had to be applied at close range. It was a neat characterization of the deadly tactic, but the cost was horrendous casualties inflicted on the vulnerable young men who had to execute it. Both Japanese generals designed defenses in-depth based on the ridges and hills that formed natural east-west defense lines across both islands, utilizing the natural caves in the coral and volcanic rock, which they augmented with miles of connecting tunnels and elaborate fortifications with interlocking and mutually supporting fields of fire. They inflicted maximum casualties at each line and, when the American pressure become overpowering, fell back to the next one.

Iwo is shaped like a pork chop. Mount Suribachi, the dominant terrain feature, is a natural fortress at the island's narrow, southernmost point. At its base a narrow neck of land widens gradually and unevenly for more than a mile to the north, to the Motoyama Plateau, then flares out to the east to the island's maximum width. Two airfields, the primary military objectives, and a third under construction were on this gradually rising plain. The northern half of the island is high ground, a rocky plateau cut by ravines and steep ridges with deep canyons and steep cliffs on the coast, described by one historian as a "jungle of stone" ideal for defense.[13] It is dominated by the island's secondary terrain features, a 382-foot hill and three others that rise 362 feet.

In addition to making walking difficult, the deep, soft volcanic sand on the landing beaches and around the airfields made excellent concrete for the Japanese fortifications. For nearly eight months prior to the landing a twenty-two-thousand-man garrison worked intensively under nightmarish conditions digging and constructing their formidable defenses. Underground volcanic fires smoldered near the area of the village of Motoyama, Hill 382, and airfield number 2, creating powerful sulfur fumes and underground temperatures as high as 160 degrees, which greatly shortened work shifts. Water was a major problem; rainfall was collected in cisterns for drinking as the island's wellwater tasted of sulfur, and a marine boiler was set up near the East Boat Basin to distill seawater into a ten-thousand-gallon concrete tank. Bathing, except in the ocean, was prohibited. Underground passages were at least thirty feet deep to protect against bombardment and were laid out to minimize blast shocks near the openings, whose approaches were angled at 90 degrees a few feet in to protect the defenders against flamethrowers and blast. Above-ground artillery, machine-gun, and mortar positions had steel-reinforced concrete roofs as thick as twenty inches. As far as intelligence teams could determine after the battle, the Japanese armament included at least 185 artillery pieces of 70-mm or larger, 1,000 antitank and antiaircraft machine guns, 350 heavy machine guns, 480 light machine guns, 30 tanks, and more than 200 rocket launchers.

Racial prejudice had blinded both sides to their opponents' fighting qualities. The Japanese were fatally contemptuous of their "blue-eyed" Anglo-American enemies, whom they scorned—including the Marines —as "cowardly."[14] The Allies returned the favor with propaganda that portrayed the Japanese soldier as a dumpy, myopic, monkey-like subhuman in a sloppy, ill-fitting uniform. This was a misjudgment not shared by the combat troops who fully came to appreciate, alas, the reality of the enemy's skill, courage, and the intensity and discipline of his training. One canard was that the Japanese were nearsighted and poor marksmen. In fact, they were excellent shots, made extensive use of snipers, and killed hundreds of Marines on the island with well-aimed rifle fire.

Prior to Iwo, the Japanese defensive tactics, combined with another factor, had proved surprisingly costly to the Marines and Army on Saipan, Guam, and Peleliu. The Japanese militarists had corrupted the Bushido code, the chivalric samurai tradition of courage, loyalty, and death before dishonor, into a doctrine of forced, mass-suicidal fighting to the death for the emperor and Imperial Japan and granting no mercy to the enemy, including noncombatants. The bloody battle for Saipan would have been even costlier if the Japanese hadn't dissipated some of their strength in ill-considered banzai counterattacks. They didn't make that mistake on Peleliu, where they stayed in their caves, minimizing the effectiveness of U.S. firepower.[15] This new tactic proved devastating to Allied infantry everywhere in the Pacific in the last year of ground combat; on Iwo the Americans lost more than a third of the landing force of more than seventy thousand men. It was devastating to both sides—almost all of the twenty-two thousand Japanese were killed— only a few hundred were taken prisoner. This made Iwo the only battle in which American casualties were greater than Japanese.

The men of 3rd Battalion, 25th Marines, on the far right flank of the landing, directly under the guns of the cliffs and ridge line, marked the nature of the battle. They dubbed themselves the "Ghouls of the 3rd Battalion" and improvised a satirical dirge to the tune of Chopin's "Funeral March," which opens, "We are the ghouls of the Third Battalion" and ends up noting that each time one of them died "ten thousand dollars went home to the folks," referring to their G.I. insurance.[16] The battalion lost twenty-six of its original thirty-six officers and nearly 600 of the 918 troops who landed on Blue Beach. When the 3rd Division landed on D+2 it took the center position between the 4th and 5th Divisions, driving north and then northeast from the airfield.[17]

Jack Lauck sailed from Hawaii on the APA *General McClellan*. The 5th Division had rehearsal landings at Saipan and Eniwetok, then sailed for Iwo. There were rumors aboard ship that the invasion force was headed for Formosa, although Tokyo Rose kept informing them that they were going to Iwo. That was confirmed when the maps were broken out and the briefings began. "The intelligence people talked about it being a three- to five-day operation at most, a learning experience," he recalls. "The Navy didn't agree, however, and the maps looked tough. I didn't think it would be easy but I don't remember feeling particularly apprehensive."

Lauck landed with a replacement platoon about 1030 on D-day, an hour and a half after H-hour; he was supposed to go in with the sixteenth wave but in the confusion his boat caught up with and landed with the twelfth. He and his platoon spent the first ten days on the island working around the clock with the division Pioneer Battalion unloading supplies and evacuating the wounded. He was hit in the hand by mortar shrapnel near Motoyama No. 1 on D+2 but returned to duty immediately after being treated at the aid station.[18] The shore parties took a lot of artillery and mortar fire because the Japanese had preregistered the entire island, but occasionally they could slip over to an LST for a hot meal and a shower. On 1 March Lauck was ordered to lead twenty-four replacements to 2nd Battalion, 27th Marines, commanded by Maj. John W. Antonelli, whom he had met while loading ships at Hilo. He was assigned to a platoon in Easy Company, which was in terrible shape from the casualties it had suffered in the drive up the island's west side.

The 28th Regiment had moved up on the 27th Marines' left after it secured Mount Suribachi on D+4, 23 February, at a cost of 904 casualties, including 209 KIA.[19] On Lauck's right, the 4th Division spent more than two weeks and suffered heavy casualties in capturing a formidable, defensive position northeast of Motoyama No. 2, which the men aptly dubbed the "Meat Grinder." The Meat Grinder complex was anchored by Hill 382, the second-highest terrain feature on the island, a grim, forbidding obstacle whose steep face was pocked by caves and undergirded by interconnecting underground tunnels and caves so deep that flamethrowers couldn't reach into them. The Meat Grinder also comprised the terrain feature known as the "Turkey Knob" and a jumble of rock and broken terrain called the "Amphitheater."

The 5th Division fought up the west coast of the island to the northernmost strongpoint, anchored on Nishi Ridge and Nishi Village. The rough, corrugated terrain of the northern part of the island, which the men of the division named "The Badlands," featured countless sandstone ridges that had been easy for the Japanese to dig into and they dug deeply. The Marines would assault the forward face of a ridge, fight their way over the crest and down the reverse slope, all under heavy fire from the positions below them and from the next ridge. They would cross the ravine between the ridges, still under fire from all four directions, and repeat the process all over again. One tactic devised by Col. Thomas Wornham, 27th Regiment commander, was to bulldoze trails into the Japanese terrain, from which his men could launch their assaults with tank support.

"Even when you were off the line, you couldn't feel secure about the caves and bunkers in the area you'd secured," Lauck recalls. "They were on both slopes of the ridges and so deep the artillery couldn't get to them. As a matter of course we'd throw grenades in them whenever we'd be near them because there was always the chance that Japanese were still hiding in them." On 7 March, D+16, Lauck's battalion finally reached the high jagged rocks of Nishi Ridge, an irregular ridge line overlooking the north coast and the ocean. After taking heavy casualties from grenades, knee mortars, and sniper fire, the battalion gained the ridge only to be forced back off because the 3rd Division unit on their right flank, 2nd Battalion, 21st Marines, was forced to withdraw, which exposed their flank.

The next day the 5th Division continued its drive to the north toward the pocket where Kuribayashi had concentrated his surviving forces for his last stand. Lauck's battalion faced the strongest positions in the area, rocky ledges where both the forward and reverse slopes were heavily defended. The Marines blasted them with tanks, rocket launchers, demolitions, and flamethrowers, but Lauck's company was halted by intense machine-gun and mortar fire from a complex of bunkers and pillboxes.

At one point in this stage of the operation, Lauck's platoon came under fire from a cave opening. One of his men on the platoon's left flank had a rocket launcher, which he held above his head, yelling, "I've got the bazooka!" Another on the right flank held two rocket rounds above his head, yelling, "I've got the ammo!" With the rest of the platoon laying down covering fire, the first man sprinted forward toward a big rock and ducked behind it for cover. The other zig-zagged over from the right and joined him. The man with the rockets loaded one into the launch tube, gave the gunner the "Up" sign—a tap on the helmet—and they put the round right into the cave entrance. All firing ceased and the two walked back to their positions, the assistant brandishing his second round above his head triumphantly. Lauck thought to himself, "If you get into a fire-fight, be thankful you are surrounded by Marines."

In return, Lauck remembered what he'd been taught about looking out for the troops—making sure they had food and ammunition, particularly the crew-served weapons, machine guns, and 60-mm mortars, that the platoon's flanks were secure, and that the men knew he was there looking out for them. "You have to worry about your people and let them know you're always there. After they set up bakeries in the rear I always tried to be sure that my men got fresh doughnuts and other things when they were available." At a 5th Division reunion in West Palm Beach, Florida, in September 2000, Lauck saw one of his riflemen, John Compton, for the first time in fifty-five years. Compton had been in Lauck's replacement draft and in his platoon all the time on the island and it was an emotional reunion. "He said to me, 'Thanks for keeping me alive there,'" Lauck recalls. "He had a flag that the guys in the platoon had signed and that really brought back a flood of memories."

One of his fellow platoon leaders in Easy Company was Lt. Jack Lummus, an All-American end at Baylor who had played with the professional football New York Giants. Lummus rose up to rally his men and was knocked down by a grenade blast. He got up, charged the position and killed its defenders with his submachine gun, and was seriously wounded in the shoulder by another grenade. He attacked another emplacement and killed its occupants. Directing the fire of supporting tanks, he again moved into the open, rushed a third heavily defended position, and killed the Japanese in it. He led his men in attacking individual foxholes and spider traps, and, twenty yards in front of his platoon, he motioned them to follow him forward again. He suddenly disappeared in a huge explosion. When the rocks and debris finished falling, his men could see Lummus and it looked like he was standing in a hole. He had stepped on a mine that blew his legs off. He yelled at his cursing, weeping men as they stopped to help him and urged them on to a three-hundred-yard advance across the area's ravines and ridges. The surgeons in the division hospital could only relieve his pain and give him blood transfusions to try to keep him from bleeding to death. They kept him alive for several hours during which he was conscious and talked to his surgeons. "I guess the New York Giants have lost the services of a damn good end," he remarked to Navy Lt. Thomas M. Brown, the battalion surgeon. "He was smiling as he closed his eyes and died," another recalled.[20] Lummus was posthumously awarded the Medal of Honor. That night Easy Company was on the last ridge overlooking Kitano Point and the ocean. They were there to stay, but they still had a long, hard way to go.

Major Antonelli won the Navy Cross the following day, 9 March. He and three of his officers were hit by a land mine that also badly wounded the 1st Battalion commander, Lt. Col. Justin Duryea. Antonelli suffered a broken eardrum and had particles embedded in one eye, but refused evacuation to the aid station until he had ordered continuation of the attack. He walked out of the division hospital and returned to the battalion. He was ordered back by Colonel Wornham, the regimental commander, and walked out again. Wornham finally ordered Antonelli off the island a week later to save him from further injury. In the interim, two days after Antonelli was wounded, Antonelli moved Lauck and his platoon into Fox Company with the intention of using what was left of Easy Company as battalion reserve. At that point, Easy Company had fewer than 40 of the 235 men who had landed on D-day. In fact, the entire 2nd Battalion was so depleted that it couldn't be used any more as a frontline assault unit and was pulled back into reserve, primarily to plug holes in the line, particularly at night.

In the final days of the battle the entire 27th Regiment was down to about five hundred effectives (out of its original strength of three thousand), about half a full-strength battalion. The remnants of the three battalions were organized into a composite battalion commanded by Lt. Col. Donn Robertson, CO of 3rd Battalion and the only original battalion commander left. The combat efficiency of all the divisions was seriously reduced by the loss of trained riflemen and their small-unit leaders, who had to be replaced by clerks, communicators, truck drivers, and cooks and bakers from headquarters units.

When Lauck and the handful of survivors of 2/27 returned to Camp Tarawa on the big island of Hawaii, Antonelli was there to greet them, and made Lauck his assistant battalion S-3 (operations) officer.

Mark Clement had a tough time just getting ashore. On D-day the Pioneer LSMs were in position several thousand yards offshore waiting to take their line of departure positions for the beach where they were scheduled to land with the eighth wave. On board the LSM-60 the troops had managed a fitful sleep during the night, rising at 0430 on D-day to eat, check their personal gear and weapons, issue ammunition, and get the armored bulldozers, cranes, and other heavy equipment undogged and ready for the assault landing. Like all the other officers, Clement was thankful for all this responsibility, which diverted him from his natural fears of what was to come; the troops didn't have that blessed distraction.

Suddenly, there was noise and activity everywhere as the Navy ship and air prelanding bombardment began at 0640 in the dawn's target-identifying light. Sections of Mount Suribachi were obscured by palls of smoke from the heavy shelling, as were the central and northern parts of the island. Aircraft strafing and bombing runs appeared to be demolishing the entire island. It seemed to Clement that nothing could withstand the pounding. As if to disabuse him of such thoughts, however, a Navy SB2U float plane that was spotting for naval gunfire was hit, slowly rolled to its left, and plunged into the ocean offshore Blue Beach. "The Japanese were still there, all right," Clement recalled. "And waiting!"

After more than three hours of naval and aerial bombardment, the Japanese dramatically announced their presence. One hour after H-hour, at about 1000, both the beaches and offshore areas exploded in an orchestrated counterbombardment whose intensity and accuracy made it clear that there would be as much resistance as the most pessimistic American could have feared. The Japanese plan was to let the first few waves ashore and then try to contain the landing with heavy concentrations of artillery, mortar, and small-arms fire on the water line, letting the following waves of Marines pile into the concentrated carnage where they could be destroyed. It was a well-executed tactic and inflicted heavy casualties, although too many Marines were already ashore for it to imperil the beachhead.

Shortly after leaving the line of departure on the initial run for the beach, things got sticky for Clement and the others on LSM-60 as they came under fire from 6-inch Japanese shore batteries. Fortunately his ship took no direct hits, although one sailor was hit by a fragment whose force was almost spent and caused only a bad bruise. These batteries had sunk or badly mauled a number of rocket-firing landing craft and destroyer escorts that had been bombarding the island earlier on D–2 and the Navy was nervous—it wanted no more disabled LSMs and wrecked heavy equipment adding to the chaos and gridlock on the beach on D-day. The armored bulldozers and other vehicles on LSM-60 were badly needed on the beach, but the tank-carrying LSMs in the third wave had taken less than three minutes to unload and still took a lot of damaging hits. The 'dozers and cranes would have taken at least twice as long to unload as the tanks, and the Navy decided that discretion was the better part of valor. The Pioneers' LSMs were told to pull up and await further orders. LSM-60 hove to and waited with engines idling, slowly coming about broadside to the beach. However, ships that had unloaded were coming back out to sea, and Clement's craft was lying broadside in their way. He was getting an early, firsthand look at how dangerous and difficult the Pioneers' beach clearing job was going to be.

"Coming straight at us was an LSM from the third wave that had dropped some tanks on the beach and was trying to get the hell out of there," he recalls. "It appeared she would hit us broadside, either in our bow or stern. While unloading she had taken so many hits in her conn superstructure and stern that . . . steerage from the bridge had been lost and her crew was operating the rudder manually under orders relayed by sound-power phones. They were trying to shout at us through bull-horns and warn us to make way. She seemed to wallow like a sick whale as she lumbered toward us listing noticeably and wavering in her heading, but . . . coming our way as fast as her engines would carry her. Her course was erratic, unpredictable, and it was impossible to tell where she might plow into us—bow or stern."

Many of the Marines and sailors were shifting back and forth from bow to stern to avoid being at the point of impact and had begun moving aft. This was complicated by the fact that the LSM's conn superstructure was located midship on the starboard side, which was the one exposed to the other LSM, and could only be bypassed using a single pipe foot rail and overhead hand rail that were set into the conn's bulkhead and overhung the cargo well deck. About this time LSM-60's skipper saw what was happening and signaled full speed ahead to the engine room. The men moving aft saw that this would expose the stern and immediately reversed direction, hastily trying to move over the foot rail back toward the bow. The damaged ship slipped by LSM-60's stern, missing it by just a few yards. Fortunately, the only casualties were bruises suffered by some of the Marines who jumped or fell into the well deck in the confusion.

LSM-60 made another abortive run to the beach on D-day afternoon with the others, but it was aborted because of the intensity of the artillery fire and the fact that the beach was closed because it was so congested with sunken and broached landing craft. LSM-60 finally landed at about

1000 the next morning, D+1. Clement's battalion operations officer jumped onto the lowered bow-ramp and shouted, "Clement, we only want to bring in the two armored 'cats' [bulldozers] and the weasel." After the vehicles were landed, Clement told his corporal that he was joining the platoon and jumped ashore. It was a reflex action, what he was trained to do, the natural thing to do. The cranes and unarmored bulldozers, along with their Marine operators, went back to sea until the next day, but the armored bulldozers were in great demand. Fortunately they drew no antitank fire, but one of the drivers later told Clement that it sounded as if he were inside a dishpan with all of the rifle and machine-gun rounds rattling off the armor. Unfortunately, the weasel, a low-slung, tracked vehicle about the size of a jeep that was used to haul light cargo and personnel, was knocked out the first evening by a mortar round that demolished the radiator and other operating parts. Its ability to negotiate the volcanic sand with its wide tracks was sorely missed.

The ordeal of the murderous Japanese artillery and machine-gun fire was compounded by the deep, soft volcanic ash, which mired even tracked vehicles and made even walking a major struggle. When it was wet, it became slippery underfoot and formed a sticky gumbo that caked an inch or two thick on the Marines' boondockers and made movement almost impossible.

The Pioneers were responsible for beach security, demolition of enemy bunkers and other fortifications, and blowing paths through minefields, broached landing craft, wrecked vehicles, and other destroyed and discarded equipment so that supplies could be brought in over the beach. Worst was the human wreckage. Both Americans and Japanese were blown apart by high explosives and body parts littered the beach. Robert Sherrod, the Time-Life correspondent who covered Saipan, Tinian, Iwo, and Okinawa, and wrote several books about the war wrote: "Whether the dead were Japs or Americans, they had one thing in common; they had died with the greatest possible violence. Nowhere in the Pacific war had I seen such badly mangled bodies. Many were cut squarely in half. Legs and arms lay fifty feet away from any body. In one spot on the sand, far from the nearest cluster of dead, I saw a string of guts 15 feet long. Only legs were easy to identify; they were Jap if wrapped in khaki puttees, American if covered by canvas leggings."[21]

For all that, Clement thinks that seeing his first wounded Marine being evacuated, that seeing the suffering of a live human, may have been more of a shock to him. "There was a constant stream of Marines with every conceivable type of wound moving to aid or evacuation stations in the Pioneer beach area," he recalls. "We tried to get them in a shell hole below ground level while they were awaiting evacuation because shell fire onto the beach often caught wounded awaiting evacuation." Coupled with this was the problem of traffic and supply on a shallow beachhead. "We were trying to move ammo, mortar shells and explosives ashore in a hand-to-hand operation while trying to keep our balance and stay out of the way of the bow ramp of an LCVP landing craft that was partially swamped [that was sometimes being] broached and tossed about by a five to seven-foot surf," he says. Amtracs, tanks, and bulldozers were trying to cross or move along a beach that was filled with people, ammo dumps, and equipment. Traffic lanes somehow had to be kept open for vehicles, most of which were drawing fire and so "buttoned up" that their drivers' vision was extremely restricted. "Keeping the traffic away from the wounded was a nightmare," Clement says. "The physical and mental horrors of Iwo were almost beyond human endurance."

By the time Clement reached the beach, his platoon commander had been promoted to company executive officer and Clement replaced him. Clement also lost his platoon sergeant that afternoon. On board LSM-60 the night before D-day, the platoon sergeant, Charles Adomitus, confided to Cpl. G. R. Lowe, the machine-gun section leader, that he was convinced that he was going to be killed on Iwo. Lowe sought to reassure him, but shortly after they landed in the sixth wave Adomitus took cover in a shell hole with Lowe, periodically popping up to check on the platoon, which was under heavy mortar and artillery fire. When he raised up to yell at one of his men to take cover, a shell burst on the edge of the hole and Adomitus fell back on Lowe, dead. The platoon guide, Sgt. William R. ("Snuffy") Smith, replaced him.

Snuffy Smith had been with B Company on Roi-Namur, Saipan, and Tinian and was a steady, knowledgeable, dependable Marine. The platoon had been badly shot up in an ambush in the last days of the battle for Saipan, and Smith was a veteran of that action. Clement couldn't tell what Smith thought about his young, new platoon commander, but to Clement Smith was the Rock of Gibraltar. And, Clement thought, very tactful with his new officer. "Lieutenant, don't you think it would be a good idea if, tomorrow, we . . . ?" He knew his NCOs were trying to help, but only with time did he come to realize how much.

The beach area was the Pioneers' chief area of operation so Clement's company tried to dig in enough there to reduce the casualties from the heavy artillery, mortar, and machine-gun fire. Shelling had been intense. The platoon radio operator had been killed by shell fire and the platoon had taken eighteen other casualties the first day from shrapnel, grenades, and rifle fire. The platoon also had been in a fire-fight with Japanese who had reoccupied some pillboxes. The original occupants had been killed by the rifle companies as they moved through the area but the Japanese reentered the fortifications through tunnels from inland.

The Marines endured what seemed to be almost continuous incoming artillery fire on the night of D+1 as the Japanese attempted to prevent the Americans' resupply of ammunition, fuel, and water. Everyone in the beach area was trying to get beach matting and other structural material and sandbags to cover their foxholes against direct mortar hits. The insidious sand also presented more problems because the Marines had to revet their foxhole walls with sandbags because the sand was so unstable. Vibrations from a nearby shell hit would cause any unsupported sides of the hole to collapse, bringing down the overlying support material and sometimes several hundred pounds of sandbags.

Clement acquired the nickname "Speed" because his long stride—he's six feet six—carried him rapidly from shell hole to shell hole under fire. One incident that contributed to the handle occurred on D+3 when he outran his runner to their covered foxhole when the platoon came under mortar fire. Clement was about two yards ahead of his runner, Pvt. Edgar Lacy, and tried to dive into the hole, which was covered by some beach matting and sandbags. However, his aim was a bit off and he didn't get his head down quickly enough. He plowed into the overhead sandbags, which slowed him only momentarily because the speeding Lacy hit him in the rear and the momentum carried them both into the hole. For a seventeen-year-old kid Lacy hit like a linebacker and Clement feared for a while that his neck would never be the same. The whole platoon, including Lacy, collapsed in laughter at the spectacle.

Late in the battle Clement also became a hero to his platoon by scrounging a gallon of ice cream from the chief cook in the officer's mess on LSM-60, whom he'd gotten to know on their eight-week voyage across the Pacific. He spotted four one-gallon containers of ice cream that the cook had scrounged from a Navy AKA (assault cargo auxiliary) while taking on supplies for the beach. "Would your guys like some of this, lieutenant?" the cook asked him. Clement allowed as how his troops probably would have killed for a lot less. "Give my regards to Gentile [the heavy equipment mechanic who had made himself popular on the voyage over with his talent for making pizza] and the rest of the guys," the cook said, giving him one of the gallon containers. There was enough for a couple of spoons full for each of the troops, who left a share for Clement and Snuffy Smith. "A grand memory of a great bunch of guys looking after us like that," Clement recalls.

His pride in seeing the flag raised on Mount Suribachi on D+4, 23 February, was one of the most vivid memories of his life. "One of my platoon yelled, 'Hey, they're raising a flag on the mountain,' and there it was, just visible atop the hill." Part of the thrill came from the powerful symbolism of the event and part from the demonstration of the rifle companies' progress the capture of this major fortress and artillery observation post represented.

On 19 March, three days after Iwo was officially declared secure, Clement and the rest of the survivors of the 4th Marine Division were on board ship bound back to Maui, where they took on replacements and began training for the invasion of Japan. His platoon had suffered more than 50 percent casualties.

8 Iwo Jima

Would Any of Us Be Left?

On 16 March, D+25, the American military brass led by Adm. Chester W. Nimitz, the Pacific Ocean Area commander, and Lt. Gen. Holland M. "Howlin' Mad" Smith, USMC, Commanding General of the Expeditionary Troops,[1] declared that organized Japanese resistance on Iwo Jima had ended and that the bloody and exhausting struggle for that island hellhole was officially over. Nearly a month after the 3rd, 4th, and 5th Marine Divisions had charged across Iwo's black volcanic ash beaches the island was officially proclaimed "secure." The most costly battle in Marines Corps history was history.

The battle may have ended as far as the brass was concerned, but a week after Holland Smith had returned to his FMFPAC headquarters at Pearl Harbor, twenty-one-year-old James Aloysius Ronayne, a platoon leader in Company I, 3rd Battalion, 9th Marine Regiment, and his fellow grunts in the 3rd Division were still on Iwo fighting as hard as ever. Ronayne's rugged features betrayed the stress of the long battle. He was haggard, bearded, and looking and feeling well beyond his years. His dungarees were ragged and caked with dirt and grease, and he looked out at his blasted, desolate world with the combat infantryman's sunken-eyed thousand-yard stare. Iwo may have been "secure" to the brass but Lieutenant Ronayne was still deeply engrossed in the business of kill-or-be-killed. Like Jack Lauck and Gordon Dibble, Ronayne had been told by his briefing officers on board ship as they approached the island that Iwo would be short and quick—"That there would probably be nothing left alive there."

As a result of the horrendous casualties the Marines suffered in the murderous struggle for the eight-square-mile island, which arguably was the most heavily fortified area yard by yard in World War II, Ronayne was leading a platoon made up of inexperienced replacements and mergers with other shot-up units. They were cleaning out the final pockets of Japanese resistance on the northern end of the island in the ridges and gullies that ran roughly east and west. The battle left a tragic carpet of dead Marines and Japanese soldiers and a steady stream of broken, bloody, and bandaged young men, many on stretchers, some walking, back to the beach and evacuation boats. Ronayne's platoon, hurling itself at the dug-in Japanese, had contributed its share to this grisly harvest.

Third row, standing, far right: *2nd Lt. James A. Ronayne, 3rd Platoon, I Company, 3rd Battalion, 9th Marines on Iwo Jima, c. 20 March 1945.*
JIM RONAYNE

As the Marines moved north in the late stages of the battle the topography changed substantially; it was up-and-down terrain broken by gullies forty and fifty feet wide, much rougher and more broken than the flat ground in the middle of the island around the airfields. As the 3rd Division swung east into what had been the 4th Division's area, Ronayne's platoon passed thirty or forty Marines who had been dead for four or five days, their bodies beginning to bloat and decay. "That really shook up some of the troops," he recalls.

Advancing northward on 22 March, six days after Holland Smith's visit, the platoon swung to its right, toward Iwo's northeast beaches, and reached a ridge line that overlooked a shallow draw about forty yards wide. There was a cave and supporting trench system dug into the far side of the draw, and as Ronayne's platoon neared the trench line a sudden barrage of small-arms fire and hand grenades from the cave and ridge above it forced them to hit the deck and take cover on the reverse side of their slope. Ronayne ordered his flamethrower operator to crawl forward and put a squirt of fiery napalm into the mouth of the cave to set it on fire. Then the platoon could rush the cave, clear it with fire or blow it with demolitions, and continue its advance, a basic tactic at that stage of the war in the Pacific.

Partly because of the hazardous nature of their occupation, which generally involved exposing themselves to an enemy that was eager, indeed frantic, to destroy them, flamethrower operators—"flamers" as they were known—often marched to a different drummer than their fellow Marines. Some were screw-ups assigned the duty by officers and NCOs who didn't want to further risk their more-reliable men. Many were simply cocky types who sometimes acted as though they could win the war single-handedly. Ronayne suspected that some were motivated to carry the lethal tanks, in part at least, because it made them exceptional. It also enabled them to swagger around with the flamethrower's personal weapon, the .45-caliber Colt automatic pistol, strapped to their waists like John Wayne.

Ronayne's flamer was a nineteen-year-old from New Mexico with a self-confident attitude and a touch of John Wayne swagger, which made him something of a hero to the rest of the platoon. It also made Ronayne wonder how he had survived the murderous combat on Iwo as long as he had. In any event, Ronayne wanted a minimum-risk maneuver, just a quick squirt into the cave mouth to enable the platoon to charge it. To Ronayne's dismay, however, his flamer got into position, stood up, and, acting as though he was out to end the war himself, directed a continuous stream of fire into the cave. Ronayne began screaming at him to get back and let the platoon attack, but to no avail. The man was killed instantly, hit in the head by rifle fire from a hill above the cave. More than fifty years later, Ronayne, a devout, straight-arrow, second-generation Irish Catholic, still found it hard to believe the curses and imprecations that came out of his mouth in his frantic attempt to save his flamethrower man. Ronayne lay on the ground looking at his dead Marine, his dismay and consternation turning to fury for several reasons: because of the tragic, senseless death, because the man had not followed orders, because the platoon was still pinned down, and because he didn't know what impact the flamethrower's death would have on his buddies.

Instead of trying to call in tanks or other fire support, Ronayne motioned his demolitions man forward and got a charge of plastic explosive known as "Composition C" and a detonator. He gave orders for the platoon to charge the cave after he blew it, and then rushed across the draw. He reached the trench, ignited the satchel charge, and threw it into the mouth of the cave. When it detonated, his men charged the cave on his command and killed an estimated thirty Japanese troops. It went just as planned, but Ronayne wasn't entirely happy with the maneuver because it appeared that possibly twice that many Japanese had managed to retreat through escape holes in the reverse slope of the ridge. At least he was able to continue his advance. "Whenever you saw a hole, you knew there was another one nearby for an escape," he says. "And sometimes the exit would be behind you."

More than fifty years later, he was still trying to understand his irrational, emotional decision to charge the cave, which easily could have gotten him killed. And he couldn't remember how he arrived at the decision, whether on his own or in agreement with his platoon sergeant and demolitions man. "With artillery there were too many short rounds," he recalls. "I liked air support, but there may not have been time to get it." However it was, he was to hear more about his decision later.

Just two days before this episode, Ronayne had said goodbye to his best buddy and fellow platoon leader in Item company: 2nd Lt. Red Qualls, who had been wounded and was being evacuated on a stretcher. Qualls, also twenty-one, had been hit in the left side of his abdomen by a hollow-point bullet. He was taken to the battalion aid station and, after passing through a series of Navy hospitals, would wind up in the United States four months later. For him, the war was over but his million-dollar wound cost him eighteen inches of intestine and took four operations to heal.[2]

Prior to becoming platoon leaders and comrades-in-arms in the same company during the entire brutal battle for Iwo, Ronayne and Qualls had been in the same platoon in the SOCS and were in the same replacement draft to the Pacific. They wouldn't see each other again, however, until the first SOCS reunion nearly fifty years later. A half century after their great shared experience on Iwo, Ronayne still marveled at how the Second World War and the Marine Corps enabled him, a native of a close-knit, somewhat insular urban community in New England, to meet and become friends with a real, live far-off Texan like Red Qualls! The U.S. Marine Corps may well be the closest, most fiercely loyal brotherhood in the world, and Jim Ronayne and Red Qualls had yet another tie in addition to the Globe and Anchor—their SOCS was unique, and in the stated view of some of their superiors, the best the Marines turned out in World War II.

Because the 3rd Division was in corps reserve on D-day, there was hope all up and down the line that it wouldn't have to be committed on Iwo; Nimitz and Smith had hoped that it might be available for Okinawa.[3] Some on board ship chose to believe this: "We were told that it [Iwo] would be a cake walk," Qualls recalls. That was the worst sort of pipe-dream, however, and as the Marine casualties escalated rapidly in the face of the skillful and desperate Japanese resistance it quickly became apparent that the division was needed. The 21st Regiment tried to land on D+1 but was thwarted by heavy seas and didn't get ashore until the following day. On 25 February, D+6, Ronayne and Qualls and the rest of the 9th Marines were awakened at 0300, fed the traditional "blitz" breakfast of steak, eggs, potatoes, toast and jam, apple pie and ice cream, then attended brief religious services. Catholics like Ronayne were blessed by a priest and given dispensation to say a silent confession, to themselves.

They then formed up at their shipboard debarkation stations. Their ships' boats circled in the heavy sea for a couple of hours while the wave formed up. Ronayne and Qualls were so engrossed with the details of what they had to do that they didn't have much time for fear. At first there was hope that the ride in might be the worst part of the day. The flag had been raised on Mount Suribachi two days before. This, along with the overwhelming aerial bombardment of the island, which was quite visible from the boats, raised a false hope that the end of the battle might be near. In the choppy waters, however, one of the great bugaboos of amphibious operations came into play—seasickness. In a small

LCVP jammed with men sitting chest to back, this almost makes the prospect of combat ashore seem like an acceptable alternative.

But that was primarily because they didn't know what was happening on the beach. The carnage and chaos there was the first of many shocks Ronayne and Qualls suffered on Iwo. Their first view as they ran down the ramp of the landing boat was of the bodies of fifty or sixty Marines at the water's edge, killed as they jumped out of their boats. Nature and the terrain aided the Japanese enormously. The fine volcanic sand made the steep terraces on the beach extremely difficult to climb and seriously impeded the movement inland. The heavy surf, whipped up by an approaching storm, broached many smaller landing craft, which made the task of clearing lanes and getting men and supplies moved forward a desperate struggle.

They learned that the human body, mind, and spirit can endure far more than they ever would have thought. They found that fear in infantry officers in combat is controlled by a couple of factors: the blessed distraction of having to keep track of developments and make quick decisions, and their training, which had well prepared them for the ordeal. It is hard to put self-preservation aside, as Ronayne would note later, but whenever they were given the order to "Move out!" there was no question that that was what they and their men would do. The knowledge that they could rely on their training and their fellow Marines was an increasingly steadying factor for them, along with the acquired realization that however scared they got, they wouldn't panic in combat. "Our training was really good in what we had to do in a combat situation," Ronayne recalls. "We believed in our training."[4]

For the first six days, their platoons furnished work details for the 3rd Division Pioneer Battalion during the day to help clear paths through the wreckage on the beach, pick up dead Marines, and move supplies inland. They provided security at night. On 2 March the two young lieutenants were ordered to report with their replacement platoons to one of the 9th Marines' battalion command posts at Target Area 200H, a two-hundred-yard-square map grid coordinate near Motoyama No. 2, the island's secondary airfield, for assignment to a rifle company. With understandable excitement and trepidation, they moved forward with a group led by Lt. Col. Robert E. Cushman, commanding officer of 2nd Battalion, 9th Marines (2/9), and a future commandant of the Marine Corps. They assumed that they would be assigned to his unit, but the CP at their map coordinate was that of the 3rd Battalion, 9th Marines (3/9).

They were greeted by Maj. Joseph McFadden, 3/9's S-3 (operations) officer, an unflappable man with a seemingly boundless thirst for Coca-Cola, who always seemed to have a cigar, often unlit, clamped between his teeth. Ronayne and Qualls came to consider him one of the best Marine officers they ever met, the epitome of the reserve officer who goes to war when his country calls, fights it, then like Cincinnatus returns to civilian life. A native of Allentown, Pennsylvania, McFadden had been a star single-wing blocking back on the powerful Georgetown University football teams of the late 1930s and the young lieutenants' view of him may have been colored by the fact that they were football players themselves.[5] They too lived up to the standard that McFadden personified, and manifested the American nonprofessional's aptitude for war.

McFadden posted his fledgling warriors and their men to Item Company, which assigned Ronayne to the machine-gun platoon, Qualls and his men to a rifle platoon. The battalion cooks prepared them a meal from what was known as "Ten-in-One" rations, so called because one ration fed ten men. It somewhat more resembled regular food than the individual C-, D-, and K-rations they carried in their packs; one delicacy, much coveted by the troops, was the canned bacon. After chow, they moved up to the line, dropping the bulk of their gear with the company supply section on one of the runways of Motoyama No. 2. Two weeks later, when the survivors returned to pick up their mail and gear, some of the battalion headquarters personnel greeted them with astonishment. A Japanese artillery shell had hit the pile of equipment shortly after they moved forward and some at headquarters assumed they all had been killed. In fact, Ronayne never did get hit on Iwo, and he and Qualls outlasted two company commanders and several other platoon leaders in Item Company. One second lieutenant, sent to the company as a replacement after they'd joined it, never showed up, and his body wasn't found until after the battle. Ronayne was told that he had been captured and tortured to death.

The headquarters personnel had good reason for their gloomy assumption. Ronayne and Qualls joined Item Company at the beginning of the most costly eight days in the 3rd Division's history. When they joined Item Company, the battalion was in reserve to reorganize and take on replacements after several days of hard fighting. The new lieutenants spent those first days on the line getting acquainted with the company and providing security for the regimental command post (CP), which was near the north end of Motoyama No. 2, roughly in the center of the island. The CP was in a U-shaped depression shielded on three sides by low-lying sandstone hills, with Ronayne's and Qualls's platoons security for the open end.

The unaccustomed cold of the north Pacific was no problem for Ronayne and Qualls at this point. They dug their foxholes in an old volcano crater near the island's sulfur-mine refinery where the ground was so hot from the underground sulfur springs that it melted Qualls's toothpaste and shaving-cream tubes and scorched the edges of a leather photo case he carried in his pack. It kept them warm, however.

The Japanese had a maze of caves and an ammunition dump dug into one of the hills surrounding the command post. Ronayne and Qualls received a spectacular welcome on their first night with the regiment. Realizing that they'd been overrun, the Japanese detonated the munitions dump in an effort to destroy the Marines in the CP. The enormous blast occurred just before midnight, and it buried all the people, tents, and equipment in the CP. Ronayne and Qualls and their platoons rushed to help dig them out and found that, miraculously, just eight Marines were injured, only one badly enough to be evacuated. They killed twenty Japanese trying to escape the area.

Because of the stalemate and casualty rate, Maj. Gen. Graves B. Erskine, commander of the 3rd Division, got permission to make one of the Marines' few night attacks of the war, on 7 March. After five days in reserve, this was Ronayne and Qualls's first combat. Their battalion was ordered to take Hill 362C, to their east, which (after Suribachi) was one of the highest terrain features on Iwo. The only preliminary bombardment was a concentration of white phosphorus shells to provide a smokescreen, which wasn't a tipoff as smoke rounds were customary in night harassment firing. Just before jump-off, however, a star shell from a destroyer burst over them, but the Navy quickly was given the word to subside. Ronayne and Qualls moved their platoons up during the night and were close enough to hear the Japanese work the bolts on the rifles during their sporadic firing. At 0500 the 1st and 2nd Battalions began a diversionary attack on the right and 3rd Battalion moved forward on a thousand-yard front. The Marines moved silently through the enemy bunkers, pillboxes, and caves for about half an hour before Japanese machine guns began firing on the battalion's left flank. It was silenced by a flamethrower and while a few Japanese awakened to what was happening they were killed before they could offer organized resistance. Aided by a cold rain and wind, the attack achieved total surprise. The enemy was caught sleeping and the battalion exacted a heavy toll with flamethrowers and machine guns. Although the Japanese managed to slow the assault after they were awakened and began putting up resistance, the Marines passed unscathed through the most heavily fortified terrain in the area in that first hour of surprise.[6] Item Company moved out with the rest, but after advancing about a hundred yards it drew heavy fire and dug in to return it. "There was mass confusion. We'd move out and stop. Move out and sit down," Ronayne recalls. This firefight freed up King and Love Companies, the other two rifle companies in 3/9, and by 0600 they were on what they thought was Hill 362C.

What they had, however, was Hill 331, the hill leading up to 362C (there were two other hills the same height on Iwo, 362A and 362B, but this wasn't the cause of the confusion). The problem was that it wasn't until after dark that Lt. Col. Harold C. Boehm, the 3rd Battalion's commanding officer, was informed that he would make the attack, moving up from reserve through the 21st Marines' lines. He and his company commanders went forward to be briefed and by the light of an illuminating shell were able to glimpse the dark outline of what they were told was the objective. It was only about three hundred yards ahead of them, which surprised Boehm, who thought 362C was farther away. He and his officers shot an azimuth to the hill so they could follow a compass course if necessary. At daylight a look at their maps and aerial photos revealed that Boehm's impression had been right—what they had seen the night before, and what they were on, was Hill 331.

Their objective was still 250 yards ahead of them, and they had lost the element of surprise. Although the Japanese resistance was fully alerted, 3rd Battalion jumped off at 0715, reduced the jumble of Japanese caves, bunkers, pillboxes, stone walls, and trenches of what came to be known as "Cushman's Pocket" one by one, and finally occupied the hill at 1400. The Marines held most of the high ground on the Motoyama Plateau. In the course of the attack, the battalion had swung around the north of Cushman's Pocket and had gotten around behind it, to the east of it.

Item Company's other two rifle-platoon leaders were wounded in the action, and Ronayne was ordered from the machine-gun platoon to replace one of them, 1st Lt. Raymond W. Ickes, son of Secretary of the Interior Harold Ickes. As he and his platoon were moving forward, Ronayne got a brief glimpse of Ickes as he was being carried to the rear on a stretcher. Ickes had been with the company in the battle for Guam the previous summer and was considered a superb combat officer by his troops; he was awarded the Silver Star as well as the Purple Heart and his men continued to talk admiringly of him after he was evacuated. In addition to Item Company's casualties, E and F Companies of Cushman's 2nd Battalion were all but annihilated during the day; Easy Company had just seven survivors, Fox Company just five.

Ronayne and Qualls and their platoons were in the assault on Hill 362C. After it was taken, Qualls was ordered to move forward and tie in for the night defense perimeter with King Company, which was supposed to be on his left. He tied in with the Japanese instead because his company commander unwittingly had sent him out about fifty yards past King Company's front. Qualls and his platoon were stopped by a pillbox and machine-gun fire from both flanks and took cover behind a berm that had a scraggly hedge on top. Qualls called for mortar fire to cover his withdrawal, but because he had advanced further than he or anyone else realized, the mortar rounds landed almost on top of him. Fortunately no one was hit by the friendly fire. Being under both enemy and friendly fire simultaneously, however, did prompt Qualls to briefly ponder how his father and brothers and sisters might receive the news if he were killed in action. This is as close as he will come to ever admitting fear or thoughts of this sort, however. A half century later, he laughingly contends that every day in the Pacific, however murderous, for him was primarily a "new adventure." "I guess I didn't really realize how horrible it was until I read a book about it some years after the war," he says. "I was too busy concentrating on my little area of it."

In the midst of all this, Qualls lost his runner, an eighteen-year-old Arkansas boy, to the stresses of war. The runner had come up to Qualls in a crouch with a message and was badly shaken when a Japanese bullet splintered the stock of his rifle. Qualls ordered the platoon to withdraw and finally tied in with King Company (learning in the process that two of its platoon leaders were SOCS classmates). The next morning, his company commander, 1st Lt. Raymond A. Overpeck, twitted him about his unexpected connection with the Japanese the night before, but this light moment ended quickly. Qualls's runner's closest buddy was hit and died in the runner's arms after he went to help him. That was the final blow for the runner, who began screaming and—in Qualls's words—"trying to crawl into his helmet." The runner was evacuated with combat fatigue, but after the war Qualls managed to track him down and they remained in touch.

Every platoon leader had runners to carry messages back to company and to the other platoons. In the Pacific, they were a primary communications medium because the Japanese monitored the radio nets and the constant shelling cut telephone lines strung on top of the ground. Being a runner was hazardous duty. Jim Ronayne's runner, a youth who had lied about his age to enlist and observed his sixteenth birthday on Iwo, was killed while dodging from shell hole to shell hole delivering a message from battalion, another victim of the merciless combat that decimated all the rifle companies. Like Gordon Dibble and many other SOCS classmates, Ronayne marveled at the youth of the Marines in the Pacific.

The lieutenants were young themselves; most were just twenty-one or twenty-two when they got to Iwo. All experienced a great surge of pride and self-confidence when they were commissioned, with the realization that their gold bars symbolized the Marine Corps's confidence in their leadership ability; for many this would affect their postwar careers and lives as well. Combat, however, was another matter, the ultimate test, and like every other young subaltern in history Ronayne couldn't tell at first what his platoon sergeant and the rest of the platoon thought about their new officer. Like the others, he imagined for a time, with justification, that they were all looking at him out of the corners of their eyes, taking his measure and wondering if he would prove to be a leader with whom their lives could be entrusted. Ronayne knew they all wanted to help, but it was only later that he came to realize how much.

Once the Marines took Motoyama No. 2, the attack became better organized, in Ronayne's opinion, in large part because of the tanks, artillery, and other supporting weapons that were landed after the chaos on the beach came under control. At one point, Ronayne and Qualls were the only officers left in the company. Overpeck, the company commander, was wounded in the 3rd Division's push against Cushman's Pocket. Qualls left his foxhole to move his platoon forward and Overpeck jumped into it behind him. Just as Overpeck raised his binoculars to monitor the action a Japanese sniper hit him in the leg and the Navy medical corpsman ordered his evacuation.

On 20 March, the day Qualls was wounded, a memorial service was held at the division cemeteries. Qualls's platoon sergeant and two Pfcs were veterans of the 3rd Division's two previous battles, Bougainville in 1943 and Guam in 1944. Wishing to minimize their risk in the final days of the battle, Qualls ordered them to attend the ceremony. His concern was well-founded—by this time the 3rd Division was mopping up the northeast sector of the island because the 4th Division, which took the heaviest casualties of the three on Iwo, began loading aboard its transports on 19 March. As they moved through the broken terrain, a defender's dream because of its many ridges and gullies, the 3rd Division men were horrified by the evidence of the 4th's ordeal. When they swung to their right into the 4th's zone, there were dozens, possibly hundreds, of Marine bodies, many dead for several days because the heavy fighting had precluded their being picked up. The bursting and putrefying sight shocked even Ronayne and Qualls's combat-hardened young Marines. Qualls led the rest of his platoon, down from its full strength of forty-four to barely more than a dozen, the size of a normal-strength squad, on a patrol to pick up dead Marines and blow up caves near the northeast beaches, site of the last fighting. While moving up, he got a message from battalion ordering him to help clear out a pocket of hills and caves where Japanese defenders were holed up.

When he arrived, another platoon from Item Company was firing into Japanese positions in a draw in front of them. Its leader, 2nd Lt. William J. McGinley, also a SOCS member, had just been hit in the face by shrapnel and, after conferring with McGinley's platoon sergeant, Qualls merged the platoon with his. He led the group down a path into the draw, where they were hit by a storm of small-arms and mortar fire. Qualls ordered his men to withdraw back to the high ground and began throwing smoke grenades on the path to cover their movement. One man disobeyed Qualls's order and ascended the ridge on the Marines' right instead. His reward was to be shot in the leg, and a medical corpsman who went to help him was hit as well. The man called to Qualls for help. Qualls threw smoke grenades to cover them and started after him while two others went to rescue the corpsman.

As he reached the man, Qualls was hit in the stomach by a hollow-point exploding bullet that also drove fragments of brass and fabric from his pistol belt into his abdomen. He took cover behind a large rock and, after making sure that the corpsman and the man he had gone after were safe, was able to work his way out of the draw. His troops put him on a stretcher and carried him to a jeep, which took him to the beach to the division hospital. As they were headed for the jeep, they met Ronayne and his platoon, and the two comrades said farewell. Ronayne's and Qualls's actions on Iwo were marked by a circumstance common to many of their SOCS classmates and other infantry officers as well: many of their most hazardous actions were to bail their men out of trouble.

The doctor who operated on Qualls in the field hospital, a converted concrete Japanese bunker near the beach, had been on his ship in his replacement draft. When Qualls came out of the anesthetic, the doctor gave him the metal from his abdomen, then tagged him for evacuation.

The ship he was on had been hit by a kamikaze and was headed for dry dock in San Francisco and departed with a load of casualties. He was in the Navy hospital at Pearl Harbor for two weeks while he underwent two more operations, then San Diego, and finally Parris Island, where he had been a boot-camp trainee just a year before he was hit. He was assigned as the base pistol-range officer but he spent a lot of time in the hospital because his wound kept abscessing; the original surgeons had left some of the foreign matter in it. He underwent his third operation at Parris Island, where the doctors finally cleaned it out and enabled him to get on with his life.

Ronayne was never hit on Iwo and stayed for the 3rd Division's mop-up. While they were finishing up, a damaged B-29 made a belly landing about a hundred yards from where Ronayne and his platoon were dug in near Motoyama No. 3, a dramatic reminder of what the battle was about.[7] His troops took off at high port to the crippled aircraft and had an emotional meeting with the grateful crewmembers. "They hugged each other and the crew members gave them their leather flight jackets and their pistols in shoulder holsters," Ronayne recalls. "I had to laugh at my kids, they were so excited."

Like most Marine infantrymen, Ronayne has grateful memories of the Marine aviators who flew close air support in their F4U Corsairs. "They'd come in so low, it seemed that you could reach up and touch their wheels. We'd call on them when we encountered caves where the Japs could run their guns out, big antiaircraft guns primarily, and fire a few rounds then withdraw them with lifts of ropes and pulleys. The fliers would put their ordnance [bombs, rockets, and machine-gun fire] right in the mouth of the cave." He called in a couple of strikes with his platoon radio, the backpack SRC-300. "You wouldn't believe the language we used on each other when they'd miss and have to come around again," he recalls, laughing. "We'd yell, 'You missed, you dumb blankety-blank,' and they'd yell back, 'Blank you, you dumb blankety-blank,' and circle around for another run." He met some of them back on Guam and they shared a laugh over their experiences; the infantry officers also teased that the flyers were really Navy men rather than Marines because of their official designation as naval aviators.

The Marines also got some help from the dog platoons in the final mop-up. The dogs, Dobermans, could sniff each hole and would bark when they smelled a Japanese presence. Nisei interpreters from Hawaii —Army men wearing Marine dungarees—would try to coax the Japanese out, but it seldom worked because all the caves and bunkers had escape exits. The Marines would blow the holes with demolitions and greatly appreciated not having to go underground themselves. "We were so happy to get those dogs," Ronayne says. On a few occasions he kept a dog in his hole with him at night, thinking that it would warn him of infiltrators, a violation of the regulations that a dog is never to be separated from its trainer. Ronayne learned first-hand why that was—the dog whimpered in its sleep one night, an obvious security hazard, and was severely punished by its trainer. He says that many trainers would have killed it out of hand.

Speaking at the dedication of the division cemeteries, General Erskine, the commander of the 3rd Division, graphically described the grim nature of the battle for Iwo. "Victory was never in doubt. Its cost was. What was in doubt, in all our minds, was whether there would be any of us left to dedicate our cemetery at the end, or whether the last Marine would die knocking out the last Japanese gun and gunner."

There was almost total quiet among the hundreds of Marines in attendance as they filed through the area looking for their friends' resting places. On the north edge of the cemetery, however, the Graves Registration men stolidly ignored the poignant ceremony, still busy registering, tagging, and preparing dead Marines for burial. Later, Jim Ronayne got the opportunity to visit the graves of two SOCS classmates, 2nd Lts. Dick Davis and John Dahl, and fallen members of his platoon. Of about 130 SOCS members who landed on Iwo, 97 (75 percent) were casualties, 27 killed and 70 wounded.

9 Okinawa

Battle of Attrition

On 1 April 1945, just ten days after Jim Ronayne won his Silver Star on Iwo Jima, more than 200 of his SOCS classmates began their chapter of the war with the landing on the northern Pacific island of Okinawa, about a thousand miles west of Iwo. It was Easter Sunday, April Fool's Day, and "L" for Landing Day all in one. Okinawa was to be the major forward staging base for the invasion of Japan and it would be the largest and most costly single ground battle the Americans fought in the Pacific. It also was the last one, but they didn't know it at the time.

The SOCS members who landed on the western beaches of Okinawa were part of one of the mightiest amphibious armadas ever assembled. With more than 182,000 soldiers and Marines and sixteen hundred oceangoing ships, the commanding general of the U.S. Tenth Army, Lt. Gen. Simon Bolivar Buckner III, had more troops and more naval firepower than Gen. Dwight D. Eisenhower's Normandy D-day force of

150,000 assault troops. Ike had more aircraft—twelve thousand—and more than fifty-three hundred ships and boats, but not the naval power of Adm. Raymond Spruance's powerful Fifth Fleet, the main U.S. Pacific Navy force.[1] This armada included forty aircraft carriers with more than fifteen hundred planes, eighteen battleships, scores of cruisers, 150 destroyers, fifty submarines, and 430 troop ships, supported by more than three hundred B-29s that bombed Japanese airfields in Japan, Okinawa, and neighboring islands in support of the landing. According to one account this flotilla covered thirty square miles of the Pacific Ocean.[2] The Japanese force totaled about 100,000 troops, 20 percent of whom were conscripted Okinawans.

Intelligence officers warned that Okinawa could be the toughest landing the Marines had made yet. In an effort to screen their intentions, the apprehensive U.S. commanders anchored the invasion fleet off the Minatoga beaches on the southeast corner of Okinawa on the eve of the landing, then sailed around the southern point of the island to the Hagushi beaches on the west during the night. At 0830 the first waves of the four assault divisions—the 6th Marine Division on the left (or northern) flank, the 1st Marine Division to its right, and the Army's 7th and 96th Infantry Divisions on the right flank—landed on an eight-mile front in the center of the island where two major airfields, Yontan and Kadena, were located. On 26 March the 77th Infantry Division had begun occupying the Kerama Islands, a group of small islands off the southwest shore; on 16 April it landed on the island of Ie Shima just west of the Motobu Peninsula. Two other divisions, the 2nd Marine Division and the 27th Infantry Division, were in floating reserve. Ernie Pyle, the famous war correspondent, landed on Okinawa with the 1st Marine Division, then joined the 77th's landing on Ie Shima, where he was killed by machine-gun fire on 18 April.

To the Americans' astonishment, the landing was unopposed. About a thousand Navy frogmen swept the shallow waters off the beaches three days before the landing and destroyed about three thousand wooden stakes that had been planted as obstacles. They found no mines, however, and one reported that when he came to the surface he startled a horse, which galloped away on the beach, an indication that it too was free of mines. Lt. Gen. Mitsuru Ushijima, commanding general of the Japanese Thirty-second Army, had chosen not to defend the landing beaches after the veteran 9th Infantry Division, which had built the beach defenses and was to man them, was transferred to Formosa in December. Ushijima also could justify his decision on the grounds that manning the defenses would have exposed his forces to the Americans' pulverizing air and naval bombardment. In retrospect some historians consider this decision a mistake, but in general he planned and executed a masterful defensive battle. Ushijima had a reputation as a man of character and integrity who inspired the confidence, respect, and loyalty of his subordinates. His chief of staff, Lt. Gen. Isamu Cho, was an outstanding officer and a fierce advocate of Japan's war goals who drove himself and his subordinates hard. He was notorious for having issued the orders to execute all the Chinese prisoners at Nanking in December 1937, the infamous "Rape of Nanking."[3] Together he and Ushijima were a formidable team.

In any event, Ushijima was carrying out the Japanese strategy for defending Okinawa. This was to allow the Tenth Army to land and the U.S. fleet to congregate offshore in support, cripple it with kamikaze aircraft and ship attacks, finish it off with an Imperial Navy task force organized around the world's mightiest battleship, the *Yamamoto,* then attack and destroy the Tenth Army on the ground. The fact that Japanese Imperial Headquarters apparently took this plan seriously indicates how out of touch Tokyo was concerning the relative strengths of Japan and the United States and how taken in they were by their own propaganda. The Japanese had no hope for victory, but the pleasant surprise of L-day turned into a tragically ironic April Fool's Day, a three-month nightmare as the Americans moved south against Ushijima's main defenses at Shuri Castle and the main city of Naha.

Among the SOCS members was Bud Morris, with the 6th Marine Division's intelligence section. Morris, an Episcopalian, attended church services on L–1 on his APA, the USS *Seabass,* an ecumenical service conducted by a Catholic, an Episcopalian, and a Jewish chaplain. It was an emotional service as everyone was anticipating a very tough landing, like Iwo. Early in the morning of L-day, he had the traditional "blitz breakfast," and landed with the third wave, ahead of the division headquarters group, at Yontan airfield. He and his observation post team followed the 4th and 22nd Marines through Yontan airfield, the first strategic objective of the landing, and north to the Motobu Peninsula. Their mission was to collect front-line intelligence from the combat units and radio it directly to division G-2, bypassing the time-consuming battalion and regimental intelligence sections.

Other SOCS class members included Phil Pearce and George Mayer, both of whom landed on L-day with a replacement battalion and spent the month of April in charge of working parties unloading supplies and moving them inland. Both would be assigned to the 5th Marines, one of the 1st Marine Division infantry regiments, the first week in May. Other members of the class such as Mo Bressoud and Bill Ditto had been assigned to mortar sections on Pavuvu with the 7th Marines, another 1st Division infantry regiment.

For a month after the landing, the Marines had a considerably easier time than the Army divisions, which immediately engaged the main Japanese defense line. The 1st Marine Division had little difficulty clearing the lightly defended center of the long island, although the 6th Marine Division had a much harder battle to clear out the northern part of the island, including the rugged and heavily defended Motobu Peninsula and its dominant terrain feature, Mount Yaetake.

The Army divisions wheeled south from the landing beaches and quickly ran into the formidable main Japanese defenses in the southern portion of the island. In that first month the Army divisions suffered seven times the casualties of the Marines. A month after the landing, around the first of May, Bud Morris and Phil Pearce would be given command of rifle platoons in the 6th Marine Division and 1st Marine Division respectively. At that time the Marines began experiencing what the Army had suffered through during the month of April.

Okinawa is about sixty miles long, generally northeast to southwest, and from two to eighteen miles wide. Ushijima established his main defense lines in the hills and ridges and draws in the southern third of the island just north of Naha, the chief port and commercial center anchored on the high ground of Shuri. The first line of defense, north of the main one, ran along the Uraseo-Mura escarpment, which stretched from coast to coast. The second, or main line, ran from Naha on the west coast, uphill to Shuri Castle, home of the Okinawan kings, then along a ridge line to the city of Yonabaru on the east coast. The third, and last, defensive line ran from just south of the Oroku Peninsula and the town of Itoman on the west coast along an escarpment to the Chinen Peninsula on the east. The briefing officers' sober warnings about the landing were wrong only in their timing—when the Tenth Army hit Ushijima's main fortifications, Okinawa became the bloodiest and most intense land battle of the Pacific war.

With the memory of the inadequate bombardment of Iwo Jima still freshly in mind, Task Force 56, with ten battleships, nine cruisers, twenty-three destroyers, 177 gunboats, and five hundred Navy aircraft, devastated the Hagushi beaches. Ushijima and his staff officers watched through binoculars from atop Shuri Castle with great interest as the storm of fire fell harmlessly on his abandoned positions in the hills and valleys behind the landing beaches. It was just as well for the Americans that the beach fortifications were abandoned; as on Iwo, the underground emplacements were essentially undamaged by the bombardment. The casualties for the landing force on L-day were twenty-eight killed, 104 wounded, and twenty-seven missing; the most suffered by any one unit was 3rd Battalion, 2nd Marines, 2nd Marine Division in floating reserve, mostly in I Company, whose LST was hit by a kamikaze, setting fire to their amphibious tractors. Eight Marines were killed, eight were missing, and thirty-seven were wounded, most suffering burn injuries.[4]

On L-day, the 1st Marine Division attacked straight east across the island against little opposition and bisected it at the end of L+3. The 6th Marine Division turned north and moved up the long, narrow Ishikawa Isthmus to the heavily defended Motobu Peninsula. The Japanese had a midget submarine base, powerplant, and other installations on Motobu, which is ten miles long and eight miles wide, about the size of Saipan, and with even more rugged terrain, mountains, and rocky ridges. It is dominated by Mount Yaetake, twelve hundred feet high, covered with dense vegetation, and cut by precipitous gullies.

A memorial on the island commemorates the 237,596 who died during the battle, an average of nearly 3,000 a day—14,006 Americans, 82 other Allied personnel, 75,219 Japanese soldiers, and 148,289 Okinawan civilians, nearly a third of its population of 450,000. The civilians died in the overpowering U.S. bombardments, either from being shot by the Americans as they moved around at night desperately seeking safety or from disease and starvation. Many preferred suicide to surrender to the Americans because the Japanese had convinced them that they would be raped and tortured and that any proffered food would be poisoned.[5] About 7,400 Japanese were taken prisoner, the most of any battle with the United States in the Pacific.

The Tenth Army lost 7,613 KIA, 3,277 of whom were Marines, and nearly 32,000 WIA, including 15,899 Marines; 55 Marines were missing in action. Another 99 Marines from carrier air and ships detachments were killed, 118 wounded, and 12 were missing in action; the grand total of Marine casualties was 19,460. In addition, 117 Navy doctors and corpsmen were killed and 442 wounded.[6] Aboard ship the Navy suffered more than 4,900 killed, the most of any of the U.S. services in the battle, and 7,000 wounded, primarily to the kamikaze attacks; this accounted for about 20 percent of the Navy's total casualties in World War II. It also lost the most ships of any of its battles, thirty-six sunk, twenty-eight so badly damaged they never returned to sea, and sixty that required extensive repairs.[7] More died on Okinawa than at Hiroshima and Nagasaki combined, but the battle received relatively scant attention in the United States for a number of reasons: the death of Franklin Roosevelt, the end of the war in Europe, and the reverberating memories of Iwo.

Like Iwo, the Okinawa defenses were underground, twenty to sixty feet down in coral rock that was harder than concrete. The main tunnel of Shuri Castle was fifty feet underground and Ushijima's men dug sixty miles of tunnels. Okinawa's terrain was far more mountainous and rugged than Iwo's and every minor crease and knob in the rocky ridges was a potential defensive position whose reduction could develop into an operation of its own and had to be dug out with rifles, bayonets, flamethrowers, demolitions, knives, and sometimes fists. Ushijima ordered exit holes in the reverse and flank slopes from which his men could emerge and counterattack the Americans when they had gained the crest.

The defensive positions were as horrible for the defenders as the attackers' exposed positions. Digging the tunnels and caves had been as much of an ordeal as on Iwo. There was little power equipment and the exhausting work had to be done by hand by the Japanese and their impressed Okinawan laborers. As on Iwo, there was a shortage of water, which only worsened when the battle commenced. The Japanese were subjected to a relentless, unending air, naval, and artillery bombardment; they could escape only at night. Their shelters became filthy, noisome cesspools of mud, human waste, festering wounds, gangrene, pus-eating maggots, and stench that finally drove some in desperation, some in madness, out into the "typhoon of steel." Many died of disease or were incapacitated by combat fatigue. Their misery was compounded by steadily dwindling supplies of water, food, and medical supplies— plus the knowledge that they were doomed to death and defeat in any event. The names of their strongpoints became part of the very beings of those who fought there—Wana Draw, Sugar Loaf, Half Moon Hill, the Horseshoe, Shuri Castle for the Marines, Conical Hill, Cactus Ridge, Chocolate Drop, the Pinnacle for the Army.

Bud Morris's rapid intelligence-gathering experiment had worked well in exercises on Guadalcanal's relatively flat topography but flunked the test of Motobu's rugged terrain where the steep, rocky hills and ridges blocked the signals of their line-of-sight

*2nd Lt. Hugh "Bud" Morris,
Intelligence Section, 6th
Marine Division, on Motobu
Peninsula, April 1945.*
BUD MORRIS

SCR 610 radios. Morris and the other division OP team tried relaying messages first through other units and then the ships lying off-shore but nothing worked. "It was a good concept, but bad equipment," he concluded. "And everyone was too busy with their own problems to worry about ours."

Nevertheless, he and his team discovered the abandoned mini-submarine base at Unten Harbor on the northeast corner of the Motobu Peninsula. It also housed kamikaze boats, small craft powered by outboard engines with a covered deck up forward for the demolition charge, and an overhaul shop dug into a hillside above the long concrete ramp where the submarines were hoisted out of the water. They found a torpedo in the repair shop with what appeared to be an enormous detonator in the warhead. Morris speculated that the Japanese had intended to demolish the base, but that the detonator had misfired. One of his men who had some experience with demolitions very gingerly attached a fuse to the detonator and they all retreated a safe distance. Just barely a safe distance as it turned out—they were spectacularly rewarded for their efforts when the explosion blew the entire top off the hill.

Shortly afterward, an enormous column of Army troops, tanks, artillery, trucks, and jeeps came winding down the only road to the base, which was little more than a wide bicycle path. The major in the jeep leading the procession informed Morris that they were from the 27th Infantry Division. The column had taken a wrong turn and was badly lost, thirty or forty miles from where it should have been as best Morris could make out, and it took a while to get all the heavy vehicles turned around and headed in the right direction.[8]

When Motobu Peninsula and Mount Yaetake were secured, Morris seized and shipped to division large numbers of documents in a Japanese headquarters building. He also disabled a primitive radar set on the hill above it and discovered a wicker basket full of condoms, presumably for the protection of the troops against the Korean "comfort women" they had imported and Okinawan women with whom they may have fraternized. He also encountered about three hundred civilians who farmed on the relatively flat land of the neck of the peninsula where it joins the main island, and he was ordered to move them out because they were suspected of passing information to the Japanese. A pretty young Okinawan woman and her husband were at the front of the crowd and while everyone was milling about, she opened her kimono, baring her breasts, and pointed vigorously to a stone hut behind her. "My first thought was, 'This is a hell of a time for an offer like this,'" Morris recalls. "But then I realized that she was pointing at their farmhouse and wanted to go get their baby, which she did." Morris had a Nisei interpreter who didn't speak Okinawan so he asked if anyone in the crowd spoke English. One man shouted that he had been a janitor in a fraternity house at UCLA before the war. "It was like one of those old movies," Morris recalls. "'I was at your university, UCRA,' he said." With his new interpreter's help, Morris got the people loaded on trucks, which was his last action as an intelligence officer—when he returned to division headquarters at the town of Nago on the southern coast of the neck of the peninsula, he was told that, partly because of the failure of the real-time intelligence experiment, the 6th Marine Division had a new job for him.

The Motubu operation cost the division 236 KIA, 1,061 wounded, and one missing before it moved south and was relieved by the 27th Infantry Division. It would suffer far worse at Sugar Loaf Hill and the Shuri Line. On 2 May the regiments of the 6th Division began heading south to join in the assault on the main Japanese fortifications. The failed intelligence operation wasn't the major factor behind Morris's being switched to a new job. "They said they were short of platoon leaders, which turned out to be the understatement of the year," Morris says. "I got it both ways, the perspective from division intelligence, and as a platoon leader, which was godawful." He was given command of 2nd Platoon, Company A, 1st Battalion, 29th Marines.[9] After hitchhiking the twenty-five or thirty miles from Nago to Machinato airfield, Morris finally caught up with the 29th Marines. The 6th Division took over the American right-flank position from the 1st Marine Division on the west coast north of Naha, and the 29th Marines were ordered to establish defensive positions against a possible Japanese landing on the beaches near Machinato airfield, three miles north of the city.

The day after Morris met his platoon, he was ordered to train it to operate with tanks. "I hadn't had any training in this, but I worked a lot of stuff out," he recalls. "You get behind the tank, right? How complicated can it get?" It didn't matter—he never got a tank to work with. His platoon had been badly shot up during the fighting for Motobu and was down to only thirteen or fourteen of the original forty-three, even though about two weeks after he took over the platoon he got five replacements. They were flown out from San Diego, four of them straight out of boot camp where they'd been on L-day. The fact that some replacements were flown to Okinawa because they couldn't move fast enough by ship is a measure of how deadly the battle was. Morris inherited an excellent platoon sergeant. "He was a hell of an NCO. He was seasoned, cool, and affable. If you set out to create a platoon sergeant, he's what you'd come up with." Unfortunately, the sergeant was wounded in the foot and evacuated three days after Morris took over the platoon. "I really hated to lose him. I tried to look him up in the hospital in Guam, but he was in a different one and I couldn't connect." As if to illustrate Eugene Sledge's contention about how quickly disposable and possibly irrelevant second lieutenants were on Okinawa, Morris's platoon went through seven leaders, three of whom were killed and three, including him, were wounded and evacuated.

A week of heavy rain began on 7 May. While his platoon was training and recuperating near the beach Morris saw a battleship hit by a kamikaze. From about a hundred feet above the beach and about a quarter of a mile inland, he had a clear view of the armada offshore and of the kamikaze plunging vertically onto the battlewagon's rear deck.[10] Shortly after that, Morris and his platoon were sent forward along a railroad line that ran south through a narrow valley between Sugar Loaf and Half Moon on the way to Naha. The cut was only about twenty or thirty yards wide most of the way, which gave the Marines a feeling of claustrophobia, particularly under sniper and artillery fire, which was inflicting casualties. Morris's platoon, however, was unscathed during the passage, although he had a close call while resting at the base of a cliff when a close-support aircraft dropped a bomb on the top of it. Rock and debris rolled down on him but he wasn't seriously injured. He had witnessed an even more harrowing episode while moving up through the railroad cut. The Marines were in two columns, one on each side of the tracks, and one of the men on the other side suddenly pulled his pistol out of its holster and held it to his head. Fortunately, a buddy behind him knocked it out of his hand before he could pull the trigger and with the help of a couple of others tied the man's hands behind his back and led him to the rear. Morris says that this was the first time he came to grips with his mortality on the island, but his attitude was considerably different from that of the despairing young Marine in the draw.

"At first, we had the feeling of the immortality of youth, that they'd never get us," he recalls. "And then in my last two weeks there we were all so miserable with the rain and mud and fatigue and shortage of men that I didn't think very deeply about personal security and safety. The second time I thought about it was when I was wounded. I didn't know how badly I was hurt but I had a profound feeling of relief when I realized that I wasn't dead, and that I was out of it [combat]."

From 13 to 18 May, one of the hardest periods of fighting in the campaign, the 6th Division hurled itself against the Sugar Loaf Hill defense complex, which was a key to the main Shuri Ridge defense system. The complex included Half Moon Hill, a major terrain feature southeast of Sugar Loaf, and the Horseshoe, a U-shaped hill just south of it. In the words of the 6th Marine Division history: "Sugar Loaf thus formed the point of an arrowhead aimed at the center of the advancing Sixth, with the two southern hills standing as the broad and sturdy base of the arrow" and able to give fire support to Sugar Loaf.[11] Sugar Loaf, about fifty feet high and three hundred feet long, rises abruptly out of a sloping plain that offers no approach cover. As one account noted, the real danger was not the hill itself but a "300-yard by 300-yard killing zone which the Marines had to cross to approach the hill from our lines to the north."

From 13 to 16 May the 22nd and 29th Marines launched a series of costly frontal assaults on Sugar Loaf, taking it and then being pushed off by counterattacks and incurring heavy casualties; 2nd Battalion, 22nd Marines was reduced to ineffectiveness and its executive officer, Maj. Henry Courtney, was killed and won the Medal of Honor on the night of

14–15 May leading the assaults in the exhausting struggle. With the 6th Division continuing its successive assaults on Sugar Loaf—and the Japanese counterattacks—16 May was probably the hardest and most costly day in its history. On 17 May the 29th Marines again assaulted Sugar Loaf and Half Moon, Morris's 1st Battalion leading the attack toward Half Moon on the regiment's left flank, the 2nd Battalion attacking Sugar Loaf on the right, with the 3rd Battalion to sweep through the center to Half Moon. Although heavy artillery fire from Shuri forced 1st Battalion to withdraw from its ridge that night, elements of 3rd Battalion remained on the slope of Half Moon Hill. With tank support, 2nd Battalion took Sugar Loaf the next day.

The capture of Sugar Loaf and the fall of Conical Hill in the Army's sector was a major turning point in the battle. With their loss, Ushijima's flanks were exposed and the main defense line anchored in by the Shuri complex was fatally compromised. The brutal attrition had worn down the dug-in defenders even worse than it had the Marines. The Japanese losses were mostly unseen by the Americans but they were severe and unlike Tenth Army's couldn't be replaced. On 22 May Ushijima ordered the beginning of a retreat to the southernmost, and last, defensive line.

Morris wasn't much aware of the big picture, however. "The only thing I knew about was the little area I had to take care of," he says. "The main thing I was concerned with was which platoons I was tied in with on the left and right. We just weren't aware of anything outside of that and I really didn't learn anything about it until after the war. I had my own fish to fry, I had complete tunnel vision."

On the night of the eighteenth on the north, or forward, slope of Half Moon, Morris was ordered to relieve a badly shot-up platoon from Company E, 4th Marines, and after getting into position was subjected to grenade attacks during the night. At dawn he saw the body of a Marine covered with a poncho lying next to him. It was the leader of the Easy Company platoon, Edward "Ned" Gaillard, a SOCS classmate, who had been shot in the back of the head the day before. Gaillard was a cousin of a man Morris had grown up with, and Morris had met him for the first time in the SOCS. When he got back to the States Morris and another SOCS member, Joseph O. Mathews, visited Gaillard's parents in New Haven to tell them what they knew about their son's death. He gave them a White Owl cigar ad that Gaillard, like Morris an enthusiastic skier, had torn out of a magazine and kept in his helmet because it was illustrated by a photo of a ski lodge. "He just had the single entry wound in the back of his head," Morris recalls. "Other than that there wasn't a scratch on him."

On the nineteenth Morris and his platoon pushed to the forward crest of Half Moon, throwing demolition charges into holes and caves they passed and taking sniper fire from the high ground in front of them. The battered 29th Marines were relieved by the 4th Marines, and first thing in the morning of the twentieth, Morris and a half dozen of his men were moving along a slope, shielded by terrace walls from snipers posted on a hill between them and Shuri Ridge. They were mopping up the area, throwing grenades into a row of Okinawan tombs, which were tall enough to stand in, had arched entrances and a small forecourt with a limestone wall, and provided excellent cover. A figure leaped out of a break in one of the terrace walls. The torrential rains had started again at this time. "With all the rain and mud everyone was a godawful mess and looked the same," Morris recalls.

> At first I thought he was a Marine. But he ran toward me and I saw that he was carrying a potato masher grenade that had a wooden handle and a ring on the end of a string which had to be pulled to activate it. It was one of the strangest experiences I've ever had. In my mind's eye I could see the page of the field manual in training at Camp Lejeune that had told us about the Japanese grenades. It had three pictures, *A* showing the grenade, *B* showing the ring being pulled to arm it, and *C* showing the tab out. I could envision that photo and I knew it was in *C* condition, that he had an armed grenade. He ran up to me and stuck it in my stomach. I had my hands full of grenades and couldn't get my pistol out of the holster. So I knocked him down and turned and ran. He fell down, he'd been shot, fatally, by one of my men when he was running at me. Like an idiot, I turned around to see if he was chasing me just as the grenade went off and peppered me with shrapnel. All up and down my body.

Two fragments lodged in his left eye, one in the lid so he couldn't close it, one broke his femur although the bone didn't displace, and his left hand was badly damaged. "I was covered with blood but looked a lot worse than I was," he says. The Japanese had been shot by one of the new replacements flown out from San Diego, a Pfc. who had been in the Corps about six months and turned out to be a good, alert Marine. "I told him I'd like to give him a million dollars but all I had was my watch, which I gave to him."

Morris was hurt badly enough that his shooting war was over, however. He was evacuated to the regimental aid station, then to division where the surgeons operated to remove the fragments, and he experienced pain in his kidneys, from the concussion, he believes. His state of mind wasn't helped much when he learned that the holes in the roof of his tent had been caused by a recent Japanese artillery barrage that had inflicted casualties on the occupants. This was quite common in the Pacific as the Japanese didn't recognize the Geneva Conventions or respect medical personnel and facilities. By the first of June he was at Fleet Hospital 111 on Guam, but still, as it turned out, not totally out of danger, although not from the Japanese. Most of the patients in his ward were fellow platoon leaders, some of whom weren't above pulling a practical joke. They told him that a SOCS class member was in one of the examination rooms, so Morris went looking for him—and found someone else: he burst in on Adm. Chester W. Nimitz, the Navy's Pacific Ocean Area commander, who was having an enema administered by a Navy hospital corpsman. Morris beat a hastier retreat there than he had on Okinawa.[12] After three months on Guam, he spent six weeks at the naval hospital at Mare Island, California, then finally to Bethesda Naval Hospital in Maryland where his mangled finger was partially repaired. His wounds entitled him to a partial disability pension, which would have a significant impact on his life five years later.

The limestone and coral ridges that run generally east-west across the island formed natural in-depth defensive positions anchored by Shuri Ridge and the Shuri Castle near the capital city of Naha. Unlike the single, unbroken line of trenches of World War I, these defenses were mutually supporting strongpoints in concentric arcs around the Shuri bastion. As on Iwo, the plan was to inflict the greatest number of casualties until American firepower made the position untenable, then withdraw to the next position. There are no major north-south ridge lines to offer approach routes for the attackers so each defensive line had to be taken by bloody frontal assaults, one after the other. Most of the caves and tunnels dug into the coral ridges were constructed to make them resistant to high-explosive blasts and flamethrowers; many had tiny firing ports, which were nearly impossible to spot but whose narrow field of view did make the defenders vulnerable to fire and maneuver by the attackers. The Americans would assault a hill or ridge line, the Japanese would counterattack and throw the Americans off, the Americans would attack the next day, and the Japanese would counterattack, over and over until the Japanese strength was worn down through attrition. Often each of these assaults cost the Americans all or most of the platoons or companies making them. The tactic of hurling men at the dug-in defenses was similar in doctrine and execution to the war of attrition on the Western front in

World War I; the big difference was that on Okinawa it worked. The Japanese weren't able to replace their losses and the Americans had the resources to prevail, albeit at terrible cost to the rifle companies. The ordeal was as horrible as that on Iwo Jima and proved even more costly. Okinawa cost twice as many American casualties, more than four times as many Japanese (plus the Okinawa civilians), and took nearly three times as long.

Phil Pearce was assigned to Company B, 1st Battalion, 5th Marines on 2 May, just as action intensified for the 1st Marine Division, which had relieved the Army's 27th Infantry Division, a New York National Guard unit that in the view of the Marines had performed poorly on Saipan and didn't do much better on Okinawa. The 27th Division had gotten off to a bad start with Marine Lt. Gen. Holland M. "Howlin' Mad" Smith, the Marines' overall ground commander. Smith considered the 27th's efforts on Makin Island in 1943 in conjunction with the Marine assault on Tarawa ineffective, and then judged its performance on Saipan as so unsatisfactory that he relieved its commander, Army Maj. Gen. Ralph C. Smith, in the midst of the battle for Saipan. The 27th didn't get the infusion of regular officers and NCOs that many Guard units did, and while it often fought courageously it suffered from bad leadership. On Saipan it was between the 2nd and 4th Marine Divisions and its slow advance had exposed their flanks. Some historians have laid some of the blame on what they consider Holland Smith's inadequacies as a corps commander, as the Army had feared, along with his gung-ho Marine's bias against the Army, but there was no question about the quality of the division's performance.[13] The Army was outraged that a Marine would presume to take such action against an Army officer, and the episode triggered one of the most bitter interservice controversies of the war. It was a good part of the reason Admiral Nimitz didn't invite Holland Smith to attend the Japanese surrender on the battleship *Missouri*. The clash also had implications for the battle for Okinawa, particularly in the deployment of the Marine divisions.

The Navy and Marine Corps were becoming increasingly concerned about General Buckner's slogging, World War I tactics, on which they blamed the excruciatingly slow advance, a protracted operation that left the naval force increasingly exposed to the kamikazes. They believed that it played directly into Ushijima's defensive strength and they pressed Buckner to use the 2nd Marine Division, his reserve force, to threaten Ushijima's rear with an amphibious landing on the southeastern coast, which had been considered as an alternative landing site for L-day. Buckner thought his logistic capabilities were marginal and the operation too risky. The Navy was reluctant to press the issue because of the sensitivity of Holland Smith's action on Saipan. However, two historians of the war, Williamson Murray and Allan R. Millett, concluded that "compared to his subordinates, Buckner was hardly fit to command a corps, let alone a field army. He rejected every suggestion that he revise the concept of the campaign, ignoring the advice of the four marine generals who had captured Guadalcanal, Cape Britain, Guam, and Peleliu. Only Spruance and Nimitz had the authority to order Buckner to change his plan, and once again the admirals shrank from conflict with the army."[14]

In fairness to the 27th Division, it was understrength on L-day and some of its units fought as valiantly and effectively as any in the first days on Okinawa. It was badly shot up in the process and was relegated to security duty for the rest of the campaign after losing twenty-two of thirty tanks in a disastrous tank-infantry attack on Kakazu Ridge on 19 April. The 27th's withdrawal appeared disorderly and the division seemed to be demoralized and disorganized to many of the Marines as they moved forward in its relief. A SOCS classmate of Phil Pearce's, Robert P. Craig, a platoon leader with Company G, 2nd Battalion, 1st Marines, noticed that many of the 27th's soldiers had no weapons and that they had left a lot of rifles and BARs strewn on the ground along their line of march. George Mayer, who had been in a replacement platoon and was moving up to take command of the 60-mm mortar section in A Company, 1st Battalion, 5th Marines, was "appalled" at seeing the bodies of men from the 27th Division still lying along the roadside several days after their deaths. One of the Marines' most powerful traditions, as Pearce was soon to demonstrate, is their care for their dead and wounded.

From the very first it was clear to the Marines that they were in for a rough time. Another SOCS member, Jeptha Jefferson "Jep" Carrell, in K Company, 3rd Battalion, 7th Marines, and his fellow officers surveyed five or six miles of the front from a high point north of the Shuri line as soon as they got into position. They could see ridge line after ridge line running east and west perpendicular to their north-to-south axis of advance. "I had a sinking feeling standing there," Carrell recalls. "My thoughts were, 'We're going to have to attack almost every ridge and there are undoubtedly many, many ridges beyond the several I can see from here.'" The reality turned out to be worse than he imagined. There were a lot of ridges and they all had interlocking defenses with nearly impervious firing ports in their coral hillsides.

Carrell got a quick initiation. His platoon was stationed on a ridge that rose on his left to a flat-topped cone and it immediately came under fire from a fortified position on the forward slope of the cone. He attacked the position with a fire team and his attached assault squad, which included a flamethrower and demolitions man. The assault units moved up to the position masked by smoke grenades and supported by suppressive fire into the aperture, which was about six feet wide and a foot high. The flamethrower operator stuck his nozzle into the aperture and emptied the tank. The demolitions man had a satchel charge, a cloth bag with pockets containing blocks of TNT and Composition C2, which were linked with primacord. He pulled the detonator's igniter and threw the charge into the cave. Two or three seconds after it exploded, a Japanese arm appeared in the aperture throwing a grenade at the Marines! The construction design and hard coral rocks had shielded the defenders from the flame and explosives. As on Iwo, the aperture tunnels in many of the fortifications had 90-degree corners a few feet in from the opening to protect the defenders against flamethrowers, demotions, and direct fire. After other fruitless assaults, Carrell had a tank open up on the position's rear exit hole with its 75-mm cannon before moving to a concealed position from which it picked off the Japanese as they fled another frontal flame and demolitions assault.

Ushijima's defensive plan grated on many of his offensive-minded subordinate officers, particularly the hot-headed Cho. He varied from it just once, when he succumbed to Cho's plea for a attack. In the early morning of 4 May the Japanese made a major counterattack and an attempted amphibious landing from the East China Sea on the Marines' west coast flank. Both were repulsed with heavy casualties, however. One group of Japanese demolition engineers in the landing was wiped out, but the Marines seized the carrier pigeon they had for communications with their headquarters and released it with the mordant message: "We are returning your pigeon. Sorry we cannot return your demolition engineers."[15] This disastrous venture cost the Japanese about six thousand first-line troops and sixty artillery pieces, and Ushijima tearfully apologized to his operations officer, Col. Hiromichi Yahara, who had strongly opposed it. After the war Yahara, the only senior Japanese officer who survived, wrote that it was the turning point of the battle. This was the last Japanese banzai attack of the war and they reverted to their highly effective defensive tactics for the rest of the campaign. It obviously was going to be very difficult, and the Marines developed an appreciation of what their Army counterparts had been facing for the previous month.

V-E Day, 8 May 1945. The day Germany surrendered in World War II. A historic event that made very little impression on Phil Pearce and his fellow Marines and soldiers on Okinawa. More pertinent to them was the cold, driving, torrential rain that temporarily immobilized both them and their Japanese enemies; ten or twelve inches of rain in a day is not uncommon during the monsoon season on Okinawa. For three miserable, chilly, wet days both sides hunkered down. The Americans reorganized for the resumption of their offensive when the weather lifted. The Japanese, relatively dry in their underground bunkers, probably had the better of it during this period. For the Americans out in the open, the storm was an unmitigated misery of flooded streams and an ocean of knee-deep mud that swallowed everything, mired tanks and bulldozers, and got into everything—food, shoes, blankets, ammunition. It was almost impossible to heat rations and coffee with fire or the "canned heat" that came with the rations. Rifles, bayonets, and anything else metal rusted, and ammunition rounds stuck together in clips and machine-gun belts. Lying in a foxhole was like being in a cold, filthy bathtub and many men scrounged empty ration and ammunition boxes to try to line their holes. These wretched conditions, in fact, only worsened as the campaign continued in the weeks ahead. The rains turned the muddy ridges into an unspeakable horror of decomposing bodies, maggots, and the other refuse of infantry warfare.

At this time the 5th Marines had just finished taking the Awacha Pocket, which it had surrounded and then reduced in a costly battle; four members of the SOCS, Duncan Crane, Bob Allen, Nick Evangelist, and Lawless Falcon, were killed there after less than a week in combat.[16] Now the regiment was overlooking a Japanese strongpoint in a deep draw just south of Awacha and Death Valley. The weather cleared on the morning of 9 May, and the Marines went at it again. On the tenth, Pearce's battalion attacked from the regiment's right flank and assaulted the far slope of the draw, with 2nd Battalion attacking from the left. Able Company, 5th Marines, George Mayer's unit, secured the ridge the next day.

Pearce and Baker Company joined Able on the ridge, which overlooked a crescent-shaped valley. The men in Baker named them Wilson Ridge and Wilson Draw in honor of their company commander, 1st Lt. Walter R. "Curly" Wilson, nicknamed in honor of his premature baldness. On 11 May Baker Company was ordered to cross Wilson Draw in support of Able Company's assault on the high ground on the other side. Wilson and Pearce, the leader of the third platoon, moved laterally along the ridge line, visually reconnoitering the draw. Pearce estimated that the floor of the valley was about seventy feet below the ridge and about three hundred yards wide, a forbidding moonscape pocked by crevices and coral upheavals and spotted with brush and scrubby trees. It appeared to be empty and Wilson ordered Pearce to move his platoon out in the lead of the company attack.

At that point, Pearce, twenty-one, had been on the front line in Okinawa for a little more than a week as a platoon leader with Baker Company. He had spent his first day with the company as the machine-gun platoon leader and on the second day was made leader of the first platoon when its original lieutenant was hit. On his third day Pearce was shifted to the third platoon, when its lieutenant was wounded in the legs by grenade fragments. Pearce remained with the third platoon for the rest of the Okinawa campaign and proved to be an outstanding infantry officer.

He quickly won the respect of his men, many of his whom, particularly the NCOs, were veterans of the bloody battle for Peleliu the previous autumn and he considered himself extremely fortunate in inheriting them. This was particularly true of the platoon sergeant, Sgt. Tommy Karr, a Texas boy who was a grizzled veteran in Pearce's eyes. In fact, Karr had just turned nineteen three months before Pearce joined the platoon, but Pearce could see that he was a good NCO who enjoyed a mutual respect and trust with the troops. Karr and the green new lieutenant quickly established a mutual admiration and friendship society of their own that holds to this day; Pearce has remained in contact with half a dozen members of his platoon.[17]

They meshed well for good reason. Pearce was an excellent combat leader right from the start. He joined the company while it was preparing for the assault on Wilson Ridge and worked side by side with the troops. He lugged water, ammunition, and rations up to the platoon's position. He helped clean and distribute new rifles, carbines, and BARs to replace those that had been damaged or were wearing out. Partly because of this, the platoon runner, Pfc. John Gartzke, an Iowa boy nicknamed "Polack" who had enlisted in June 1944 upon graduating from City High School in Iowa City, somehow didn't get the word that Pearce was an officer. Gartzke recalled that Pearce "just showed up" one day, and since he was working alongside him, Gartzke assumed that he was a replacement NCO awaiting assignment or maybe even a deserter from another unit. Finally, the day before the action in Wilson Draw, Gartzke mentioned to Pearce that the platoon needed a lieutenant and was astonished when his new friend "Phil" said, "I'm him." More than fifty years later Gartzke still contends that Pearce had sergeant's stripes stenciled on his dungaree jacket sleeves, at which Pearce smiles; he did have his lieutenant's bars pinned to the underside of his collar, as all the officers did, so he wouldn't be a target for Japanese snipers.[18]

Pearce told the third platoon that his first concern was for their lives and well-being and that while the platoon would do everything necessary to accomplish its mission, he would try to lead them in a way that would minimize casualties. He said that his standard procedure was to be at the front of the platoon with just a four-man fire team ahead of him and he quickly won their trust. An Illinois farm boy who took naturally to soldiering, Pearce says he never worried about leadership: "We were taught leadership, to take care of the troops and keep the boys from getting killed. I enjoyed it and thought it made a lot of sense." To him small-unit tactics were a challenge "like hunting rabbits or squirrels without a dog." The Marines knew the Japanese could lie patiently in wait for a long time "like a rabbit in a cornfield." To Pearce the key was to "try to figure out a good place where they'd [the enemy] get you. It's kind of a knack in finding and recognizing the hidden indications. And at night, not getting lost." He says he never worried about getting hit. "Oh, everyone's scared. Not while you're being shot at, but afterwards. I guess I really didn't realize it even though we were taught that that was what would happen."

Like several of his peers, Pearce improvised on his Marine Corps issue equipment. He carried a .38-caliber Smith and Wesson six-shooter revolver given to him by his great-uncle. The platoon came to appreciate the weapon in the cave warfare on Okinawa. The standard issue M-1 "Garand" rifle was unwieldy in tunnels and its muzzle velocity was too high—the rounds ricocheted wildly, which posed an indiscriminate threat to friend and foe alike. So, whoever went head-first into the tunnels to check them out carried the revolver, which was an excellent close-combat weapon. It didn't have the great stopping power of the standard-issue Colt .45 automatic pistol, which is something like being struck with a blunt axe, but it was more reliable in the dirt and grit of combat situations—it would fire even when it was very dirty. Karr recalls killing a "couple of Japs" in the tunnels with it.

Pearce also won the trust of Curly Wilson, who had been the platoon's commander on Peleliu the previous September, and in Tommy Karr's estimation was an exemplary combat officer. This was because of Wilson's and Karr's relationship on Peleliu. Karr landed on Peleliu as a BAR man in third platoon and was promoted to squad leader during the battle. However, he had some bad moments during his second day on

Peleliu when the 5th Marines were ordered to capture the airfield, the primary rationale for taking the island. This involved charging across the open airstrip, which was swept by Japanese fire, and Karr was wondering what a nice eighteen-year-old Texas boy like him was doing in a place like that when he got some inspiration from his platoon leader. One of Wilson's toes had become so badly infected that he had to cut the end out of his boondocker in order to walk, but he led the charge across the runways anyway, limping and dragging his bad leg. Karr figured that if Wilson could do it, he could too. After Peleliu, when the 1st Division returned to the Russell Islands to stage for Okinawa, Wilson was promoted to first lieutenant and made company commander. When the platoon sergeant, Frank Ball, was wounded on Okinawa while helping string concertina wire in front of their position, Karr was promoted to sergeant to replace him.

When Pearce joined the company on Okinawa, Wilson quickly recognized him as a kindred soul. To the men of the third platoon, however, this was not necessarily a blessing. After Pearce's first couple of weeks with the platoon, some of them pointed out that the unit had been on the company point for the entire time, which Pearce says hadn't occurred to him until then. When he mentioned this to Wilson, the company commander's response was, in effect, yes, that's right, Pearce, and it's not by accident. That was all the explanation he gave and the third platoon remained on point for the rest of the battle.

Wilson Ridge and Wilson Draw were north of Shuri Castle, the anchor of the Japanese main line of resistance on Okinawa. The 5th Marines, on the left flank of the Marine sector, had been fighting in the Awacha Pocket and were ordered to take Wilson Ridge, which they did on 10 May, but couldn't hold it. They returned the next day, however, and did secure it.

They were part of Buckner's general offensive of 11 May with all of his line divisions, the Army on the left (east) flank, the Marines on the west, all prompted by the Navy high command's pressure on Buckner to speed the campaign up and reduce the supporting fleet's exposure to the kamikazes. Descending into Wilson Draw on that day, Pearce, as usual, moved out with a four-man fire team (the fire-team leader, a rifleman, the BAR man, and the assistant BAR man, who was both ammunition carrier and rifleman) on the point, with himself and Gartzke just behind it and the rest of the platoon in a column behind him. The platoon snaked down a narrow trail toward the floor of the valley, covered by Baker Company's other platoons, machine guns, and mortars. Before they reached the bottom they were hit from all sides by a storm of rifle, machine-gun, and mortar fire. Undetected by Pearce and Wilson, the Japanese were burrowed into caves in the forward slope of the ridge the platoon was descending. The enemy charged out of the caves and into the Marines' midst. One shot Pearce's hand-held SCR 536 radio ("walkie-talkie") out of his hand and when he raised his carbine to defend himself he hit the magazine release button by mistake in his excitement. Gartzke, who considered safeguarding his lieutenant a primary duty, discharged this responsibility by killing the Japanese soldier with his Thompson submachine gun.

The platoon took cover in the brush and outcroppings and returned fire. Pearce saw that any advance was impossible. With his radio destroyed, he ordered one of his men to work his way back up to the ridge line to get a smoke screen to cover their withdrawal. However, this first messenger was hit by a round that also disabled his rifle before he could get out of the draw, so Pearce dispatched Gartzke, who made it. The company lobbed smoke grenades and 60-mm mortar smoke rounds into the valley to cover the withdrawal and sent down stretcher bearers to help.

This took nearly four hours of desperate, close-in fighting. Constantly exposing himself to enemy fire, Pearce directed the withdrawal and supervised the stretcher bearers in removing the wounded. He gave first aid to five walking wounded and then personally helped them to safety through the climb. In the process he also threw smoke grenades to help screen the movement and killed several Japanese who tried to charge his wounded men. Pearce knew that if he survived the ambush his first responsibility was to ensure that all his men were out, dead or alive, so after the last man reached safety on the ridge, he and Gartzke, who had rejoined the platoon, remained behind to scout the area, just to make sure. No Japanese were in evidence by this time; they either had been killed or retreated. Pearce and his platoon had succeeded in bringing all twelve of their wounded comrades out with them; miraculously, no one was killed. After he reached the ridge top, Pearce and two of his men lay on their stomachs on the top of the ridge and hurled "satchel" charges down into the Japanese cave mouths, which were eight or nine feet wide, only four or five feet below the ridge line. The concussions so disoriented one of the men, the oldest man in the platoon, old enough to be Phil's father and known in the platoon as "Pappy," that he had to be helped back by a corpsman. "Those blasts were so strong they'd lift you right off the ground," Pearce recalls. Then he had concertina wire strung in front of their position. The next morning Baker Company crossed the valley and occupied the other side without resistance. The Japanese survivors had withdrawn to the Shuri defense complex.

After Baker Company reached the ridge on the other side, it spent the next two and a half weeks with the other Marine units fighting south toward the Shuri defense complex. With bloody frontal assaults, they reduced one grim objective after another—Dakeshi Ridge, Wana Draw by the 1st Division, Sugar Loaf and Half Moon Hill by the 6th. It was bitter, heartbreaking going. The rifle companies would storm ridge lines and cave lines at great cost and then, with their weakened strength and while subjected to heavy fire, be counterattacked and forced to withdraw, only to have to attack the objective again—and sometimes yet again. Companies in both Marine divisions were reduced to such shadow strength that they had to be pulled from the line to be reinforced and refitted for combat effectiveness. On the left flank, the Army's three front-line divisions, the 7th, 77th, and 96th, fought as hard and well as the Marines and suffered the same catastrophic casualty rates in their rifle companies.

By 21 May Pearce's battalion was on high ground east of Half Moon Hill near Wana Ridge and Hill 55 on the approach to Shuri. Baker Company was ordered to establish an outpost on one of the two hills out in front of the battalion and Pearce's platoon, as usual, drew the assignment; the other hill was occupied by a platoon from Charlie Company commanded by 2nd Lt. Alex Agasse, an All-American football lineman at the University of Illinois after the war. The two platoons were isolated for two days by strong Japanese forces to the left and right of them and had to subsist on the rations, water, and ammunition they had humped in with them; attempts to parachute supplies from Marine "Avenger" torpedo bombers missed the mark. One lesson Pearce learned on that hill was not to be surprised by what the troops might bring into the field. One of his men happened to be carrying a kettle, which the troops made good use of after they caught a hapless rooster that had somehow survived the fighting. They boiled it and augmented their rations with chicken soup. Pearce's concern was more about ammunition and water than food, however. He finally got resupply when he was able to lead a fire team back to hook up with a detachment of black Marines from one of the Corps's segregated Depot and Ammunition Companies.[19]

When its flanks were secured, the platoon advanced across a rice paddy to a hill about five hundred yards from Shuri Castle, the keystone of the Japanese defenses. Reaching the crest unopposed in the late morning, they caught an unsuspecting Japanese unit taking a break on the reverse slope, killing some and routing the rest. On that hill, Pearce encountered Capt. Harry Leonard Ziegler, who was leading his company up to the front. Ziegler was a senior at Carmi (Illinois) High School when Pearce was a freshman and is now a lawyer in nearby Fairfield.[20]

On 22 May, after the fall of Sugar Loaf and Conical Hill, the Japanese began their withdrawal from the Shuri complex south to the Kiyamu Peninsula, which took several days with American artillery, air, and naval gunfire pounding the retreating columns despite having their observation hampered by the heavy rains and bad weather. As a result, the Marines were able to make a comparatively rapid advance and on 29 May Pearce's battalion captured Shuri Ridge, which was eight hundred yards west of Shuri Castle. The castle was to the east of the battalion's operational zone in the Army's area. The 77th Infantry Division was ordered to capture the castle, but Pearce's battalion, in violation of basic infantry doctrine, crossed the operational boundary line and took it instead, to the Army's understandably deep displeasure—and to the Marines' peril. The 77th Division had scheduled air strikes and artillery bombardment of the bastion in support of its assault and learned of the Marines' move just minutes before it was made. Working frantically, the Army was able to contact all the supporting arms barely in time to avert disaster. Maj. Gen. Pedro del Valle, commanding general of the 1st Marine Division, justified this glory-grabbing move with his desire to seize the high ground behind Wana Draw, which had been such a bloody and dispiriting obstacle, and his belief that it would be a few days before the Army division could capture Shuri.[21] In fact, Capt. Julian Dusenbury, commander of Able Company, 5th Marines, which took the castle, had encountered only light resistance, which he reported, and then got permission to press his advance. He planted a Confederate flag that he carried in his helmet on the castle. Dusenbury and Able Company were the first Americans to reach the castle itself, but Pearce thinks his platoon was the first on the defensive complex on the ridge. He had set up on the right of the castle, which had been nearly pulverized by 16-inch naval shells, near the radio tower that functioned for the Americans as an artillery aiming point. Dusenbury's company was on his left.[22]

During the last week in May all the combatants were subjected to several days of driving, torrential rains and stalemated before the approaches to Shuri such as Half Moon Hill. The combination created a slimy, reeking nightmare of mud, decomposed corpses, maggots, stench, and other horrors, which sometimes seemed worse than combat itself. Eugene Sledge, who described the area as a vile and revolting "garbage pit," related his attempt to dig a foxhole on Shuri Ridge. In the process he dug into a Japanese corpse left from the American artillery bombardment, which he concluded had been very effective, judging from the overpowering stench of decomposed bodies in the area.[23]

During the fighting around Shuri Castle, Tommy Karr was making a head call when he was lifted off the ground by a Japanese mortar explosion that wounded him in the right shoulder. He was evacuated to a field hospital near Kadena airfield. It was the subject of constant shelling and night air raids, however, and after three days he decided that he was better off with his platoon. He sneaked out of the hospital and fought the rest of the battle with a bulky bandage on his shoulder. He and Gartzke considered the capture of Shuri and the action in Wilson Draw as the highlights of their epic battle on Okinawa.

The battle for Shuri also was the most memorable Okinawa experience of George Mayer, who commanded the 60-mm mortars in Able Company, 5th Marines. In the struggle for Wana Draw, leading into Shuri, George managed to get smoke rounds to screen the riflemen when the artillery was unable to provide support. "They'd take a position, then get hit by the Japanese coming out of exit caves in the reverse slope and sides of the hills and would need smoke cover if they had to withdraw," he recalls. When the tubes are firing, the primary responsibility of the mortar officer is to go up with the rifle companies as the forward observer because estimating distance is of crucial importance, leaving his section sergeant to lay the guns and run the section. "I had a very good sergeant from Watertown, New York."

In the next forty days of the grueling battle for Okinawa, Pearce and his men fought for Knob Hill, Wana Draw, the Shuri complex, Mezado Ridge, Kunishi Ridge, and other Japanese strongpoints on the island. On 4 June the 6th Division made a land-to-land amphibious landing on the Oroku Peninsula just south of Naha. They embarked on LCTs (landing craft tank) near Machinato airfield the night before and made the two-hour run to Oroku in the morning. The general advance from Shuri south to the town of Itoman was relatively rapid because of the Japanese withdrawal, and Mo Bressoud (Item Company, 7th Marines) voiced the frustration the Americans felt with the brutal, slogging drive to the Shuri complex. "On the road to Itoman we fought my kind of war," he says. "At least it was the war for which I had been trained at Camp Lejeune." In other words, it was a war of fire and maneuver against the Japanese snipers and light machine guns that harassed and tried to delay the relatively rapid American advance south. This kind of war was short-lived, however, as the Americans soon hit Ushijima's last defense

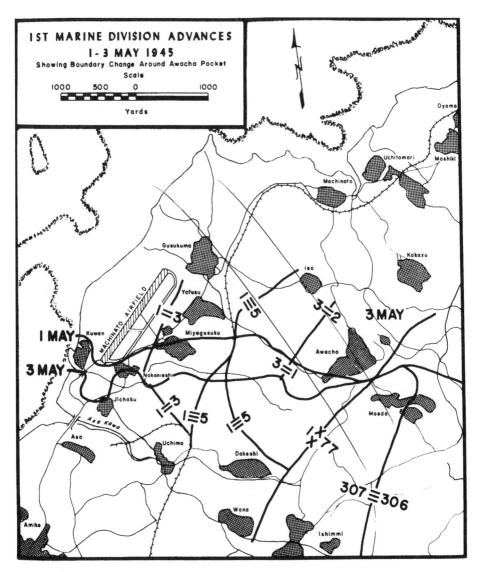

1st Marine Division advances, 1–3 May 1945. From Col. Joseph H. Alexander,
U.S. Marine Corps (Ret.), The Final Campaign: Marines in the Victory on
Okinawa. HISTORY AND MUSEUMS DIVISION, HQMC, WASHINGTON, D.C.

line, on Kunishi Ridge, which was like Dakeshi and Wana. It took the 1st
Division several days to secure Kunishi, a process that was marked by
Marine bodies being stacked several feet high like cordwood and a
steady stream of walking wounded and stretchers to the rear.

Bill Ditto with a Japanese bunker directly behind him, near the southern end of Okinawa, June 1945.
BILL DITTO

The Marines also encountered another horror show with the accumulation of Japanese and Okinawan bodies in the area. The murderous advance south was measured by the degree of decomposition of the Japanese and Okinawan bodies—they changed from fresh kills nearest the front to bloated corpses to skeletal remains in the rear areas. As Mo Bressoud noted, "They marked the distance from the fighting almost as accurately as yard markers on a football field." One result was the attraction of swarms of blow flies, which settled immediately on the Marines' rations and made it almost impossible for them to eat.

The Okinawa civilians suffered terribly during the entire campaign, but their ordeal was worst in the final days partly because the southern third of the island, where the Japanese defenses were concentrated, was also the most densely populated, four times that of Rhode Island. Mo Bressoud had to deal with civilians on several occasions. In one village, either Dakiton or Hanja, he encountered a dead mother with a live, healthy baby boy lying beside her. The solution to his problem was to give the child to a Japanese prisoner being escorted to the rear by a Marine rifleman. "In the other direction I went forward with my platoon—looking for other enemy soldiers to kill," Bressoud recounts.

Near the village of Shichina just south of Shuri on the way to Itoman on 8 June, Bressoud encountered civilians who were hiding in a cave near his position, not knowing whether they were Japanese troops or not. Women and children screamed when his demolition man tried, unsuccessfully, to blow the entrance shut, but he didn't know if there were troops with them or not. There weren't, but the Marines learned it through an act of heroism. "One of my squad leaders did what I consider one of the bravest acts I ever witnessed," Bressoud recounts. "He grabbed his rifle and a flashlight and dropped into the cave. It wasn't the kind of act for which the Corps gives out medals, but one of a totally unselfish individual trying to prevent further wanton destruction. It was exceedingly dangerous." The corporal prodded the people to climb out and Bressoud evacuated fifteen or twenty men, women, and children, who were escorted to the rear by one of his Marines who was suffering from severe dysentery. One young woman had a broken leg and the Marines rigged a litter that two of the men could drag.

A mother, grandmother, and child had been seriously wounded and were comatose and near death. After conferring with his platoon sergeant, Bressoud determined that the humane course was to end their suffering rather than leave them unconscious on the ground. It wasn't something he could order someone else to do, so he shot each of the three comatose victims in the head with his carbine as his platoon moved on. He used three rounds on each because he feared he'd botched it with the first two and left the scene "thoroughly ashamed." At the time he was ashamed primarily because he'd been so unprofessional, but as a deeply religious and spiritual man he underwent a great deal of soul-searching on the matter later. He never wavered in his conviction that it was the most humane option at the time, but he thought a lot about war and killing in general. "Is it always wrong, regardless of the circumstances, to kill another human being?" he asked. "Yes. Is it always more wrong to kill another human being than to take some other action which is itself also wrong? Ah . . . now I cannot answer 'yes' or 'no.' . . . It is a question unanswerable in theory, answerable only in the midst of a concrete real life dilemma."[24]

Pearce and Baker Company fought up to the bitter last hour of the struggle for Okinawa. The 1st Battalion, 5th Marines, spent the last four days of the battle trying to take Hill 79, a high point on the southern tip of Okinawa which had been a Japanese artillery spotting post. On 18 June the battalion assaulted the hill with Baker Company on the right flank. On the nineteenth the assault had Baker on the left, Able in the center, and Charlie on the right with antiguns and three tanks per company in support; George Mayer's 60-mm mortars in Able Company fired more than a thousand rounds on those two days, but the attempt failed both times. On the twentieth, Able Company got to the top of the bill but was driven off the crest by heavy mortar and artillery fire, although the battalion kept possession of most of the rest of the hill.

Because Pearce's third platoon had been on the point constantly during the campaign, Wilson promised before the battle to keep it in company reserve while the other two platoons took the hill. After his first reconnaissance, however, Wilson ordered Pearce to saddle up his platoon for the first assault on the eighteenth. That failed, and the next day, with a tank in support, the second platoon tried and also failed, suffering heavy casualties in the process. The first platoon tried the next day and also failed, with severe losses. Finally, Pearce suggested that they combine the three weakened platoons for the assault, and on the fourth day, under his leadership and with tank support, his company along with Able and Charlie Companies finally secured Hill 79. It was 21 June, the day Okinawa was officially declared secure. About nine thousand Japanese died in those last three days of the campaign.

One of the regiment's special action reports noted that the enemy had heavy and accurate artillery and mortar fire and that his tactics were "excellent," obviously hoping to make the operation prohibitively costly. It called for better use of supporting arms—citing the effectiveness of the 4.2-inch mortars and recommended assigning a battleship in direct support of each battalion—for the frontal assaults on the defensive lines. It also recommended the "delay of attacks until tanks are available . . . to reduce casualties," varying the time of attacks, and using more night attacks and patrols to reduce strongpoints that held up the advance during the day.[25]

When Hill 79 was secured, Phil Pearce could see dogfaces—probably of the 96th Infantry Division—on his left, playing volleyball in the valley below Hill 79, about half a mile to his left. Even though Okinawa had been declared secure, the killing went on and Pearce still had to contend with Japanese defenders who were in tunnels they'd dug in Hill 79. A hole five feet in diameter in the top of the hill led to the tunnels below and came out about 150 feet away, at the bottom of the south slope of the hill, away from the Americans' direction of attack. Pearce's men fired flamethrowers and dropped hand grenades into the hole to flush the defenders out. Tragically, they also got some innocent victims. With their machine guns they inadvertently killed twenty-nine women, whom the Japanese had impressed as "comfort women," or prostitutes, and had tried to escape during the night. In addition, a nine-year-old Okinawa boy was burned by the flamethrowers and taken to an aid station. Pearce never learned whether he survived.

After its attack on Hill 79, the second platoon leader, an older lieutenant who had been a detective in the Los Angeles police department, was evacuated with combat fatigue. Then, the first platoon leader, William C. Peterson, a SOCS classmate of Pearce's, was wounded during his attack when a Japanese bullet hit the wooden stock of his carbine; he went to the aid station after the assault was called off. After the battle Pearce recommended one of his men, Cpl. Donald "Jesse" James, a fireteam leader, for the Silver Star; Karr thought James was a tiger in combat. In fact, the overwhelming majority of the Marines on Okinawa, and in the entire Pacific for that matter, were heroes.

In the evening of 21 June George Mayer was wounded by a Japanese grenade while his company was assaulting Hill 69. He was lying on his stomach when the grenade landed next to him, but he was able to crawl about six feet away before it exploded and peppered his back and the rear of his legs with shrapnel. Not wanting to risk moving at night, which could get him shot by Marines who might think he was an infiltrator, he lay there until morning, when he could safely walk to the battalion aid station. His wounds weren't serious, primarily because Japanese grenades exploded into much smaller fragments than American

2nd Lt. George N. Mayer, Company A, 5th Marines, A-1-5 Compound, Okinawa, August 1945. GEORGE MAYER

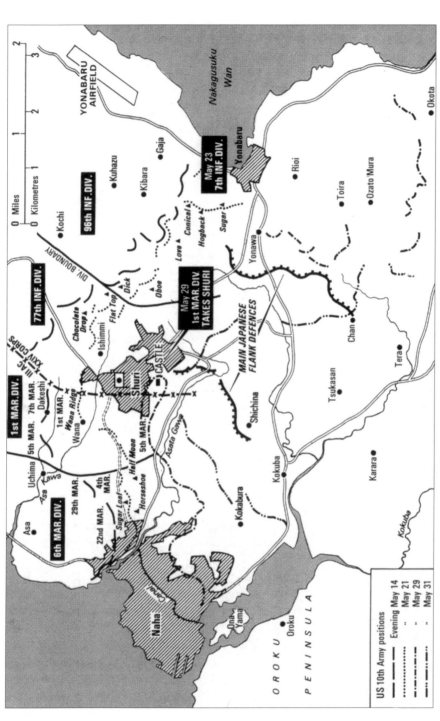

Tenth Army positions, 14–31 May 1945. From Col. Joseph H. Alexander, U.S. Marine Corps (Ret.), The Final Campaign: Marines in the Victory on Okinawa. HISTORY AND MUSEUMS DIVISION, HQMC, WASHINGTON, D.C.

grenades and were less lethal as a result. "They had too big an explosive charge," he explains. The medics dug the fragments out of his rear end using a local anesthetic, but because of the number of wounds they feared the possibility of infection and George was evacuated to Guam. Released from the hospital, he was on an LST at Saipan on his way back to Okinawa on 6 August, the day the *Enola Gay* dropped the atomic bomb on Hiroshima. He rejoined the 1st Marine Division at its camp on Okinawa as it was staging for the invasion of Japan.

General Buckner was killed on 18 June when he went forward to observe the 8th Marines, which had just been committed to relieve exhausted 1st Division units. A Japanese shell drove a piece of coral into Buckner's chest, wounding him mortally. Geiger, a Marine aviator who was commanding III Amphibious Corps, was promoted to lieutenant general and replaced Buckner. He was the first Marine general ever to command a field army. This didn't sit well with the Army, which immediately dispatched Gen. Joseph ("Vinegar Joe") Stilwell to replace him. Stilwell arrived five days later, after the battle was over. The furor over Holland Smith and the 27th Division still reverberated.

In all the cruel and disheartening bloodletting, Pearce, miraculously, was never hit. His platoon, however, whose normal strength was forty-four men, suffered more than ninety casualties, 200 percent including replacements. Many of these came in the exhausting final four-day struggle for Hill 79. All the rifle companies of the 1st and 6th Marine Divisions and the four Army divisions on Okinawa were similarly decimated in the battle, just as those on Iwo Jima were.

The Tenth Army lost almost 40,000 men killed, wounded, and missing plus 26,000 to accidents and disease and the Navy suffered its heaviest losses of the war. U.S. casualties in the Pacific per thousand, measured in days of combat, were three times those in Europe in 1944 and 1945.[26] For his contribution to this slaughter, a grateful Japanese government posthumously promoted Ushijima to General of the Army, only the second in Japanese history. The appalling losses on Iwo and Okinawa cast a black cloud over the relief the combatants felt that those desperate struggles were finally over and deepened their fear about what lay ahead. They had lost the belief in the immortality of youth they had brought on the beach with them. The Japanese hope that such battles of attrition would gain them bargaining points was futile. What they won instead was the atomic bomb.

10 The Atom Bomb and the Invasion of Japan

You Second Lieutenants

Are Expendable

When Okinawa was declared secure on 22 June 1945, the SOCS class's losses were 48 members killed in action—27 on Iwo Jima, 21 on Okinawa—and 168 wounded, a casualty rate of 58 percent.

However, they faced the prospect of much worse to come. The Japanese strategy of attrition on Saipan, Peleliu, Iwo, and Okinawa foretold an even worse struggle for the home islands. Many Army and Marine rifle companies suffered more than 100 percent casualties in those battles. One battalion on Iwo lost 95 percent of its original officers and 98 percent of its enlisted men, as well as 70 percent of its replacements; one Marine platoon on Okinawa had seven different lieutenants. One member of the SOCS, John Pittman, recalls of Okinawa that "all forty-five in my rifle platoon [in the 1st Marine Division] that went ashore on April 1, 1945, Easter Sunday morning, were either wounded or killed. Six of us [were] wounded twice. When I left the island on June

22nd with my second wound, nineteen of the twenty-two replacements I got on June 19 were already wounded or killed. Fortunately, my other memories of the Corps are far more positive."

The effectiveness of the kamikaze attacks were equally sobering. Intelligence reports indicated that the Japanese could put five times as many aircraft in the air over Japan as they did at Okinawa, which triggered alarms about what suicide airplanes and ships—including small manned submarines and swimmers—could do to heavily loaded troop transports off the home island shores. There were seemingly endless sources of potential disaster—about 2.3 million regular troops in the home islands alongside a Home Guard of 28 million men and women—if, indeed, not the entire civilian population of Japan—being mobilized to fight the invaders, plus the presence of more than 1 million troops in China and another million in Manchuria, Korea, and Formosa. Then there was the often violent northern Pacific weather—Typhoon Louise hit Okinawa and then Japan between 9 and 11 October 1945 and wreaked heavy damage. Even without storms the heavy seas in the area are a threat to heavily loaded landing craft; an amphibious landing is a hazardous undertaking under the best of circumstances. All this prompted Adm. Ernest King and other Navy planners to consider the possibility of substituting fire-bombing and blockade for the amphibious assaults, but the need to put an end to the protracted war overrode this.

Their island battle victories inspired little elation among Americans of all ranks in the Pacific, particularly the veterans of the grisly final battles on Iwo and Okinawa. Their relief in surviving was tempered by the awful cost their pilgrimage had exacted, and they were infused with dread of even worse to come. As usual, Pfc. Eugene Sledge, a 60-mm mortar man with Company K, 3rd Battalion, 5th Marines, on Peleliu and Okinawa, expressed most eloquently the troops' reaction when they were told of the Japanese surrender on 15 August:

> We received the news with quiet disbelief coupled with an indescribable sense of relief. We thought the Japanese would never surrender. Many refused to believe it. Sitting in stunned silence, we remembered our dead. So many dead. So many maimed. So many bright futures consigned to the ashes of the past. So many dreams lost in the madness that had engulfed us. Except for a few widely scattered shouts of joy, the survivors of the abyss sat hollow-eyed and silent, trying to comprehend a world without war.[1]

Six members of the SOCS were platoon leaders in Sledge's company on Okinawa, one of whom, Duncan M. Crane, was killed and four others wounded.[2] Their fates appeared to support Sledge's theory that modern warfare may have made infantry second lieutenants obsolete, and they shared his foreboding about an invasion of Japan. One, Soterios John "Sam" Menzelos, recalled a briefing by their regimental commander at the end of July 1945. The 1st Marine Division was part of III Amphibious Corps and would have been in Gen. Courtney H. Hodges's First Army, which was slated to land on the Kujukuri-Hama beaches east of Tokyo in Operation Coronet on 1 March 1946.

"There would be cliffs to climb on rope ladders," Menzelos recalled. "He said, 'You second lieutenants will lead the way. You will climb fast. Tell your troops, "Follow me!" You second lieutenants are expendable!' That night Sam Dunlap and I got drunk at the unfinished O-Club." Jep Carrell, Company K, 3rd Battalion, 7th Marines, expressed a universal belief shared by most of the American infantrymen in the Pacific: "Those of us who survived Okinawa were thoroughly depressed. I don't think any of us thought we would escape being killed or wounded in the next landing scheduled for the Japanese homeland." Carrell had excellent reason for this feeling—he was the only one of twenty-seven platoon leaders in the 7th Marines to last the entire operation on Okinawa.

The invasion of Japan, code-named Operation Downfall, would have been in two stages: Operation Olympic, the landing on Kyushu in November 1945, and Operation Coronet on the Plains of Tokyo the following March. The two landings would have involved a total of 1.3 million men. Planning for Olympic included fourteen divisions, including the 2nd, 3rd, and 5th Marine Divisions in V Amphibious Corps, a total of nearly 574,000 troops and about fourteen hundred ships. Coronet, "this much dreaded operation" in the words of the official Joint Chiefs of Staff history, called for fifteen divisions already in the Pacific, including III Amphibious Corps—the 1st, 4th, and 6th Marine Divisions—plus a dozen more Army divisions from Europe as follow-on and reserve forces and five British Commonwealth divisions. The fortifications on the Plains of Tokyo appeared so fearsome that the Army mounted its 240-mm howitzer—its largest artillery piece—on a modified Pershing tank chassis to give it a mobile weapon that purportedly could penetrate five feet of reinforced concrete before exploding. Planners on both sides considered the use of poison gas. Both Olympic and Coronet would have been supported by as many as five thousand aircraft, including a thousand B-29s in Maj. Gen. Curtis LeMay's XXI Bomber Command, more than a thousand Navy aircraft in Adm. William Halsey's Third Fleet, plus Army Air Force B-24s, B-17s, fighters, and Marine aviation.[3]

The Japanese were stockpiling kamikazes and mobilizing the entire population in a program government propagandists starkly dubbed "The Glorious Death of One Hundred Million" (exercising a bit of poetic license as the nation's population was about seventy million). They had no realistic hope of defeating the invasion force but, consistent with their central and northern Pacific island defenses, planned to concentrate their strength on the beaches in the hope of inflicting such cataclysmic losses that the Allies would negotiate a peace settlement. Some Allied casualty estimates ran as high as five hundred thousand killed and wounded; in a controversial article in *Harper's* magazine in 1947 Henry L. Stimson, the secretary of war under Presidents Roosevelt and Truman, cited now discounted estimates at possibly more than one million. The Allied planners also noted that in 1944 and 1945 their casualty rate per one thousand combat troops in the Pacific was three times that in Europe.[4] When the troops landed on the home islands for the occupation, they found that the estimates of the Japanese fortifications and weapons were by no means exaggerated. The Japanese planners had calculated—almost to the day and man—the grid coordinates, timing, location, and force levels of the Allied invasion plan.[5]

These horrendous figures, given credibility by the battles of the last year of the war, and uncertainty about the Soviet Union's postwar intentions in Asia, entered into Pres. Harry S. Truman's decision to use America's new nuclear weapons to hasten the war's end. The dropping of the atomic bombs on Hiroshima and Nagasaki, however, precluded the invasion and the planned two-hundred-thousand-man British landing on the Malay Peninsula to retake Singapore. One incidental result was that at the war's end the Pentagon had about half a million Purple Heart medals on hand that had been struck in anticipation of the invasion. Most of these have been awarded to the 370,000 casualties the country has suffered post–World War II.[6]

It also triggered a vigorous debate about the necessity and morality of Hiroshima and Nagasaki that continues to this day. One school of historians in the 1960s and 1970s argued that the Truman administration was convinced that Japan was ready to surrender but dropped the bombs to send a political and diplomatic message to the Soviet Union, in effect the opening shots of the Cold War. Probably the most vigorous exponent of this argument is Gar Alperovitz, who argued that the Joint Chiefs were convinced that Japan would have surrendered without the bombs, that they were dropped for diplomatic rather than overriding military reasons, and that the administration actually ignored Japanese surrender initiatives.[7] These critics argue that the Japanese, led by Emperor Hirohito, who realized that the war was lost and wanted to avoid any further suffering by his people, were on the verge of surrender and would have done so in a very short time.[8] Other historians believe that the Allied insistence on unconditional surrender and the Japanese fear of losing their emperor were major factors in their seemingly irrational and suicidal intransigence.

Truman's defenders counter that even after the second A-bomb at Nagasaki there was strong resistance to the emperor by Defense Ministry and Army officials who wanted the nation to fight to the death. There was the threat of a coup against the emperor and attempts to stop his surrender broadcast to the Allies and the Japanese people.[9] Truman and his advisers also had considered the probable fates of Allied prisoners of war and subject populations in the event of an invasion. Unlike the Germans, on the Western front at least, the Japanese scorned the Geneva conventions on warfare. Allied medics in the Pacific, unlike in Europe, were armed and didn't wear the red cross on their helmets and medical packs because it was just a bull's-eye for the Japanese. The same was true for hospital ships. The idea of a temporary ceasefire to retrieve wounded, as the western Allies and Germans occasionally agreed to, was never entertained for a moment.

Allied leaders had profound worries about the fate of Allied prisoners in Japanese hands. Downed B-29 airmen were subjected to brutal torture and execution and only a small percentage survived. Whereas 4 percent of the more than 235,000 American and British prisoners of war died in German captivity, nearly 40 percent of the 132,000 who fell into Japanese hands were killed or died of starvation, torture, and other maltreatment.[10] The growing public impatience with the war was another concern, manifested by the rapid demobilization of the divisions in Europe. The concomitant result was that those slated for the invasion of Japan were being filled up by inexperienced recruits, promising an even higher casualty rate. Finally, given the nature of the final negotiations leading up to Pearl Harbor, how much trust could Truman place in Japanese diplomacy? Whatever has been learned in hindsight, it is hard to see how Truman could have justified a continuation of the war at that point when he had the weapons in hand to end it. Even after the major battles on Okinawa and Luzon ground to a close, the casualty toll, primarily among airmen and sailors, continued to mount during the summer of 1945, averaging about 7,000 per week.[11]

Paul Fussell, now a literary scholar and an eloquent essayist, was an infantry platoon leader who had been wounded with the 103rd Infantry Division in Europe and then was transferred to the 45th Division, which was staging for the Pacific in August 1945. He speaks eloquently for the Allied servicemen already in the Pacific and those slated to go there, for whom the sudden end to the war meant that they would live out their expected life span, the traditional three score and ten: "When we learned to our astonishment that we would not be obliged in a few months to rush up the beaches near Tokyo assault-firing while being machine-gunned, mortared and shelled, for all the practiced phlegm of our tough facades we broke down and cried with relief and joy. We were going to live. We were going to grow to adulthood after all."[12]

Not surprisingly, there were few members of the SOCS who didn't applaud the dropping of the atomic bombs at the time along with Fussell, and this feeling hasn't diminished over the years. Joe Clement probably puts the case as strongly as anyone in the class: "My prior basic feeling as a Marine Corps junior officer has changed little over the past fifty-plus years. I should not, I could not, and I would not have sacrificed the life of one of my men for all of those Japanese who died from the A-bombs." One of the few who questioned it is Craig "Tuffy" Leman, who won the Silver Star and Purple Heart on Iwo with Company H, 3rd Battalion, 26th Marines:

> I regret that we dropped the A-bomb on undefended cities and incinerated civilians, just as I regret that we firebombed German and Japanese civilians as a matter of policy. I believe we should have used it on a truly military target . . . the Japanese and German governments had both committed this kind of atrocity many times over, but I am not proud that we descended to their level of barbarity and I was appalled when I saw Sasebo, burned to the ground in a single B-29 fire raid, and Nagasaki. . . . But it is done, and I may owe my life to the fact that it was done. . . . My daughter has been in Kagoshima for the last two years teaching English to Japanese students. If we had landed there, she probably would not exist.

Except for the belief that the bomb probably saved his life, Craig Leman was in the minority in his class.

But for all this, postsurrender analyses of the Japanese defenses revealed that the home islands army was poorly trained, equipped, and supplied, and that many of the forward beach defenses on Kyushu were incomplete and unmanned. American air and naval attacks had devastated the Japanese. These studies estimated that the occupation of Kyushu would take two months, at a cost of 75,000 to 100,000 Allied killed and wounded. They also concluded that Operation Coronet, the invasion of Honshu, probably would not have been necessary because the battle for Kyushu would so deplete the Japanese forces.[13]

After Iwo was secured, Jim Ronayne and the 3rd Marine Division returned to Guam for outfitting and training for the invasion of Japan; the division was to be part of Operation Olympic. In July the 9th Marines scheduled a regimental parade and ceremony and on that morning, Ronayne's battalion adjutant instructed him to be sure to wear a clean set of dungarees and have his web gear in immaculate condition. Why? Ronayne inquired. Because there's going to be a medal ceremony to award you the Silver Star, was the reply. Ronayne was getting the third highest award for valor in combat for his assault on the cave on Iwo. That was the first he'd heard that his battalion commander had put him in for the medal. After the ceremony, Ronayne noticed a difference in Item Company: the troops seemed to snap to with considerably more alacrity when he gave an order. The medal apparently indi-

2nd Lt. James A. Ronayne, right, *receives the Silver Star from Brig. Gen. William E. Riley, Assistant Division Commander, 3rd Marine Division, at an award ceremony on Guam, April 1945. Ronayne won the Silver Star for gallantry on Iwo Jima, 22 March 1945, with Company I, 3rd Battalion, 9th Marines.*
JIM RONAYNE

2nd Lt. James A. Ronayne in the village of Yona, Guam, sometime after Iwo, 1945.
JIM RONAYNE

cated that the young shavetail may have done more and learned more on Iwo than they thought. Modest to a fault, Ronayne maintained fifty years later that the medal was a tribute to the SOCS class, not him, an assertion that inspires his classmates to smile faintly and shake their heads in disbelief.

Despite the respite from combat, this was not an uneventful time for Ronayne. In enjoying the newfound respect that went with his Silver Star, he began casting a critical eye on the new replacements in his company. One of the new platoon leaders was an Annapolis graduate who was proud of his big blue class ring, which Ronayne eyed with askance. It didn't seem to him that a man needed a fancy education at the Naval Academy to lead a rifle platoon. Ronayne's ordeal on Iwo persuaded him that strength of character was the fundamental prerequisite for leading men in combat.

He was more impressed by some of the other replacements. When a replacement draft for his battalion arrived in late April, about a month after the division had returned to Guam, Ronayne went down to meet the newcomers and found to his surprise that his new platoon sergeant was to be none other than one Sergeant Brinkerhoff, his drill instructor at Parris Island. Brinkerhoff had spent the war training recruits and was in the Pacific for the first time. When he saw the lieutenant approaching, Brinkerhoff called the detail to attention, did an about face, and gave Ronayne a crisp salute in the best Marine tradition. After introducing himself, Ronayne reminded Brinkerhoff of their past relationship. Also in the best Marine tradition, Brinkerhoff betrayed not a flicker of movement nor a whit of emotion: "Did the lieutenant feel that he got good training, sir?" he inquired. Indeed Ronayne did and he enjoyed what he considered an excellent working relationship with Brinkerhoff.

Also in the draft and assigned to Ronayne's platoon was Cpl. Thomas Donovan, who had been Ronayne's roommate in the V-12 program at Dartmouth. A former football player at Manhattan College, Donovan had busted out of the officer program because he expended more effort on football at Dartmouth than on his studies. Ronayne knew what a screw-up Donovan could be and got him transferred to the motor transport platoon so he could be Ronayne's driver, an act that almost had disastrous consequences.

One day they drove across the island to see Ronayne's cousin, a supply officer in the Marines' 1st Field Service Command, and Ronayne unwisely loaned Donovan a set of lieutenant's bars so the three of them could have a drink at the officers' club. A major in the bar had had a few more than he needed and, unfortunately, Donovan managed to catch up with him. Even more unfortunately, he took umbrage at the loud and drunken major and ended up punching him out. Behavior like this can lead to a long stretch of hard time in a military prison like Leavenworth. Fortunately, in the uproar Ronayne and Donovan were able to slip out and escape in the jeep. Also fortunately, blood turned out to be thicker than Marine green; Ronayne's cousin held up under hard questioning and didn't waver in his insistence that he'd never seen the two culprits before in his life, that they had just sat down beside him at the bar, and so they were never fingered. Ronayne probably wouldn't have gone to Leavenworth or the naval prison at Portsmouth, New Hampshire, but his life would have been a great deal less pleasant and his military career could have come to an ignominious end. Abetting the impersonation of an officer is a serious enough offense and the physical assault of a superior officer is a major military crime.

Also in the replacement draft was another Donovan, a big, genial corporal named Arthur Donovan Jr. (no relation to Tom), who was made a squad leader in the Item Company machine-gun platoon. "Artie" Donovan also was a football player, at Notre Dame and Boston College, and went on to the professional football Hall of Fame as a defensive tackle with the Baltimore Colts. He had spent most of the war in Ireland as a Marine guard at the U.S. submarine base on Londonderry Island. His father, Arthur Donovan Sr., had been a leading prize-fight referee before the war and coached and managed service boxing teams during the war. After his son joined the 3rd Division, Donovan *père* arranged matches between his teams and those on Guam, which afforded him a wartime reunion with his son. The 3rd Division boxing team was outstanding and cleaned up on most of its opponents, as did the division baseball team, led by Dodger shortstop Pee Wee Reese.

With the Japanese surrender, the Marine divisions began to scatter and disband. The 1st and 6th were posted to China and the 2nd and 5th to Japan for occupation duty. The 3rd Division, which was supposed to accompany the 2nd and 5th Divisions to Japan, was replaced at the last minute by the 32nd Infantry Division because the Joint Chiefs wanted to keep one Marine division in the central Pacific for security and mop-up. One battalion of the 21st Marines was sent to occupy the Japanese fortress at Truk and a battalion of the 3rd Marines was posted to Chichi Jima in the Bonins. Many recent low-point replacements were transferred to the divisions in North China. Ronayne and the 9th Marines remained on Guam patrolling and mopping up the remnant Japanese troops who were hiding out in the hills. Finally, in December 1945, the high-point combat veterans, including Ronayne, boarded ship for return to the States and civilian life.

Ronayne's troop ship was the APA *Bunker Hill,* and his buddies duly noted the gold plate on the ship that informed them that it had been built at Fall River, Massachusetts, about thirty-five miles from Ronayne's hometown of Milton. This inspired considerable kidding about the likelihood that it would sink on the voyage home. Ronayne arrived back home in Milton in February, in time to enroll at Holy Cross for the spring semester. He thought about returning to Dartmouth, but his strong-willed mother objected. She wanted him to remain near his neighborhood of Jesuit high schools and nearby Jesuit Boston College, where he had started as a freshman, but when he pointed out that Holy Cross, which was in Worcester about forty-five miles west, also was Jesuit, she relented. Ronayne knew he had to get farther away from home than Boston College. The first summer he was back, he was out after 12:30 A.M., his mother's curfew hour, and she locked him out. A war hero in his officer's uniform and the Silver Star on his chest slept on the porch that night.

Red Qualls was awarded his Purple Heart while still bedridden on the hospital ship that transported him from Pearl Harbor to the United States. In addition to finally getting the wound healed, he realized another benefit at Parris Island. On Christmas Eve, 1945, he met Ruth Rentz, a pretty young civil service payroll clerk who had just been transferred to the Parris Island hospital from the Naval Air Station at Beaufort, S.C. They celebrated their golden wedding anniversary in 1996.

At the Naval Air Station at Corpus Christi, Texas, where he was the rifle range and ordnance officer, his final assignment before being discharged in May 1946, Qualls was informed that he had been awarded the Bronze Star for his heroic conduct in the action in which he was wounded. He had been recommended for the Silver Star but somewhere along the line the award was reduced a grade to the Bronze Star. There was no award ceremony for Qualls; the Marine Corps mailed a certificate for the medal to his home in Cisco after he had returned to civilian life.

After tours in hospitals on Saipan and Tinian, Dan Hurson was evacuated to Pearl Harbor where he was assigned to a transient barracks until pronounced fit for duty. While there he went to the Navy hospital looking for friends and found a couple of them, including John Hyndman, a SOCS classmate who had been in Baker Company, 28th Marines and evacuated with a severe head wound. The 5th Division returned to the big island of Hawaii on 12 April and after Dan caught up with his unit, Charlie Company, 27th Marines at Camp Tarawa, he was reassigned to the machine-gun platoon, and began training for the invasion of Japan.

The division had received heroes' welcomes in Hawaii with a Navy band playing and civilians lining the route in Hilo as they debarked and moved back up to Camp Tarawa. They were cited by the Territorial legislature and paid a visit by Commandant Gen. Alexander A. Vandegrift. In April the XXI Bomber Command on Saipan informed the division that more than three hundred B-29s had made emergency landings on Iwo by then and that the command intended to name a new Superfortress for the division. On it would be inscribed the division insignia and its battle name, "The Spearhead." While they were at Iwo, a huge outdoor theater named "Kama Rock" had been built in the 26th Marines regimental area. It was played by the USO and stage shows starring bandleaders Ray Anthony and Dick Jurgens, and playwright Moss Hart, and featured two movies nightly. In addition to the movies, the USO organized dances, beach parties, athletic events, and canteen services. There were post exchange facilities and athletic facilities, featuring baseball,

basketball, and softball games. There were parades and medal cere-
monies for the division's 1,308 decorated members, including fourteen
Medals of Honor, ten of which were posthumous; ninety-four Navy
Crosses, thirty-nine of which were posthumous; and 337 Silver Stars.

Their major preoccupation, however, was the next order of business:
the invasion of Japan. Before leaving Iwo, the division was alerted to
another operation, a landing on Miyako Jima in the southern Ryukyus
as part of the Okinawa campaign. This was called off, but just after its
return to Hawaii the division got another false alarm, an alert to assault
the China coast in the Chusan Archipelago. The cancellation of this was
immediately followed by the real thing—an order to be ready by 1 September for the landing on southern Kyushu as part of V Amphibious
Corps, D-day of which would have been 1 November 1945, had the invasion of Japan been necessary.

The division took on replacements and new weapons and began an
accelerated training program. It incorporated the lessons learned on
Iwo, but because of the large number of replacements it began with individual training of those slated for the rifle units and infantry training for
service and support troops. The level of training worked up through
squad, platoon, and company exercises to battalion, regimental, and
finally division-level training. The battalion landing teams conducted
amphibious exercises during the summer and there was increased
stress on assaulting fortified positions, house-to-house combat, mines
and demolitions, and intensified swimming on the beaches. The swim
drills emphasized rough water in the event of disaster at sea at the
hands of Japanese kamikaze aircraft, submarines and other ships, torpe-
does, and frogmen, or storms.

On 15 August the Japanese surrender was announced. Dan was the
battalion officer-of-the-day and got the word of the surrender while a
movie was in progress. He entered the theater, turned on the lights, and
ordered the movie halted while he made the announcement. "There
wasn't that much reaction at first and there were some calls to start the
movie again," he recalls. "It took a little while to sink in." One reason for
the delayed reaction was that the troops had already celebrated the end
of the war twice, once on the sixth when the first atom bomb was
dropped on Hiroshima, then on the ninth with the second one on
Nagasaki. The actual announcement came as something of an anticli-
max. But react they did, and a few moments later the men came stream-
ing out of the theater whooping and yelling. Dan exercised his authority
to bend the rules and break out the beer in celebration.

Talk of going home was quickly extinguished when the division got orders to be loaded and embarked in twelve days. Disappointment over not going home immediately was offset by the profound relief that at least they wouldn't have to make the invasion. In many cases, the young soldier's historical conviction that someone else would get it but not him, which most of the Marines carried onto Iwo and Okinawa, were left behind on those islands. "We were very happy just for the surrender because many were convinced that we were going to die in the invasion," Hurson recalls. On 27 August the division sailed from Hilo to Pearl Harbor on forty-three ships of the Navy's Transport Squadron 22 and after four days at Pearl embarked for Saipan. The next day, 2 September, Allied and Japanese representatives signed the surrender documents on the battleship *Missouri* in Tokyo Bay. The division was given training in occupation duties aboard ship—customs, courtesies, Japanese history, psychology, appearance and conduct, and Japanese phrases. They would invade Japan after all, but as diplomats as well as conquerors.

The reborn 4th Marines, the successor to the regiment that had been forced to surrender on the beaches of Corregidor, were the first Marines to land on Japan. On the day of surrender the regiment loaded into transports at Guam and sailed for Japan the next evening. It was the point of the Fleet Landing Force, a near-divisional formation that also included a provisional regiment of 2,000 Marines from ships of the Third Fleet, a Navy regiment of 956 sailors, and a battalion of 450 British Royal Marines. It occupied the big naval and air base at Yokosuka, on the west side of Tokyo Bay, while the 11th Airborne Division occupied Atsugi Airfield southwest of Tokyo. The Marine unit landed on 30 August, three days before the surrender ceremonies on the *Missouri,* and began the inventory and destruction of military equipment and installations. About 120 members of the newly liberated "Old 4th Marines" were brought down from Yokohama to meet their victorious brothers-in-arms and be prepared to return home.

On 22 September the 5th Marine Division arrived at Sasebo, Japan's third-largest naval base, on the northwest coast of Kyushu, not far from where it would have landed in Operation Olympic. As the early morning mists on the sheltered bays began to lift the men saw Japan for the first time, with neat, cultivated terraces on the steep, green hillsides, from a distance seemingly untouched by the war. But it had been—Sasebo is just thirty-five miles north of Nagasaki and after they'd settled in the Marines discovered small local hospitals whose patients included horribly burned and injured victims of the A-bomb and fire bombings. Sasebo, a city of about two hundred thousand, was an expanse of burned-out rubble; three quarters of the city had been leveled by B-29 firebomb raids that killed and injured thousands.

The Americans were grateful for the docile Japanese acceptance of the occupation, which was due in great part to the influence of the emperor, especially after they learned the extent of the preparations to resist the Allied invasion. While many structures above ground at the Sasebo naval base were in ruins, war plants, including submarine assembly facilities, warehouses, repair and machine shops, and command and communications centers were in underground bunkers and caves, in pristine condition. Similar underground defense positions and thousands of kamikaze aircraft and boats were all over the island—Kyushu was a gigantic arsenal, loaded with arms, munitions, and installations to repel the American invasion, including 178 kamikaze aircraft at Kanzaki. The Marines' mission was to enforce the terms of surrender and their first action was to place guards on ammunition dumps and storehouses, gun emplacements, and other military facilities, which they then proceeded to destroy. Then they turned to repairing roads and buildings and putting up telephone lines. With this and the wearing off of the strangeness, fear, and uncertainty, the attitude of the people began to change from apprehension and reserve to curiosity and acceptance.

On the morning of the second day, Hurson's company embarked on a thirty-mile trip by DUKW, those big amphibious trucks known as "Ducks," to occupy the airport at Omura, the only one large enough to accommodate U.S. military aircraft. The narrow, muddy roads made it an eight-hour ordeal but the Japanese were entranced by the seemingly miraculous vehicles. "They watched as we marched through town to board the Ducks and they went wild when they saw the drivers deflate the tires to cross a stream, and then re-inflate them on the other side," Hurson recalls. After about ten days, Charlie Company was relieved by elements of the 2nd Marine Division, which was based at Nagasaki, and rejoined its battalion.

A typhoon had struck less than a week before the Marines had landed, destroying hundreds of kamikaze aircraft on the field in the Fukuoka area, an estimated 75 percent of the strength there. The typhoon (the "Divine Wind," which in Japanese legend had saved Japan from Kublai Khan in the thirteenth century) proved to be a two-edged sword. Another hit Okinawa on 10 October and Kyushu on 11 October, heavily damaging barracks and other facilities, and destroying tons of mail and packages bound for the 5th Division. However, a load of turkeys arrived on 1 November and the division made that its Thanksgiving Day, with gratitude that it wasn't assaulting the beaches south of Sasebo as had been planned for that day.

In late November Hurson's battalion was sent to two heavily fortified islands, Kamino Shima and Shimono Shima, about forty miles offshore to the northwest of Sasebo, to destroy the military stores and installations. Over the course of two weeks they blew up or dumped everything in the ocean. Their haul included two 12-inch battleship guns, which were supposed to have been destroyed under the terms of the Washington Disarmament Conference of 1922. The Japanese bitterly resented this agreement because it didn't give them naval parity with America and Britain and they scrapped the ship but not its guns. "We had a casualty there," Hurson recalls. "We were blowing up some installations and we'd posted a Marine as sentry to keep people out of the area and he was hit by a piece of four-by-four from an explosion. It came down like a spear and hit him in the head and killed him."

The Marines learned a lot about their enemy in the occupation. The people on Kyushu were subjected to the same fanatical discipline and devotion to the emperor that had cost so many American lives in the Pacific. It appeared to the Marines that the people and their level of development was about fifty years behind America's, and they hadn't been kept informed about the course of the war. They didn't know until three days after the surrender that it had taken place, and the Marines learned to their astonishment that the people thought they had won on Iwo. They were told that their forces were "progressing daily" toward the northern part of the island, that they had lost only three thousand men to twenty thousand Americans, and that the Marines had been allowed to invade the island so they could be trapped and killed.[14]

Jack Lauck returned to Camp Tarawa from Iwo with 2nd Battalion, 27th Marines. The battered, decimated unit took on replacements and new equipment and began training for the invasion of Japan. Because of his experience, the battalion commander made him the assistant operations officer (S-3) as they filled the platoon-leader billets with new lieutenants fresh from the States. When the division went to Japan, Lauck's battalion was sent to Saga, about 40 miles east of Sasebo, where there was a large fighter base, Kanzaki airfield, a huge ammunition dump, and an internment camp for Dutch, British, Italians, Portuguese, Swiss, and Belgians. Lauck was transferred to the battalion S-2 section, where he organized and led an intelligence platoon whose duty was to search for contraband and weapons, help dismantle ships in the nearby bay, and destroy ammunition and airplanes. He didn't have to search very hard.

Kyushu was loaded. Lauck spent most of his occupation tour searching out and destroying these supplies. When the 5th Division began returning to the States in late November 1945, Lauck was one of the low-point men who were transferred to the 2nd Marine Division and wound up his tour with 2nd Battalion, 6th Marines. He was awarded a second Purple Heart on 2 January 1946 when he was injured destroying a collection of airplanes at Saga. After the Marines had cannibalized them for seats, compasses, and other useful items, the engineers would push the planes together with bulldozers and set them on fire. On this occasion they lit the bonfire on top of a store of buried artillery shells, which cooked off with a spectacular explosion. Lauck was hit in the leg by a shell-casing fragment, which was removed on the ship that took him back to the United States in March.

After returning to Camp Pendleton, Lauck made his first liberty in Los Angeles in dungarees because, like the others, he'd sent his dress greens and summer uniforms home before going overseas. The MPs gave him no trouble, and his mother sent his uniforms to an aunt in Los Angeles. She sewed the 5th Division patch on the shoulder of his shirts and blouses for him. Lauck was sent to the hospital at the Great Lakes Naval Training Center at the end of March where he was an outpatient for two months while his leg and an operation on one of his fingers healed. He was discharged and returned home to Indianapolis in June 1946.

Joe Clement in Charlie Company, 2nd Marines, 2nd Marine Division, went ashore at Nagasaki on Kyushu in the early afternoon of 23 September: "We were loaded for bear with everything we could carry. I carried the only automatic weapon in my mortar section, a Thompson submachine gun. On returning to Saipan from Okinawa one of my men found it on one of our numerous patrols and I had refurbished it. I was carrying two thirty-round clips taped back to back in the weapon, five twenty-round clips in a pouch on my belt, and a drum of fifty rounds in my pack. This was in addition to the three illuminating mortar rounds and the normal field gear. My section sergeant and squad leaders were also carrying extra rounds of 60-mm ammunition."

The LCVPs slid smoothly onto the beach, the coxswain dropped the bow ramp, and the Marines charged into the friendly cheers of sailors lounging around the beach who banged their beer cans together or on anything that would make noise. "Had it been six weeks later, against Japanese resistance as originally planned, many of us wouldn't have reached the beach," Clement says. His battalion was sent to an old POW camp on the outskirts of Nagasaki.

"I particularly remember the devastation from the A-bomb at Nagasaki. Only a few things remained which were more than a foot or two above the ground, three or four smoke stacks which had been guyed internally with cables, the steel skeleton of a three story factory, a very large, globular petroleum storage tank, and the stone archway to what had been the jail. Stone rubble covered the ground. Everything else was gone! It was awesome and staggering to the imagination to view what had happened there."

One of Clement's major assignments in Nagasaki was commanding a guard force of about a hundred men in the huge dock area. He and another second lieutenant set up their headquarters in the small interior building that had housed the ticketing facilities within a huge building that had been the center for arriving and departing passengers. The officers dropped their gear on the concrete deck of the ticket building and the troops occupied one side of the large structure, which had large multipaned glass areas in the ceiling. Their job was to guard the enormous amounts of material being stockpiled every day, from frozen sides of beef, which were immediately trucked out, and seemingly unlimited cases of beer, to ammunition, tires, clothing, and other equipment. It was stored on a broad open area that covered several city blocks (there were many broad, open areas in Nagasaki then) and were stacked in ten-by-twenty-foot piles, protected from the rain and snow by tarps.

Clement designated a separate room, at one end of his domicile in the passenger ticket station, as an aid station for his three corpsmen, who manned it round-the-clock although the guards' jobs were not particularly dangerous. The most peril stemmed from the natural instincts of young men. They were granted liberty during off-duty hours and there were young females in the area. The Corps had a strict regulation that anyone who contracted venereal disease without a record of getting treatment by a corpsman after exposure could be subject to court-martial. Often, the corpsman's business picked up in the early morning hours on days when no one was returning from liberty. It appeared to coincide with the changes of the guard.

Clement had noticed this and so had his battalion executive officer, a major. One afternoon the major appeared at Clement's office to inform him that he knew what was going on with the guard detachment. "There was no doubt in his mind that some of the little gals had been meeting some of my men while they were on duty at their posts during the night," Clement recalls. "Silently, I agreed, but had been unable to catch them." The major told Clement that he wanted the corpsmen's list of the men treated and the times of treatment during the previous two weeks, plus the guard schedule. Clement could tell that the executive officer had court-martial on his mind.

"As I had learned previously on Saipan, there are times that you don't comply with orders from a field-grade officer and this was one of them," Clement recalls. "I told the major that I was not permitted to give him the list for the purpose of prosecuting my men. I reminded him that such information was available only to refute charges of contracting a venereal disease without taking proper preventive measures and in such cases it was admissible strictly as evidence to prove a man's innocence. Such records were inadmissible for prosecution purposes. Had their names been listed for future punitive action, none of my other men would have visited the pro-station. In turn, we would have lost control over giving them preventive treatment."

This obviously didn't sit well with the major and he stalked furiously out of the office, but Clement didn't see him again for several days. "Apparently, he had checked on my comments and found them to be justified. Anyway, the subject was never broached again. I was now twenty years old and learning about many varied responsibilities regarding things of which I was totally ignorant when I received my gold bars a short twelve months previously." Clement had experienced a similar encounter on Saipan with his battalion commander, who passed a sentry patrol one night while returning to his billet from the officers' club. He was outraged that the men were patrolling in the clearing and not in the jungle, which was not in their orders and was dangerous, and threatened a court-martial. Clement told the colonel that they were operating under his orders and endured a long dressing down in front of the men and the battalion sergeant major. This was an egregious violation of leadership principles by the colonel, but it made Clement a hero in the battalion.

Several weeks later Clement's unit boarded LSTs and sailed from Nagasaki to Takusu. From there they traveled by train to Miyazaki on the southeast coast of Kyushu. The officers were billeted in what had been a hotel. Since most of the men in Clement's mortar section were rotated to the States from Nagasaki he was transferred to Able Company. In Miyazaki the Americans were first able to attend a Catholic Church, which was an occasion of welcome by the Japanese. "As I entered the church, I encountered a custom which I did not see again until attending Mass in a small church in southeastern Montana some years later—all the women and children knelt on one side (I think the right) and the men knelt on the left. Many of the Marines did not catch on to the system and ended up out-of-pocket. Nevertheless, everything proceeded smoothly. Mass was celebrated in Latin on a world-wide basis in those days so we did not feel completely alienated."

The local bishop was on hand to deliver the Gospel, which he gave in Japanese. After a few words to the congregation, he turned to the several dozen Marines. "In understandable, but a long ways from fluent English, he read a greeting to us. He concluded by wishing us a happy and prosperous stay in Japan. He must have practiced his short talk for some extended period because he knew little or no English. It was obvious that he had memorized the entire text and pronunciation. We were all impressed with his efforts as well as with his greeting."

The Marines wanted to express their appreciation, which they did in the universal manner—through the collection baskets. The custom in Miyazaki was to bring the baskets to the front of the pulpit where the bishop could bless them. "Looking down at the collection baskets full of money, the poor man was almost overcome," Clement recounts. "I was close enough to see the tears well out at the corner of his eyes. The Marines had stuffed the baskets with one hundred- and two hundred-yen notes until they were full and overflowing. It was probably more money than the church had collected the previous year."

At that time, the rate was fifteen yen to the dollar, which made the two-hundred-yen notes worth about fourteen dollars each. A haircut cost two sen—about one-eighth of a cent, but most Japanese were unable to put even one-yen notes in the basket. Inflation came to the country almost immediately, however, and the most effective method of purchase became barter—cigarettes, chocolate, or soap—rather than two-hundred-yen notes. "If you offered a store owner yen, [he] would shake his head, pull out a wad of two-hundred-yen notes, thick enough to choke a horse, and wave them under your nose," Clement says. "Then he would light a cigarette and hold it up in front of you. There was no need for wasted conversation about money."

In Miyazaki the Marines conducted daily patrols searching the countryside for contraband weapons but found none. They blew up planes and suicide submarines. Ammunition was collected and dumped at sea. Clement can still picture Japanese workers on the wharves shoveling all types of loose ammunition into wide wooden boats about thirty feet long. When loaded, they would take the boats offshore a couple of miles and dump them, once again with shovels as there was abundant manpower. There was lots of ammo and many boat trips. "The Japanese doing the work seemed undisturbed by their dangerous job," Clement noted.

"We were privileged to observe many interesting places and customs in that part of Japan" he recalls. One day in November he had gotten horses to use on patrol and some distance from Miyazaki the patrol discovered a small temple that had a large seated statue of what appeared to the Americans to be Buddha. There was room for a few people although none were there at the time.

> We didn't enter as we didn't know if it would have been in bad taste. However, it was completely open and we could observe everything inside by merely walking around it. The building looked just like something out of a story book. The curved ridges on the roof, the tile, the wood carving and everything else was exquisite. We were there for about fifteen minutes but saw no Japanese. Their care of the temple and the surrounding grounds was impeccable. I don't remember any buildings for a couple of hundreds yards or so in any direction. The temple was at the center of a park-like area. Trees, about ten to twelve inches in diameter, were growing in any direction one went from the structure. They were about sixty or seventy feet apart, and precisely located to form a symmetrical pattern. We were all impressed with the beauty of the small temple and the neatness and preciseness of the tree pattern around it. It was a very pleasant afternoon.

In late January Clement was ordered to check out a town about fifty miles south of Miyazaki, where he was to billet with a squad for a month to search for munitions. "The trip probably took ten years off my life," he says. The road was carved out of the almost vertical side of the mountain by hand and was barely wide enough for the Jeep. It also featured rickety bridges over steep ravines, which the driver managed to negotiate. "If he had driven off the edge we would have fallen for thirty minutes," Clement says.

When they arrived at the town they were greeted by the Mayor and many of his "court." "Our welcome by the citizens of this small town was overwhelming." The Marines were taken on a tour of the town with an interpreter provided. "Anyplace we wanted to go or anything we wanted to see was available. . . .We were shown a lovely one story building which was to be our quarters. . . . I couldn't believe that my future was going to include spending a month in this place. . . . Lunch was fabulous with lots of fish and cakes, fruit and nuts, along with sake."

"Such dreams don't end," Clement ruefully concluded. "They explode or disintegrate from some drastic cause." The end of Clement's dream was posted on the battalion bulletin board in the mess hall when he returned to Miyazaki that evening. There was a list of lieutenants who would be sent back to the States in two days. Clement's name was at the top.

"I was crestfallen. Try as I might, I could not get my shipping orders changed so that I could delay my departure for a month or two. Our group of 'evacuees' left for Sasebo shortly thereafter." He arrived back in the States in April, given two months leave, and was released from active duty at Naval Air Station Corpus Christi in July. Like the other SOCS members, he was promoted to first lieutenant, reduced to his permanent rank of platoon sergeant, and discharged. "The entire process took about fifteen minutes and I didn't have to move fifteen feet," he recalls. He also joined the Marine Corps Reserve and was restored to his rank of first lieutenant. Being in the reserves would be very important when the Korean War broke out four years later.[15]

Mark Clement's 2nd Platoon, "B" Company, 4th Pioneers landed at Iwo with two officers and fifty-two men. Only twenty-two of them returned with it to Maui, along with eight replacements who had joined it during the first week on Iwo. Clement has a picture of the 4th Pioneer Battalion officers taken about three months after their return to Maui.

2nd Lt. Mark Clement, Company B, 4th Pioneer Battalion, Maui, Hawaii, May 1945. MARK CLEMENT

Of the thirty-two company-grade officers, twenty are replacement second lieutenants and another (Breck Breckenridge) is a returned WIA.

The Pioneers began training for Operation Coronet, the landing on the main island of Honshu scheduled for 1 March 1946. They got a lot of training in mine disposal and building assault (Bailey) bridges (the same type bridging equipment that was air-dropped five years later to the 1st Marine Division in its withdrawal from the Chosin reservoir in Korea). "The general feeling was one of apprehension about an operation on the Japanese mainland . . . after our experience on Iwo and our reports from Okinawa," Clement recalls. "Thus, we felt the enormous psychological sense of relief when the atomic bombs were used and Japan finally surrendered. At first, many just had difficulty believing and coping with the reality! They all felt that they had been given a new lease on life. One thing for sure, I didn't know anyone in my unit who spoke out against the concept of dropping the atomic bomb."

After V-J day, Clement was sent to Oahu and then to Hilo, where he was assigned to an engineer unit that dismantled the 5th Marine Division camps and returned the area to its pineapple and sugarcane fields. One of his additional duties was camp fire marshal and one day his fire brigade NCO informed him that they had received a shipment of a new firefighting "foam" and they wanted to try it out. They drove out to one of the small bays and broke out the five-gallon "jerry" cans that contained the foaming agent. The procedure utilized a nozzle on the fire-hose, which also had a suction line extension that was inserted into the can. "The effect was marvelous, with foam everywhere, mostly in front of us in the bay. We returned to camp convinced that we had the best thing going to fight gasoline and similar type fires." That is, until the next day when Clement was called into the battalion commander's office. "Lieutenant, what the hell's going on?" the colonel shouted. "I have a hundred Hawaiian fishermen at the camp gate shouting that the Marine Corps has ruined their fishing grounds." The foam had difficulty dissolving and the surface tension had formed a thin layer of "gunk" over the entire surface of the protected bay. It was an embarrassing day for a young, "experienced" engineer second lieutenant, but fortunately, in less than a week wave action had helped dissipate the foam and Clement was able to get on with business.

The war had gone out with a bang, a big bang, and he returned to the mainland from Hawaii in March 1946. He was promoted to first lieutenant and after two months leave was discharged at Naval Air Station Corpus Christi. He didn't say goodbye to the Corps; however, he also signed up in the reserve. "We all knew we had just fought the 'war to end all wars,' didn't we?" he notes sardonically.

In early December Dan Hurson and the other high-point combat veterans began loading aboard APAs at Sasebo to return to Camp Pendleton. The low-point newcomers were transferred to the 2nd Division, which assumed the 5th Division's occupation duties. The transports carrying the 5th Division docked in San Diego every day between 20 December and 1 January 1946, and the Marines went to Pendleton, where they were processed and discharged and their units disbanded. The 26th Marines had been ordered to Peleliu in October to help with repatriation there. The 1st Battalion, 26th Marines was the last to return to Pendleton, in March, and was the last unit to be disbanded. A year and a month after D-day on Iwo, the 5th Marine Division was history.

The occupation of North China by the 1st and 6th Marine Divisions proved considerably more complex for them than that of Japan because of the major civil war between Mao Tse-tung's Communists and the Nationalists under Chiang Kai-shek; the Communists had an army of about one million, and Chiang's forces totaled about three million. The Japanese troops that had to be disarmed and shipped home proved to be the least of the Marines' problems. On their way to China, the Marines were trained in occupation duty, street fighting, and crowd control of a civilian population, but the major problem was the Communists, who were not inclined to acquiesce in the U.S. desire to reestablish Nationalist control of China and prevailed over Chiang four years later.

The Americans were warned of this before the first Marine unit set foot on China. On 20 September, ten days before the 1st Marine Division landed at Tanku, the port for Tientsin, an advance party from III Amphibious Corps, now commanded by Maj. Gen. Keller Rockey, met in Shanghai with the Japanese commanders and Gen. Chou En-lai, the Communists' leading spokesman. In a heated session, Chou warned the Marines that the Communists would fight any American attempt to move inland to Peking and he proved true to his word. The Americans wanted Chiang to control Peking, which was not only a symbol of national power, but had two first-class military airfields. The Marines pointedly told Chou and everyone else who was listening that the two Marine divisions were combat-hardened and ready to fight if necessary.

Phil Pearce and the rest of the 1st Marine Division, which had been slated for Operation Coronet, embarked from Okinawa for North China in mid-September 1945. After encountering a typhoon on the way they landed at the port of Tanku on 20 September. The 6th Division, minus the 4th Marines, arrived at Tsingtao on 11 October, a day late because its convoy was on the edge of another typhoon, which devastated Okinawa and southern Japan, and which the Marines sardonically viewed as an appropriate introduction to peacetime for them, given their recent experiences.

The 1st Division accepted the surrender of the Japanese occupation troops and were posted near Tientsin and Peiping as bridge and railroad guards against the Chinese Communist Army, with which they had frequent clashes in what turned out to be the opening rounds of the Cold War. Ironically, some of them wound up serving alongside some of the surrendered Japanese units, which were assigned to help them with this duty. Jep Carrell in Company K, 7th Marines knew the world situation had changed one day shortly after arriving in Tientsin when he was battalion officer of the deck, in charge of the MP detachment. A crowd of three thousand Chinese were threatening a small group of Japanese troops, who still were armed but had orders not to shoot. Carrell's battalion commander approved his recommendation of using two squads with fixed bayonets in wedge formation against the crowd, which enabled him to break up the crowd and disperse it in several directions.

The Marines encountered no resistance at Tsingtao and Tientsin, where fifty thousand Japanese troops surrendered to General Rockey, but when Marine engineers tried to remove roadblocks on the route from Tientsin to Peking, they were fired on by the Communists and three were wounded. A rifle company supported by tanks pushed through the next day and the 5th Marines moved into Peking. In the ensuing months periodic fire fights broke out between the Marines and the Communists along the railroad and other communications lines between Peking and the ports. Japanese troops were assigned to guard some bridges and stretches of track because the Marine commanders needed more manpower and didn't want to expose vulnerable small units to the Communists' attacks.[16]

Guarding the bridges and railroads that ran between the ports and Peking, to the coal mines and industries east of Peking, and into Manchuria was cold, boring, and dangerous, but the Marines in Tientsin and Peking enjoyed a touch of civilization after months and years on Pacific islands. There were restaurants and some elaborate banquets by the Chinese and European business communities—the young Marines were introduced to delicacies such as Peking duck—beds and hot baths. Bill Ditto, the 81-mm mortar section leader in 2nd Battalion, 7th Marines, and some of his fellow officers cast around for uniforms other than their dungarees and khakis, and hit on the idea of giving a local tailor some Marine blankets and having him fashion a number of the waist-length jacket adopted during the war. It was known in the Army as the "Eisenhower jacket," after their creator, and as a "battle" jacket to the Marines. There also was a booming prostitution industry and one of the duties of the officer of the day was to clear out the red-light district at 2300 and put the curfew-breakers in the brig overnight.

In October 1945 the 1st Marine Division scheduled a parade and review in Peiping at the Polo Grounds, which was in the area where the ambassadors and other foreign diplomats lived at the time. That morning, Phil Pearce was summoned by his battalion adjutant, who instructed him on what he was to do at the ceremony; after the battalion had formed up Pearce would be ordered "front and center." When Pearce asked why, the adjutant informed him that he was to be awarded the Navy Cross for his action back in Wilson's Draw. As with Jim Ronayne on Guam, that was the first inkling Pearce had that he had been recommended for the prestigious medal. After recounting the action, Pearce's citation concluded: "The last man to leave the area, [Lieutenant Pearce] served as a constant inspiration to his men and, by his unfaltering courage and determination, was responsible for

2nd Lt. Harry P. "Phil" Pearce, B-1-5th Marines, receives the Navy Cross from Brig. Gen. Louis Jones, Assistant Division Commander, 1st Marine Division, at an award ceremony in Peiping, China, 26 October 1945. Pearce was awarded the medal for heroism on Okinawa.
PHIL PEARCE

saving the lives of at least twelve men. His gallant leadership through-out was in keeping with the highest traditions of the United States Naval Service."

From Peking Pearce's battalion went over to the port cities of Tanku and Taku to process the return of Japanese troops to the home islands. His company was the MP unit for the operation, with a full platoon on duty each day and the platoon leader as officer of the day. He had no clashes with the Communists but one of the other companies in the 5th Marines that was guarding the Marines ammunition and supply dump at Tanku had occasion to fire on Communists who attempted to raid the dumps. The Marines put Japanese troops to work erecting quonset hunts and other buildings for barracks, mess halls, and warehouses, and one of Pearce's major problems was protecting the Japanese work-ers from vengeful Chinese. Some of the Japanese worked on a wharf in the harbor and when they would take a break, Chinese would sneak up behind any of the Japanese who were having tea or were relieving them-selves over the side off the dock into the water. "We lost a few to drown-ing that way," he says. Tanku, of course, had bars and restaurants, and on one of their days off Pearce stood his platoon to a full day of eating and drinking in one of them. The other problem in Peking was the port town's red-light district, which was visited by the Marines as well as sailors and Seabees.

In March 1946, Pearce and the other combat veterans who had enough points from their combat service were loaded aboard the USS *Roi,* an escort carrier. At Tangu it picked up members of the 6th Divi-sion at Tsingtao and also took them back to the United States. The pleasure of going home was enhanced by the luxury of space a carrier afforded compared to the packed troop transports. Pearce spent a week in San Francisco undergoing administrative processing and being issued dress greens and summer uniforms and other missing equip-ment and enjoying stateside liberty, then took the train for St. Louis and home to the farm at Carmi, Illinois. After a month's leave, he went to the Naval Training Center in Chicago where he was reduced to his perma-nent rank of platoon sergeant and released from active duty. Like many of his SOCS classmates, however, he did not bid adieu to the Marine Corps. A few minutes later he was signed up in the reserves as a second lieutenant.

11 Postwar

When Johnny Comes

Marching Home Again

In late 1945 and early 1946 the United States demobilized the enormous war machine it had built up over the previous four years. About 13 million American servicemen and women began returning to civilian life and among them were the 325 members of the SOCS who survived the war. More than half the SOCS members had been wounded, some severely enough to require evacuation to hospitals in the United States. After the surrender, many of the class were with the divisions that went to Japan and China on occupation duty before they returned to the United States.

Some SOCS members had completed their degree requirements in the V-12 program before they were ordered to active duty and the rest had finished most of their work before they were ordered to boot camp at Parris Island. Nearly all of these completed their bachelor's degrees on the G.I. Bill of Rights, after they were discharged, with many going on to graduate and professional degrees. They became doctors, lawyers, judges, engineers, dentists, journalists, college professors, teachers and coaches, FBI agents, scientists, ministers, farmers, and businessmen of every description. Some made the Marine Corps their career. At least two studied at the Sorbonne.

Some of the class members became famous. Wally Westfeldt became a television journalist and was executive producer of the *Huntley-Brinkley Report* on NBC television. Jay Hebert, who won the Purple Heart on Iwo with Company E, 26th Marines, became a top golf professional, winning the PGA Championship in 1961 and serving as captain of the 1971 Ryder Cup team. Jim Landrigan, a star lineman for Holy Cross before the war, played professional football for the Baltimore Colts before being recalled to active duty for Korea, when he integrated into the regulars and retired as a colonel. Their successful postwar careers are representative of the World War II generation.

Joe Clement estimates that nearly one-third remained in the reserves, that about fifteen took regular commissions and retired after twenty or thirty years service. Most who joined the reserves when they were released from active duty after World War II were recalled for the Korean War in 1950 or 1951. About thirty of these remained in the active reserve, many retiring as lieutenant colonels. Some were at the Chosen Reservoir, including Horace L. "Sonny" Johnson Jr., who had been wounded on Iwo as a platoon leader with Company H, 3rd Battalion, 26th Marines. Probably no one had a more spectacular run in Korea than Sonny Johnson, who was awarded the Navy Cross, two Silver Stars, a Bronze Star with combat *V*, and a second Purple Heart there. He won the Navy Cross as executive officer of Company G, 3rd Battalion, 1st Marines, when the Chinese hit it on the night of 28–29 November 1950, near the Chosen Reservoir. He received his Silver Stars the following March and April as company commander of George Company. After release from active duty he joined AT&T in engineering and management.

Gordon Dibble had made a concentrated effort to finish his degree requirements in the V-12 program before he was ordered to active duty because he didn't think he'd want to return to school after the war. After his discharge in December 1945 he went back home to Topeka and job-hunted briefly before going to Chicago with Marshall Field, the big department store, as an assistant buyer in men's clothing for about three years. He went from Chicago to Marietta, Georgia, for two years as marketing director for a hosiery manufacturer. In 1951 he started a women's wear wholesale firm in Los Angeles, but like so many other SOCS members his life was rudely interrupted by the Korean War.

In February 1952 Dibble was ordered to active duty and to a three-month junior staff school at Quantico. The class was "somewhat rambunctious," he recalls, partly because some like him were forced to sell their businesses or were losing money through their absence. Others were restless because they wanted to go to Korea. "They told us they might need staff officers for an extended war and another big expansion of the Corps, but they never explained how they selected those of us who were recalled," he says. "For many, morale was bad. The guys like me who had businesses were unhappy. I had written the Corps asking if I was to be recalled because I had contracts to renew and got an answer back that, no, I wasn't. About thirty days later I got my orders to active duty." Dibble, a first lieutenant by then, fell into both camps of the discontented—"I wanted to go to Korea," he says. Instead, he was sent to Camp Pendleton after completing the course. The Corps was organizing a brigade commanded by Chesty Puller, which became the core of the reactivated 3rd Marine Division. Dibble was promoted to captain and made assistant S-4 of the regiment that was the core unit of the brigade.

The recall profoundly changed his life. Before his release he was recruited for the Central Intelligence Agency (CIA). Dibble had been interested in the agency right after World War II but he was informed that there would be a two-year screening and waiting period and that was too long for him. As he was about to be released from active duty in March 1953, however, his regimental headquarters posted a notice that a CIA recruiter was coming around because the agency wanted people with a military background. Dibble asked for an appointment. The agency told him to come to Washington, which he did as soon as he was discharged. He spent several months being screened and interviewed and supported himself by driving a cab in Arlington. He resigned his commission in August 1953 and began training with the CIA. "They were worried about World War III at the time and needed people with military training." He remains close-mouthed about what he did, but some of it apparently involved military training of Cold War allies.

Dibble was with the CIA from 1952 to 1985 and spent thirteen of those years overseas, mostly in the Middle and Far East, including tours in Taiwan and Laos. The postings were for two or three years at a time, and he was able to take his wife, Margot, and their two oldest children with him; he has two daughters, one a doctor, the other a lawyer with the Environmental Protection Agency, and a son who is an investment consultant in the Washington, D.C., area. After retiring in 1985, Dibble was a consultant with the agency for recruiting and personnel for three years. "Many of my classmates went into business," he says. "I didn't make as much money, probably, but it was interesting and I was lucky to be able to continue serving my country. The Marine Corps experience affects you in discipline, outlook, and commitment to country."

Jack Lauck also tried to complete his degree requirements before being ordered to boot camp, but he was twenty-three hours short. After being discharged at the Great Lakes Naval Training Center in June 1946, he spent the summer working in his family's funeral home in Indianapolis, then reentered Notre Dame in the fall. He completed his degree in one semester, graduating at midterm in business administration. Lauck returned to Indianapolis, got into investments with his brother, and resumed work in the family business; as did his three older brothers and two sisters he attended and completed funeral directors' school. In 1948 he and Mary Ann Bush were married and have seven children and nine grandchildren. He had remained in the inactive reserve, however, and was recalled to the Korean War. Lauck's first notification, in the fall, was that Marine Corps policy was that no one who had two Purple Hearts, as he did, would be recalled. The second communication he received a few months later informed him that the policy had been changed. The third contained his orders to report to Camp Pendleton.

He arrived in the summer of 1951, a newly minted captain, and was given a replacement company to train at one of the tent camps at Pendleton. It was the last company formed for his replacement battalion and the night before the ship sailed from San Diego for Japan, the MPs pulled up to the pier with one last load of troops—they scoured the AWOLs and other minor offenders and misfits out of the Camp Pendleton brig and put them on the boat to Korea. Some of the AWOLs had gone over the hill precisely in the hope of avoiding the war, or at least delaying it. The draft landed at Kobe, where they left their seabags and locker boxes for storage and were greeted by liaison officers from Camp Pendleton and the 1st Marine Division in Korea who decided what their assignments would be. From Japan Lauck landed on the east coast of Korea, where the division was operating at the time, and was trucked up into the hills to the units. On his arrival he was given command of Company D, 2nd Battalion, 1st Marines. It was late December and he got his first introduction to Korea's infamously cold winters.

Because so many inexperienced new replacements became casualties almost immediately, the new arrivals were given several days training and orientation before going into the line. The Marines fought over outposts on the hills from a trench line known as the Main Line of Resistance (MLR) in what had become a static war. Lauck had received a Purple Heart on Iwo and another when he was injured blowing up Japanese armaments while on occupation duty. He got his third Heart in Korea when he was hit in the hand by shrapnel during a bombardment in January and his fourth when he was wounded in the leg by shrapnel. Neither was severe enough to require evacuation.

In March 1952 the division was moved to the tidal plains of the Han and Imjin Rivers estuary on the west coast to block a possible move against Seoul by the Chinese. He participated in the battle for Bunker Hill, a bitter struggle over a piece of high ground that both sides wanted as an outpost and which, in his estimation, wasn't worth the cost. "You had better observation from the higher ground behind it on Hills 181 and 157," he contends.

Lauck also won the Bronze Star and Letter of Commendation, both with the combat *V.* He received the Bronze Star in April 1952 when one of his platoons was manning an outpost on Hill 181, about five hundred yards in front of the MLR. The Chinese hit it hard about midnight, inflicting several casualties—"They seemed to take those things (U.S. occupation of the outposts) personally," he observes—and Lauck took a two-squad reaction team out to cover the withdrawal, with artillery support. The platoon leader, who was severely wounded, was carried out on a litter, and a half dozen troops were wounded, but no one was killed. Lauck got everyone safely back to the MLR. "The platoon leader had to be evacuated, but the others who were wounded kind of sneaked around to the corpsman to get bandaged up and come back to the company," he remembers. "Marines don't like to leave their buddies."

Lauck received the Letter of Commendation for his service in his tour. He was supposed to be rotated home in July 1952 along with several other company commanders, but the new regimental commander was worried about losing all his experienced officers and extended some, including Lauck. He had been transferred back to the battalion S-2 section for his last days, but was returned to Dog Company for six more weeks. He finally returned to the States in September.

Lauck was in Korea for ten months, from December 1951 to the end of September 1952, and with the exception of his week with the S-2 section, was with Dog Company the entire time. He elected to take a regular commission and retired in 1969 as a colonel after twenty-seven years service. "We saw how hard and intransigent the Russians were and thought World War III was a real possibility," he recalls. "I decided I didn't want to be called up and have my life disrupted a third time."

He taught at various schools at Quantico, the Basic School, the Junior School, Command and Staff College, the communications officers school, and women Marines' courses in 1952 and 1953. In the summer of 1953 the Marine Corps created the Fiscal Division at Headquarters Marine Corps under then-Colonel David Shoup, the deputy quartermaster general, who had won the Medal of Honor on Tarawa and became commandant in 1960. Lauck was one of the ten original officers in the new office.

During tours of duty at Headquarters Marine Corps Lauck was able to take night courses at George Washington University. He received a master's degree in business administration in 1963 and a Ph.D in business administration in 1968. He wrote his dissertation on military survivors' benefit plans, a subject on which he was expert; he helped draft the current plan. After retiring from the Corps he taught business policy and other courses for sixteen years at Ball State University in Muncie, Indiana, and is the author of *Katyn Killings: In the Record,* an exhaustively researched account of the massacre of fifteen thousand Polish prisoners of war, mostly officers, by the Soviet secret police.

Jim Ronayne enrolled in Holy Cross, where he received a degree in education in 1947. In 1948 he married Mary Maley, a cousin of a Boston College friend who had been a Marine lieutenant with him on Guam after Iwo. They have two children, a son who is a policeman in Falmouth, and a daughter who is raising a family in Fall River. Thanks to the G.I. Bill, Ronayne went on to get a master's degree in education in 1953 and a Certificate of Advanced Graduate Study (CAGS), a nondissertation doctorate in education in 1957, both from Boston University. "I couldn't have gotten those degrees without the G.I. Bill," he says.

"I set out to be a baseball coach because that was my best sport," he says. He was a catcher at Holy Cross, which had a strong baseball program. In those days the Crusaders played exhibition games with the Braves and the Red Sox in alternating years; in his senior year, 1947, Ronayne played against Ted Williams. Like the other starters, Williams took one time at bat and then turned the game over to the rookies who were on their way to the minors for the season. Ronayne remembers that Williams came to Worcester in a Cadillac rather than on the team bus; he also remembers the ease with which Williams hit batting practice pitches over a six-foot wall on top of a hill that rose up in right field. "It had to be at least four hundred feet, and it just seemed like a flick of his wrists," he says. "I couldn't even hit to the base of the hill. We all tried to copy his style, which was to drop his hands straight down just before he swung, but we couldn't do it."

Holy Cross also was scheduled to play Yale and its captain and first baseman, George H. W. Bush, that year in a playoff for the College World Series in Omaha. However, a funny thing happened to the Crusaders on their way to New Haven—a Connecticut state trooper stopped their bus and told them that since it was raining at Yale the game would have to be rescheduled. When they got back to Worcester they learned that Yale had been invited to Omaha and to this day Ronayne thinks the fix was in from the start. "Up here the Ivy League has such a presence, with Harvard and Yale and Princeton," he says. "Us Catholic kids didn't have anything like that." Holy Cross did get to the series a few years later, however. Ronayne also helped work his way through grad school playing semipro baseball in an industrial league, on a team in Hopedale. He was paid fifty-five dollars a week for three games, two at night during the week, one on Sunday.

Ronayne taught physical education and coached high school football, hockey, and baseball at St. Bernard and Boston English from 1947 until he was recalled for Korea. When he returned he coached football, baseball, and indoor track for six years at East Boston, then moved to Newton. The Newton North High School football team he coached was undefeated and won the state championship in 1968. "The parents sent us to Bermuda as a reward," he recalls laughing. "They raffled off a bottle of whiskey in every bar in town to finance it." His graduate work enabled him to move into administration and he quit coaching football in 1972. He wound up his career as director of physical education and athletics for the Newton school district and since 1981 has been manager and teaching professional at the golf club in Pocasset, Massachusetts. He was the summer golf pro there from 1953 to 1980, and in 1959 was admitted to the PGA, of which he is a lifetime member.

When he was recalled for the Korean War, Ronayne was sent to Camp Pendleton, where he was assigned to a replacement draft for Korea. A friend from the 3rd Division on Iwo, an MP captain named Bob Mangene, intervened, however. Mangene had been a star running back and teammate of Ronayne's both at Boston College as freshmen, then on the V-12 team at Dartmouth, and worked for a colonel in personnel at Pendleton. "I told him I thought my orders from Headquarters Marine Corps couldn't be 'short stopped' because they were for 'duty beyond the seas' or something like that," Ronayne recalls. "But he suggested that the colonel take a look at the orders and send some of the second lieutenants who had been commissioned too late to get overseas in World War II instead. That sounded fair to me." Ronayne wound up as a training officer in the Infantry Training Regiment at Tent Camp 3 for several months and ended his year at Pendleton in special services as the golf course officer. "Justice wasn't always done, however," he says ruefully. "There'd be cases where a guy would have his wife and children outside the personnel office in his car and couldn't get his orders changed."

Like many others, Ronayne's military experience opened his mind to the possibility of broader vistas than he had envisioned prior to Pearl Harbor. And, like so many others, Ronayne learned from the Marine Corps that he was capable of much more than he had thought, which led to the realization that he could aspire to higher goals than his upbringing had led him to assume.

It sometimes seemed to Red Qualls that getting out of the Marine Corps after World War II was harder than getting into it. He was held at Parris Island for six months on limited duty while the doctors worked on the injuries to his intestines and he was finally separated in June 1946; the time wasn't completely lost, of course because he and Ruth were married there on 9 March 1946. Even then, he spent about two weeks at a Navy installation at McAlester, Oklahoma, because the Marine Corps misplaced his records, as well as those of several other SOCS members. He then spent eight months in Cisco as a bookkeeper with the West Texas Utility Company, training to be a district supervisor before moving back to Beaufort, South Carolina, where Ruth's parents lived. He worked for a year as a bookkeeper for a Ford dealer, then moved to Coastal Chevrolet, a big General Motors dealer. He was business manager there until his retirement in 1983.

Qualls joined the reserves and in March 1951 was recalled for the Korean War even though he was still bothered somewhat by his wound —certain foods gave him indigestion, a condition that cleared up, seemingly by magic, while he was in Junior School at Quantico. He had made first lieutenant in the reserves and his physical for active duty also served for his upcoming promotion to captain. After the four-month Junior course the Corps sent 78 of the more than 150 class members, including Qualls, to Korea. They flew from San Francisco to Hawaii, and just before they took off Qualls and one other officer got their promotions to captain, which meant that they got the choicest seats on the plane. After overnighting at Barbers Point Naval Air Station, they took

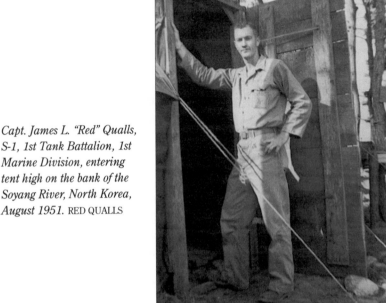

*Capt. James L. "Red" Qualls,
S-1, 1st Tank Battalion, 1st
Marine Division, entering
tent high on the bank of the
Soyang River, North Korea,
August 1951.* RED QUALLS

off for Tokyo on a Marine R4D (DC3), with a stop in Guam when one of the two engines went out. From Japan they flew to Kimpo airfield in Korea and on 1 August 1951 Qualls was assigned to the 1st Tank Battalion. He wasn't a tank officer—his primary MOS was 0302, infantry—but he had a secondary MOS for administration so he became the S-1. He arrived just in time for the Marines' big and inconclusive battle for Bunker Hill, an outpost in front of the MLR, where the tanks were used primarily as artillery.

He was joined in the tank battalion by Milt Raphael, a SOCS classmate who had been in his battalion on Iwo and had joined a reserve tank unit in Louisiana. He also got a Christmas card from one of his flamethrowers on Iwo, who was from Arkansas. There apparently was a grapevine on his activities and whereabouts because his runner on Iwo, also an Arkansas boy, called Ruth to see if Qualls had been one of the Marine reservists called up. He said he called because he assumed that Qualls would have been one of the first to volunteer to go. "I guess I managed to fool at least one of my boys on Iwo that I knew what I was doing," Qualls laughs.

As the battalion adjutant he prepared two courts-martial for possession of marijuana, which grew in profusion and was free for the picking.
One, a black Marine reservist from Houston, had been under suspicion
and surveillance for some time, and when it was time for him to rotate
back to the States, his seabag and other gear was searched after he'd
packed up. He had two Prince Albert tobacco cans of marijuana, which
he reportedly said he was going to sell back home. The court sentenced
him to twenty years. The other, a white Marine from Louisiana, had a
civilian lawyer provided by his family but was acquitted because, Qualls
says, the Provost Marshal "screwed the case up royally."

Qualls sailed back to the States from Kobe and was released the day
the ship docked in San Diego. It turned out that he and a number of others had qualified for a higher pay scale and there was a delay of a couple
of hours while the paperwork was processed, which caused him to miss
his 7 P.M. plane. One of his comrades had his car delivered from Los
Angeles, however, and by great good fortune was going to Texas. Four of
them drove night and day and Qualls was delivered at the doorstep of his
dad's home in Cisco. From there he returned to Beaufort and Coastal
Chevrolet.

After spending the spring and summer of 1946 working on the family farm, Phil Pearce reentered Milliken University in the fall, moved
back into the SAE house, and completed his degree in industrial engineering with the class of 1947. After graduation he operated the Standard Oil bulk fuel station in Carmi, selling fuel to farmers and other
business customers, and acquired the Massey-Harris farm implement
dealership.

Along with many who had signed up in the reserves, Pearce was
recalled to active duty in 1951 after the outbreak of the Korean War. He
wasn't sent to Korea, but he paid a price, nevertheless. His recall forced
him to sell the Massey-Harris dealership and the bulk fuel plant. Like
many of his colleagues, Pearce was assigned to Junior School at Quantico to train as a staff officer.

After Junior School he spent six months training troops at Camp
Pendleton, then a year in Toledo, Ohio, reactivating the 8th Reserve
Infantry Battalion. He had decided to make the Marines his career and
was on his way to Camp Lejeune to accept a regular commission but
changed course when his mother asked him to take over the 1,500-acre
family farm three miles from Carmi, which he'd grown up on and had
been in her family since 1808. He still lives on the farm, raising pacers
and harness horses and 150 acres of alfalfa. He ran it for more than forty

years but in 1995 he started renting the corn, wheat, and soybean land to another farmer. He has a daughter, a stepson, and two stepdaughters. After Korea, Pearce and about thirty others from the Carmi and Evansville, Indiana, area joined a reserve unit, an air-control squadron in Columbus, Ohio. Pearce served for five years, then transferred to another at Glenview Naval Air Station for another five years. He left the active reserves as a lieutenant colonel and was promoted to full colonel in the inactive reserve.

George Mayer also went to China with the 1st Battalion, 5th Marines and was rotated back to the States and released from active duty at the same time as Pearce. He had completed his B.A. degree in the V-12 program and a postdischarge conversation with a friend persuaded him to apply to graduate school in business. He applied to Harvard, one of four thousand applicants for four hundred openings, was accepted, and began the MBA program in the summer of 1946. He finished in November 1947 and took a job for a brief period with a storm-window company in Chicago. Mayer went from there to a job in market research and analysis with U.S. Steel in Pittsburgh and in 1949 joined a business consulting firm in Cleveland, Robert Heller & Associates. In 1950 he married Jane Peet, who then was an American Airlines stewardess, but was also a whiz at math and physics and ended up working for an industrial gear designer. They have a daughter and three sons.

Mayer also had joined the reserves and was recalled to active duty shortly after the Korean War erupted in June 1950. He had orders to Parris Island but stopped at Headquarters Marine Corps in Washington where an acquaintance introduced him to a colonel who was impressed by his MBA and association with Heller and got his MOS changed to supply. He spent his thirteen months as special assistant to the quartermaster general, traveling the country on procurement and supply matters, including the new body armor and insulated winter-boot programs. In 1951 Mayer returned to Heller, then went to Crown Cork & Seal Corporation in New York, and the Arvey Corporation in New Jersey.

Mayer was with Xerox from 1959 to 1977 in program and sales management, planning, and marketing, specializing in photographic and micrographics development programs. He also consulted in railroad, food, and government areas. He was in Los Angeles and Chicago briefly as a regional manager, but spent most of his time with Xerox in Rochester, then the corporate headquarters, as marketing director. In the early 1960s Xerox sent him to Huntington, West Virginia, to shape up a Women's Job Corps training center it operated there. He soon had it training, graduating, and placing more women faster than any other of the centers except one, and returned to Rochester, where he retired in 1977. Mayer formed an executive recruiting and placement firm in Findlay, Ohio, and moved to Beaufort, South Carolina, near Parris Island, in 1987; after a lifetime in the north he wanted warm weather and access to the PX and commissary. He retired from the Marine Corps reserve as a lieutenant colonel and spends much of his time writing for the *Marine Corps Gazette* and other military publications.

Joe Clement enrolled in Southern Methodist University as part of the huge wave of veterans who flooded the nation's college campuses in the fall of 1946 and got his B.S. in geology in 1948. He worked for a year in Buffalo, Wyoming, for the Carter Oil Company, part of Standard of New Jersey, then returned to SMU for a master's degree, which he finished after his release from active duty in the Korean War.

Like many other SOCS members, Clement went to Junior School at Quantico. Half of his class was sent to Korea, but Clement was assigned as a rifle company commander in the 3rd Marine Brigade at Camp Pendleton. About two months after his arrival, while driving back to Tent Camp 2 from mainside, he and another officer, a fellow Texan named Weberneck, also a geologist, saw a sign that read "Office of Ground Water Resources." Curious, they drove up the hill to a Quonset hut, where a lieutenant there told them the office was engaged in research for litigation involving the Corps's legal right to Pendleton's water supply. When he learned that they were geologists he asked if they'd be interested in joining the unit. They were and they served in it until released from active duty in July 1952. One afternoon in the fall of 1951 they were mapping an area used for field problems and came across a small clearing in the woods that was strewn with cardboard boxes and other junk. "It reminded us of a small trash dump," Clement recalls. "Web got a little carried away with his disgust and about halfway across the clearing he kicked one of the cardboard boxes out of his way." The box exploded and flew into the air and so did Weberneck. "The intervening years had not robbed Web of his training and experience gained on Iwo," Clement says. "That lanky bean pole critter must have gone five feet straight up in the air and came down running." They were in a training area for booby traps and had set off a small charge, probably controlled by a pressure fuse. Clement was some distance away and immediately realized what had happened. They lit up cigarettes and Weberneck joined in the laughter but, as Clement concluded, "had we been under combat conditions such an insignificant act would have been disastrous."

After completing his M.S. at SMU Clement returned to Carter Oil doing field work in a number of states—Nevada, Louisiana, Mississippi, and Utah—and set up a geology laboratory for the company in Denver in 1955. Several years later, he bounced to Salt Lake City, Midland, Texas, and on to Houston before taking early retirement in 1980. Since then he has had his own consulting firm, has worked with his twin brother, Mark, and done a number of consulting, exploration, and geological projects for various oil companies, including Arco, for whom he wrote a study on strata and fossil formations along the Gulf Coast.

He and his wife, Marie, live about six blocks from Mark in Dallas. The have five children. The oldest son, Paul Awtry, was a Marine lieutenant in Vietnam, an artillery forward observer for sixteen months. One daughter is a veterinarian with the 6666 Ranch horse-breeding operation near Guthrie, Texas, and the other taught biology and raised a family in McAllen, Texas. He and Marie have eighteen grandchildren.

Mark Clement also enrolled in SMU and received a B.S. degree in geology in June 1948. He went on for a master's degree in geology two years later and worked for Pan Am Southern Corporation before being recalled for Korea in February 1951. Clement was slated to report to Camp Pendleton to pick up an engineer company going to Korea, but after taking his physical in Dallas he received orders to the Navy photo-intelligence school in Washington, D.C. After completing the five-month course he was sent to Fleet Marine Force Atlantic (FMFLANT) headquarters in Norfolk, Virginia, to head up the photo-intelligence unit in the G-2 section. The CG of FMFLANT at that time was Lt. Gen. Graves Erskine, who had commanded the 3rd Marine Division on Iwo.

Some of the field-grade officers at FMFLANT had been battalion commanders at the Chosen Reservoir. "On a fleet landing exercise, I often was able to be in the command plot or shore headquarters where I was involved with the maintenance of the FMFLANT intelligence maps and at the same time could watch the Corps Commander as he made decisions on maneuvering his units," Clement recalls. "On one occasion I had a twenty-one-year-old second lieutenant report in to my section. In a moment of total forgetfulness, I thought, 'What am I going to do with this young kid?' Then I thought, 'What did Captain Pearcy think when he found out he was getting a nineteen-year-old second lieutenant to go with his second platoon into Iwo Jima?' I never again worried about any problems resulting from that lieutenant's age." Mark spent eighteen years in the Marine Corps Reserve after World War II and Korea, resigning his commission in 1961 as a major. He married Gretchen Griffith of Ennis, Texas, in 1958. "My time was cut short when Gretchen and

I went to South America for three years and I couldn't keep up with the annual reserve attendance requirements," he says.

After returning to civilian life in 1952, Mark Clement joined Sun Oil Company, which sent him to a dozen different places in the United States and Venezuela between 1952 and 1970. He left Sun in 1970 and wound up establishing his own oil consulting firm in Dallas. He semi-retired in 1987 but after eight months of complete inactivity, he and two other geologists formed a computer software company that still occupies him today. He has written software programs for analyzing drilling and exploration projects and helped develop a database management program that can locate every oil and gas well in the world. He also got back into consulting on oil and gas exploration deals, and has taught courses and given lectures on computers and software in the oil business for Arco and at SMU and community colleges in Dallas.

He and Gretchen have two daughters. Hilary, the oldest, is married to Jon Olson, a professor in the petroleum engineering department at the University of Texas. Margaret, the youngest, was married in 1999 to Michael Slawin, technical director for a staging company. In Chicago. "Fishing, golf, and hunting dove and turkey get a whole lot less time than I think I would like, but I do like my participation in the computer business and wouldn't trade the pure enjoyment of the oil and gas business for anything."

Hugh "Bud" Morris on his 77th birthday, April 2000.
BUD MORRIS

Like many of his SOCS classmates, Bud Morris joined the reserves as a second lieutenant when he was released from active duty. He spent a year getting a master's degree at Columbia University, then put in three years in law school on the G.I. Bill of Rights at the University of Virginia, where he also coached the Marine reserve rifle team. He was taking the bar exam on 1 July 1950, when he got a telegram from the U.S. Marine Corps: Report for active duty at Camp Lejeune immediately. North Korean troops and tanks had invaded South Korea on 25 June and the United States was at war again after less than five years. He was assigned to the 8th Marine Regiment, part of the 2nd Marine Division, and for a month didn't do much of anything except coach the regimental football team.

Morris had become friends with a battalion executive officer whose unit was preparing to go to Korea in early August. Late one evening at the officers' club he received a call from his friend. "Bud, great news! I managed to get you on board. We're shipping out in two days. Go draw your 782 (field) gear and meet us at the railhead Friday morning." Morris's heart sank as he thought of leaving his comfortable billet in the BOQ with a complete bar and hi-fi setup. He was a bachelor and his parents and sisters were out of the country and he had no way to notify them. As he started to board the train, the officer taking the muster stopped at his name. Aren't you drawing a pension for partial disability? he asked Morris. Yes. Sorry lieutenant, but you can't join this draft then. After a moment of disbelief Morris had the presence of mind to wave at the departing train and shout, "Go get 'em, guys!" His friend, the major, never made it to Korea either. He was hospitalized on the West Coast.

Morris then was ordered to a two-month multiservice, multinational intelligence school at Fort Riley, Kansas, and while on liberty in Kansas City, Missouri, met his wife, Dorothea "Dee" Meriwether, a native of that up-to-date city. They were married 14 April 1951, and Morris was sent back to Lejeune to the 8th Marines as regimental intelligence, legal, and public information officer. Shortly after that, he was deployed to the Mediterranean with a battalion landing team (BLT) from the 8th Marines. They landed on the French coast, had maneuvers on Cyprus with elite Greek "Evzone" troops, and went on to Athens, where Bud made plans to fulfill his dream of finally seeing the Acropolis. At the port of Piraeus, however, he was greeted with the news that two Marines were in the brig charged with breaking into a jewelry store in France and stealing wristwatches. They were to be tried under the new Universal Code of Military Justice (UCMJ) and Bud was going to be involved.

Bill Ditto at the Camp Lejeune rifle range theater, standing next to a plaque of SOCS members killed in World War II. BILL DITTO

He was to fly immediately to Izmir, Turkey, where he would be schooled on the new military justice system by a Navy lawyer. All he saw of Athens and the Acropolis was what he could glimpse from the sedan to the Athens airport. He had a pleasant enough time drinking Turkish coffee, playing tennis, and learning the UCMJ from the companionable Navy commander—but it wasn't the Acropolis.

After being promoted to captain, Morris was sent to psychological warfare school at Fort Riley on his return to the States. In June 1951, after a year of active duty, he was released back to the reserves and resigned his commission a year later. He and Dee moved to the San Francisco area and while he was studying for the California bar he noticed that he kept falling asleep because he was bored with the law. So he took a job with a company called Magna Power Tool, which manufactured a popular woodworking tool called ShopSmith, and began a career in advertising and public relations. He went from Magna to Kaiser Aluminum in Oakland with the advertising department and then to Kaiser's advertising agency in San Francisco, Young & Rubicam, where he became a vice-president and head of the San Francisco industrial division. After twelve years at Y&R he went to American Microsystems (AMI), a computer-chip manufacturer in Silicon Valley, where he was director of advertising and public relations for eight years. "That was the first wave of the high-tech industry, I guess," he says. He turned down an offer from Intel, the computer-chip giant, and wound up his career with Signetics, another chip and electronic firm, a subsidiary of Phillips Radio, the big Dutch electronics firm.

Morris retired in 1982 and moved to Carmel. During their four years there he and Dee remodeled old houses and built new ones. Always fascinated by the Southwest and Mexico they designed and built a hacienda-style home in Santa Fe, N.M., where they lived for ten years before moving to Shawnee Mission, Kansas, near Dee's former home. They have two sons and four grandchildren.

Epilogue

Fifty Years Later

Since the late Bill Carter contacted the commandant in 1984 with the request that the Marine Corps research the SOCS members who were killed in World War II, the class has had several reunions. The first was in 1990 at the Camp Lejeune rifle range where they had been commissioned, when the plaque bearing the names of their comrades was dedicated. They have had a reunion every other year since then, in San Francisco in 1992, Camp Lejeune again in 1994, which was the fiftieth anniversary of their commissioning, and in San Diego in 1996, Quantico in 1998, and Hawaii in 2000. In 1995 some attended the fiftieth-anniversary commemorations of their battles on Iwo Jima and Okinawa. Many also attend division, regiment, company, and other reunions.

Mark Clement has been to four of the SOCS class's five reunions and about a dozen reunions of B Company, 4th Pioneer Battalion, and the 4th Marine Division Association. In March 1995 he and Gretchen went to

Iwo Jima for the "Reunion with Honor." They flew to Hawaii and then on to Saipan, which was the base for the 4th Marine Division group for four days; the 3rd and 5th Division contingents were billeted on Guam. "At every fuel stop, we were greeted by honor guards of Marines," Mark recalls. "What a wonderful experience. Everyone was ready to 're-up' for another four years." They flew up to Iwo one morning and returned after dark that night. At Iwo each flight of veterans was greeted by young Marines who eagerly shook their hands and thanked them for what they had done fifty years before. From the airport they were trucked to an area just behind Yellow Beach to await the arrival of the other flights.

"We were early so I walked down to the Yellow Beach/Blue Beach area [the 4th Division's landing beaches], stopping at the remnants of an old knocked-out pillbox on the way," Mark recalls. "All of the area in which I was walking was covered with low-lying plants and vines. About halfway to the beach a perplexing thought crossed my mind: 'I wonder if anyone has swept this area for mines and other ordnance?'" But, as he was halfway there he kept on walking.

"I still had an eerie feeling the rest of the way down to the beach. I felt a sense of awareness as I approached the surf area. There are certain memories that engender an awful quiet in the heart of man. There was no one else for a hundred yards up and down the beach. The weather was good, with excellent visibility and slightly cool temperature. At the beach, I turned to the right to look at Suribachi, then swinging further to the right, looking inland, to the old location of Motoyama No. 1 airfield, moving on to the area of Charlie Dog Ridge and Turkey Knob, and finally to the cliffs overlooking the Boat Basin on the right flank of Blue Beach. My reflections meandered through many names in that moment in time. Many good thoughts mixed with the sad. Lots of memories of those thirty days in 1945 and of the Marines with whom I shared them. Bless them all!"

Clement watched the mild surf as it broke over the beach and observed the swash as the water receded after the waves had reached their high point and started falling back. It was mesmerizing for a veteran geologist. He took some samples of the beach material which, when examined back home under a binocular microscope, "revealed a poorly sorted, very coarse-grained sand, composed predominantly of well rounded grains of obsidian (black volcanic glass), an unusual sand composition associated with volcanic areas. I also took some sand samples from the offshore area beyond the swash area looking for foraminifer (tiny, pinhead-sized sea animals with calcareous shells) for my daughter Hilary who is a micro-paleontologist. The offshore material was similar, but better sorted and not as coarse."

Clement was amazed at the items still on the beach—many rounds of badly encrusted, unfired .30-caliber rounds and old 37-mm shell cases. "The surf was modest, but the beach sand at the terraces was still just as difficult to navigate on the way back as it had been fifty years earlier, if not more so. A young Marine corporal appeared at my side the moment I started back. I thanked him but declined his offer of what I considered unnecessary assistance. Nevertheless he 'walked' me all the way back to the top of the last terrace. The Marines all had orders that not one of these veterans would make the climb back unattended. Smart thinking. It was a pretty good trek. The terraces seemed to slow both of us . . . (although) it might have been unwarranted . . . to think that the terraces should have had any effect on him."

They then circled the island in five-ton trucks. In the northwestern segment they inspected old Japanese hospital tunnels that had been preserved, with lighting by Marine engineers, then ascended Mount Suribachi. "It was both engrossing and chilling to finally see the observation

Mark and Gretchen Clement on Mount Suribachi in 1995, the fiftieth anniversary of the Iwo Jima landing.
MARK CLEMENT

the Japanese had on all of the beach areas! The observation was truly amazing! Not one of our positions was hidden from observation."

To Clement the only problem was that the time on Iwo wasn't long enough. "The Marine Corps was absolutely outstanding in their preparation, efficiency and courtesy for the entire trip. We were really proud and grateful. I never in my wildest dreams thought that at some point in time I would be standing in the area of Motoyama No. 2 airfield enjoying wine and hors d'oeuvres."

One of the highlights of the tour was Clement's reunion with Paul Berry, one of the men in his platoon who had ridden the LSM-60 with him all the way from Maui to the beach, and who was wounded and evacuated at the end of the first week. Berry, who settled in El Paso, where eighteen members of their company had a reunion, also was on Saipan, which he showed to Mark and Gretchen Clement. "He, Pat his wife, and two of his children drove us on a guided tour of Saipan, showing us the cliffs at Marpi Point [where several thousand terrified Japanese civilians committed suicide by jumping off the cliffs in the final horror of the battle]. . . . The lagoon was magnificent. His son Patrick and I swam out to two old Sherman tanks which have been in over five feet of water for fifty years. Many parts of the tank showed surprisingly little deterioration. In the ruins of an old amtrac, knocked-out in the lagoon about thirty feet from shore, we snorkeled and dug around finding several unfired .50-caliber rounds. For both Gretchen and me, it was a really meaningful trip."

Robert C. Euler, another SOCS member, who won the Purple Heart with Company B, 1st Battalion, 24th Marines, also was there: "For our arrival there were dozens of active duty Marines from Okinawa, lined up to shake our hands and thanking us for coming and for what we did for the Marine Corps. It brought tears to many eyes, including mine. . . . I couldn't get back to the beach where I had landed nor to the gully where I was shot and evacuated. . . . I did, however, kneel on the black sand and say a prayer for our comrades who lost their lives during that battle."

Also in 1995, Phil and Carol Pearce were among a group of about three hundred American servicemen, including a number of SOCS classmates, who went to Okinawa for five days for their fiftieth anniversary. They were taken by bus to areas where they'd fought and Phil revisited Wilson Ridge and Wilson Draw, where he'd won the Navy Cross. He descended into the draw and could look up to the ridge line and see a row of houses where his company had been dug in. "There are houses on the ridge now and trees and other growth have covered the caves in the slope where the Japanese jumped us." He also visited Shuri Castle, which was demolished by bombing and heavy artillery during the fighting, but much of which has been rebuilt. "The two radio towers that we sighted in on are gone." He revisited Hill 79, the site of his last battle, near where Lt. Gen. Simon Bolivar Buckner was killed just four days before the island was declared secure. "My main reaction was how enormously the island has been built up," he says. "We stayed in a brand-new motel just north of Naha which had room for a thousand people and there is a four-lane highway just like one of our freeways from Naha down to the southern tip of the island."

From Okinawa Phil and Carol went to China, where they spent twelve days in Beijing, Tsingtao, Shanghai, and Tientsin. Beijing also has changed enormously. A large area around the Polo Grounds, where the 1st Marine Division held his Navy Cross ceremony, was closed to the public. "They told us it was pretty run down," he says.

In the half century since their war the members of the SOCS have devoted considerable time to thinking about various aspects of warfare in general and their experiences in particular—the nature and comradeship of infantry combat, the process of being decorated for valor in combat, and the Marine Corps and their pride in being part of it.

As one of the most decorated Officer Candidate Classes in the war, they ponder the random process by which medals are awarded. Everyone interviewed for this book has expressed the opinion that the only true heroes are those who never returned and some have been initially reluctant to talk as a result. There is agreement that those who were decorated fully warranted it. But some have reservations that the system doesn't reward many who deserve recognition. Jep Carrell lists two regrets:

> The first is that there were many other men equally deserving, but either they did something no one else saw or got around to reporting, or the person who did see it was killed or wounded and the deed was unreported for that reason. The second concerns the men who provide courageous, consistent, first-class service day-to-day, but do not have a spectacular example of performance, and thus do not receive a medal for valor. It is possible to seek a medal for the consistent high performer, but few are written up for that kind of service. . . . Senior officers, rather than the men at the platoon level, get these awards. . . . I just wish my two platoon sergeants, Winfred Jones and Don Oettinger could have been honored that way. They were brave, energetic, tireless, excellent leaders. They frequently jeopardized their own safety to protect their men, or to move the attack forward.

Jack Bradford (A/1/23), who was awarded a Letter of Commendation and Purple Heart on Iwo and was the one who discovered Morg De Mange's body, had a machine-gun section leader with him for the twenty-six days he "remained vertical" on Iwo who "did something exceptional each day he was on the lines. For this he earned a Commanding General's Letter of Commendation. I always regretted being gone for three months (wounded and in a Navy hospital) after the campaign and not being able to push his case. Another obvious thing, a lot of the riflemen and assault platoon guys are out front and they are fighting isolated episodes in many cases, and die, get hit, or come back unobserved, [whereas] the officer is generally in a position where he is observed."

Joe Clement notes that "the promotional pyramid becomes acute at the top" and the presence of combat awards is considered a valuable asset for promotion at or near the top. In addition, he continues, "there is a tendency to allocate many awards proportionately, i.e., your unit is entitled to so many of these specific awards. . . . This is similar to grading 'on the curve' in school."[1]

Overriding all these matters, however, is their love and pride in the Marine Corps. Jack Bradford listed the blessings of his life—his wife and family, his career teaching history and international relations, his community (Laguna Beach, California) and church, his friends, and golfing and tennis companions. He also spoke for his classmates and all other fellow Marines:

> There is one association, however, which defies description and which certainly must stretch the understanding of many of my friends and family, and that is the deep, continuing loyalty I feel toward the U.S. Marine Corps and concomitant feeling I have in turn about my country. What I feel seems to be mirrored by almost every other Marine of my era with whom I come into contact. What is it that produces such strong feelings, when a great deal of the experiences we all had were hard, difficult, unpleasant, dangerous, and scarring?

Bradford had an answer to his question.

> The Marine Corps is small. It is cohesive. It builds its traditions on loyalty to your comrades (for example: the smallest unit in a rifle company is a fire team, four men). . . . [T]here is no tolerance for poor performance, but every effort is made to develop good performers. Marines also take care of their wounded and this leads me to mention the special relationship with

their naval corpsmen who save lives all day. . . . A Marine thinks of a corps-man as a fellow Marine. . . . As I get to the latter part of my happy journey on this planet I get great comfort and companionship from communicating and associating with men who know exactly what I am trying express—*My fellow Marines!*[2]

Mark Clement expressed similar feelings:

There is a bond which develops between individuals who have shared the same experience, who have shared the exposure to life-threatening danger in times of military involvement. . . . In the Marine Corps, it is at the company and platoon level, where individuals have shared the memory of the same incoming fire or, whether they knew each other or not . . . that the bond really appears to manifest itself. Individuals may not have seen each other for many, many years, yet the strength of that original shared experience is all-powerful. Only they truly know the exposure which they shared and uniquely for many, only they are the ones with whom they share its details.

Individuals may sometimes feel guilt over the fact that others in their unit were casualties while they were not. They may feel guilt over something which they did not do even though a detached observer can readily tell them that such action was impossible or, more objectively, useless.

I consider the Corps to be unique, a truly outstanding group of people. I have developed friendships with Marines and former Marines which were initially founded on one trusted value—*Marine!* They are like a second family. I cherish my many memories of the Corps, my platoon, my companies, the many Marines with whom I served, the many friends I made, and last but not least the associations with my fellow SOCS officers. Semper Fi!

About sixty-five of the SOCS class members and their wives attended a three-day reunion in San Diego in September 1996, one of the highlights of which was a day at the Marine Corps Recruit Depot (MCRD), the Marines' West Coast boot camp. This was the first time most of them had seen the big San Diego base, as they had all gone through Parris Island. MCRD San Diego is a handsome collection of neo-Moorish buildings with red Spanish tile roofs built around three sides of a huge parade ground known as the "grinder," with the recruit barracks forming the fourth. The installation wasn't their major source of interest, however.

The highlight of the day was a poignant memorial ceremony in the base chapel. One class member, George Mayer, a handsome, vigorous man who looks as though he could still go on active duty if called, read a tribute to the class. "The Special OCS was one of those rare happenings in the scheme of things that was at the right place at the right time," he said. "For the United States of America it was one more memorable contribution of a few for the benefit of all." Jack Lauck, who publishes the class's newsletter and is the clearing station for information on the members and their whereabouts, read off the names of the forty-eight who were killed in action on Iwo Jima and Okinawa, a powerfully emotional presentation.

They also were guests of honor at a Friday graduation ceremony for a company of young recruits, 471 strong, who formed the parade and formal pass-in-review. They had lunch at the former officers' club, which is now a restaurant, along with about three dozen gunnery sergeants who were students at the senior NCO school and were about as impressive a collection of military professionals as anyone could imagine. After lunch they watched a company of recruits undergo pugil-stick training, a drill in bayonet-fighting techniques, and another being taught to rappel from a hundred-foot tower, a training for helicopter assaults. This was a tactic unknown to them in World War II, but what really amazed them was the youthful appearance of both the superbly conditioned recruits and their instructors. Their conclusion was that the New Corps appeared to be in very good shape.

The SOCS members, in their early seventies, graying, balding, some with varying degrees of infirmity, watched with rueful admiration and envy. "Were we ever that strong and young-looking?" one asked another. The answer, first revealed by their old photographs and confirmed by their war records, is yes, they certainly were. And they always will be to those who know and appreciate the magnitude of their accomplishments.

Notes

Chapter 1. Pearl Harbor: A Date Which Will Live in Infamy

1. The Redskins won 20–14 with Sammy Baugh, their Hall of Fame quarterback, throwing two touchdown passes. Baugh was granted a draft deferment to stay on his Texas ranch and raise beef cattle. Nick Basca, a rookie Philadelphia halfback out of Villanova who kicked both the Eagles' extra points, enlisted three days later and was killed in action as a tank driver with Gen. George Patton's Third Army in France on 11 November 1944.

2. One result of the war that saddened Bud was that two popular Japanese American students at Dartmouth became *personae non grata* overnight.

3. Red went out for football as a walk-on. He went to Abilene Christian because his father, who had some oil income in the 1930s, had bought a piece of property from the university as an investment and sold the lot back to the school to pay Red's room, board, and tuition costs of $225 per semester.

4. J. Fred Clement, *The SOCS 400* (Dallas, 1996), 460–61.

5. His son, Charles Krulak, who was commandant of the Marine Corps from 1995 to 1999, told members of the class how he remembered sitting on his father's lap as he and other Marine generals, including the legendary Holland M. "Howlin' Mad" Smith, talked about the class.

6. Lt. Col. George N. Mayer, USMCR (Ret.), "The Marine Corps 400," *Marine Corps Gazette,* October 1990, 72–74.

7. Shortly after Pearl Harbor, James "Jimmy" Roosevelt was commissioned as a captain in the Marine Corps and, as executive officer of the 2nd Marine Raider Battalion under Lt. Col. Evans Carlson, participated in its famous raid on Makin Island in the South Pacific eight months later.

8. Doris Kearns Goodwin, *No Ordinary Time: Franklin and Eleanor Roosevelt: The Home Front in World War II* (New York: Simon and Schuster, 1994), 288–99.

9. The author was in high school after the war with several youthful veterans who finished their diplomas on the G.I. Bill of Rights. Later, in the Marine Corps, I had a first sergeant who had observed his sixteenth birthday chest-deep in water in the lagoon at Tarawa. His case wasn't particularly unusual; the average age of a Marine in the Pacific was twenty, compared to the service-wide average of twenty-six.

10. William Manchester, *Goodbye Darkness: A Memoir of the Pacific War* (New York: Dell, 1982), 291.
11. William L. O'Neill, *A Democracy at War: America's Fight at Home and Abroad in World War II* (New York: Free Press, 1993), 127.

Chapter 2. Brass Hats and Gold Bars: Warriors and Leaders

1. Williamson Murray and Allen R. Millett, *A War to Be Won: Fighting the Second World War* (Cambridge, Mass.: The Belknap Press, 2000), 336–37.
2. Benis M. Frank and Henry I. Shaw Jr., *Victory and Occupation,* vol. 5 of *The History of U.S. Marine Corps Operations in World War II* (Washington, D.C.: Historical Branch, G-3 Division, U.S. Marine Corps, 1968), 10–13. Bill D. Ross, *Iwo Jima: Legacy of Valor* (New York: Vintage Books, 1986), 12–17. Robert Leckie, *Okinawa: The Last Battle of World War II* (New York: Viking, 1995), 1–4.
3. Ross, *Iwo Jima,* 12–17.
4. C. L. Sulzberger and the editors of American Heritage, *The American Heritage World History of World War II* (Boston: American Heritage Publishing, 1987), 593.
5. Stephen E. Ambrose, *American Heritage New History of World War II*, rev. and updated (New York: Viking, 1997), 566.
6. Henry Berry, ed., *Semper Fi, Mac: Living Memories of the United States Marines in World War II* (New York: Berkley Books, 1983), 172.
7. Ibid., 308. Some historians are critical of Puller's command of the 1st Marines on Peleliu where his frontal assaults resulted in such high casualties that the regiment was incapacitated for combat and had to be pulled from the line. They argue that the 5th Marines, employing fire and maneuver, finally carried out the mission with fewer casualties. As a Marine infantry second lieutenant in Vietnam, Puller's son, Lewis B. Puller Jr., lost both legs and several fingers to a booby-trapped artillery shell. He went on to law school and ran for the Virginia state legislature but subsequently committed suicide after bouts with alcoholism.

Chapter 3. The V-12 Program: Passage into the Marine Corps

1. Sources for this chapter are: James G. Schneider, *The Navy V-12 Program: Leadership for a Lifetime* (Boston: Houghton Mifflin, 1987), passim; Clement, *The SOCS 400,* 5–18; and author's interviews of the SOCS class members.
2. On 1 November 1943, 480 enlisted Marines entered the program and another 323 were enrolled in March 1944. Between 1 July 1944, and the end of the war another 1,333 enlisted Marines were enrolled. Most were combat veterans and NCOs; the Corps was looking for regular officers for the postwar force.
3. Bernard C. Nalty and Lt. Col. Ralph F. Moody, *A Brief History of U.S. Marine Corps Officer Procurement, 1775–1969,* rev. ed. (Washington, D.C.: Historical Division, Headquarters U.S. Marine Corps, 1970), 10.
4. He was wounded at Wana Ridge on Okinawa with Company I, 7th Marines, won another Purple Heart and a Silver Star and Bronze Star in Korea, and a second Silver Star in Vietnam.
5. Most of the commanding officers worked out fine but a few had trouble adjusting to an academic setting. The COs at two other large programs, Northwestern and Yale,

also were relieved. Another, College of the Pacific, was even less fortunate because Commander Burton E. Rokes, a regular Navy officer who had been commissioned out of the ranks, loathed everything that had to do with higher education, starting with Naval Academy graduates and including college students and faculty in general, and the COP president, Dr. Tully Knowles, in particular. Dr. Knowles failed in his attempt to get Rokes transferred and had to settle for having another official of the college stand in for him in dealings with the commanding officer.

Chapter 4. Parris Island: All Hope Abandon, Ye Who Enter Here

1. A Marine Corps study has shown that San Diego recruits achieve a somewhat higher level of training primarily because there are fewer interruptions of training by inclement weather in San Diego's benign climate.
2. Anyone who has associated with and/or led young Marines knows that, actually, boot camp doesn't erase individual identity, it enhances it.
3. Thomas E. Ricks, *Making the Corps* (New York, Scribner, 1997), 238–47, 274–97. Ricks expresses the fear that the U.S. military in the post-Cold War has become more politically conservative and more isolated from a civilian society that seems to be increasingly undisciplined, culturally coarsened, and with relatively few leaders and members who have served in the military. At a Smithsonian Institution seminar on the Marine Corps on 17 September 1999, he had a spirited debate on this with former commandant Charles Krulak.
4. At the beginning of the chapter on boot camp in his oral history of the SOCS, *The SOCS 400,* Joe Clement has a drawing of a drill instructor with Gunnery Sergeant chevrons, arms akimbo, glowering menacingly from under his campaign hat. The caption is: "God! (1944 version)."
5. Jim has two nieces who are nuns and teach in Catholic schools in Kenya. "They'd have been great Marines if they'd chosen to be," he says.
6. After Iwo Jima Jim was to encounter his senior drill instructor, Sergeant Brinkerhoff, who was in a replacement draft to the 3rd Marine Division on Guam; Brinkerhoff was assigned as his platoon sergeant and he recalls that Brinkerhoff was "great to work with."
7. The first time the author approached Denebeim about this book, he broke up in laughter over his snafued entrance into the Marine Corps even before the first question. However, he concluded, "I have considered myself lucky that a series of foul-ups allowed me to experience for a short while the life of a D.I."

Chapter 5. The SOCS 400: A Lot of You Are Not Coming Back

1. Edwin P. Hoyt, *The Marine Raiders* (New York: Pocket Books, 1989), 22. The four-man fire team was a new concept at this time. The Corps adopted it as its basic maneuver unit for all its divisions in 1944 and first deployed the teams in combat on Saipan. The fire team was built around the Browning automatic rifle (BAR) and consisted of the BAR-man, assistant BAR-man who carried extra magazines for the weapon, rifleman-scout, and the fire-team leader. The firepower of the BAR and the semiautomatic M-1 rifle made such a small and flexible maneuver unit possible. The Marine Raiders had first used a three-man fire team; the concept was introduced to

the Corps by Lt. Col. Evans F. Carlson, organizer and commander of the 2nd Marine Raider Battalion. Carlson's fire team had a BAR, a Thompson submachine gun, and an M-1 rifle. Consistent with the "triangular" organization of American infantry divisions, there were three fire teams to a squad, three squads to a platoon, three platoons to a company, and so on.

2. Unlike the Army, which often assigned KP (Kitchen Police) duty for several hours or a day as punishment, the Marines would assign men for full-time mess duty for a month. It is onerous duty with long hours, generally beginning at 0330, and little liberty. It is supposed to be assigned on a rotating basis but first sergeants do tend to give priority to the troopers who have incurred their displeasure. The system is disliked by everyone, including officers and NCOs, in large part because it interferes with training. There is a current trend to contract food services out to private contractors.

3. Richard W. Johnston, *Follow Me! The Story of the Second Marine Division in World War II* (Nashville: Battery Press, 1987), 305. Carl W. Proehl, ed., *The Fourth Marine Division in World War II* (Nashville: Battery Press, 1988), 235.

4. Nalty and Moody, *Brief History of U.S. Marine Corps Officer Procurement*, 14.

5. Kenneth W. Condit, Gerald Diamond, and Edwin T. Turnbladh, *Marine Corps Ground Training in World War II* (Washington, D.C.: Historical Branch, G-3, H.Q. U.S. Marine Corps, 1956), 233–47. Lt. Col. Charles A. Fleming, USMC, Capt. Robin L. Austin, USMC, and Capt. Charles A. Braley III, USMC, *Quantico: Cross Roads of the Marine Corps* (Washington, D.C.: Historical and Museums Division, Headquarters U.S. Marine Corps, 1978), 75.

6. Like most of the officers and NCOs involved in the program, they had a direct stake in its effectiveness. Snedeker wound up as commanding officer of the 7th Marines on Okinawa. Schmuck, who had been wounded as a company commander in the 3rd Marines on Bougainville, all five of whose platoon leaders were killed or wounded, was one of the young veterans rotated back to the states. He wasn't at Lejeune to see the class be commissioned; on that day he was on Peleliu with the 1st Marine Division. He was lieutenant colonel by war's end and was one of seven Marine officers on the Tenth Army G-3 staff on Okinawa, where he was wounded again.

7. Fawcett, who died in December 1996, was fondly remembered by the class members by his nickname, "Spigot." An Annapolis graduate, he had been a seagoing Marine and got his nickname from his Navy friends, who informed him that there was no such thing as a faucet on board ship, only spigots.

8. Brig. Gen. Donald M. Schmuck, interview by George Mayer, July 31, 1997.

9. Brig. Gen. Donald M. Schmuck, letter to the author dated April 5, 2000.

10. Named after a musical instrument that resembled a length of two-inch pipe, which was invented by radio comedian Bob Burns and used as one of his props.

11. Mayer, "Marine Corps 400," 74.

12. E. B. Sledge, *With the Old Breed: At Peleliu and Okinawa* (New York: Bantam Books, 1983), 222.

Chapter 6. To Westward: For Duty Beyond the Seas

1. Clement, *The SOCS 400,* 53–58.

2. Ibid., 60–61.

3. Camp San Onofre was still the home of the Infantry Training Regiment (ITR) for

troops fresh out of boot camp during and after the Korean War; graduates of San Diego went there. The Parris Island recruits were trained at a similar facility at Camp Lejeune.

4. He was in 1st Battalion, 7th Marines, commanded by the also-legendary Lewis B. "Chesty" Puller, when the Japanese made a major two-day attempt, primarily at night, to breach the Marines' defense perimeter around Henderson Field. Basilone ranged along his company line, keeping his guns in operation and bringing up ammunition, fighting his way through infiltrators with his .45 pistol. More than eight hundred dead Japanese were found in front of his position after the battle and his action was considered a major factor in the Marine victory in what was one of the pivotal battles of the campaign.

5. As noted earlier, De Mange was killed on Iwo and to many of the class members became a symbol of the SOCS.

6. Proehl, ed., *Fourth Marine Division in World War II*, 235.

Chapter 7. Iwo Jima: Red Blood and Black Sand

1. Bernard Nalty and Danny J. Crawford, *The United States Marines on Iwo Jima: The Battle and the Flag Raisings* (Washington, D.C.: History and Museums Division, Headquarters, U.S. Marine Corps, 1995), 21.

2. Col. Joseph H. Alexander, USMC (ret.), *Closing In: Marines in the Seizure of Iwo Jima* (Washington, D.C.: History and Museums Division, Headquarters U.S. Marine Corps, 1996), 7–8.

3. Richard Wheeler, *Iwo* (Annapolis, Md.: Naval Institute Press, 1980), 36.

4. The last American casualties, 53 killed and 119 wounded, were inflicted in a Japanese attack on the night of March 26, D+35. One of the KIA was 1st Lt. Harry Martin of the 5th Pioneer Battalion, who was awarded the Medal of Honor for organizing and leading the defense and defeat of the raid. He was the last Marine to die on Iwo.

5. About 75 percent were casualties, with 27 KIA and 70 wounded. Bob Holmes was killed on D-day in the fight for the airfield.

6. He got the submachine gun after a drinking bout with a Navy pilot whose new .38 revolver he bought for ten dollars. He then traded that to a Marine captain for the Tommy gun.

7. Clement, *The SOCS 400*, 187.

8. An Army quartermaster study reported that the average load of the U.S. infantryman in World War II was 83.4 pounds.

9. Like many of his fellow lieutenants, Dibble also improvised a little with his personal weaponry. He carried a .32-caliber "police special" revolver that his father had given him, which he thinks was taken by one of the corpsmen who evacuated him when he was wounded.

10. Another SOCS member, Bob Humphrey of the 26th Marines, who was his platoon's sixth leader and was wounded himself, learned another lesson about Marines in combat. He urged his men to keep their heads up out of their holes while on guard at night or else they would be very unpleasantly surprised by Japanese infiltrators. An NCO gave him a tip: "You're saying the wrong thing, lieutenant. Don't tell them that they will get themselves killed. You have to tell them that the Japanese will crawl by them and *kill us others.*" That approach worked.

11. The section leader was in a cast from the waist down, which somewhat inhibited his

plans to put some serious moves on the nurses on the hospital ship and at the hospital in Hawaii.

12. Alexander, *Closing In,* 49.
13. Ibid., 3.
14. Wheeler, *Iwo,* 39.
15. Murray and Millett, *A War to Be Won,* 365.
16. Maj. Gen. Clifton B. Cates, the 4th Division CG, was quoted as saying, "If I knew the name of the man on the extreme right of the right-hand squad of the right-hand company of 3/25 I'd recommend him for a medal right now."
17. Richard Wheeler, *A Special Valor: The U.S. Marines and the Pacific War* (New York: Harper and Row, 1983), 151–55.
18. Jack was awarded another Purple Heart while on occupation duty in Japan. He had a platoon in the battalion S-2 (intelligence) section and was injured while destroying kamikaze aircraft with demolitions at an airfield on the island of Kyushu in January 1946. He won two more Hearts in Korea in 1952 along with the Bronze Star and a Letter of Commendation, both with the combat V.
19. Howard M. Connor, *The Spearhead: The World War II History of the 5th Marine Division* (Nashville: Battery Press, 1987), 57–68.
20. Ross, *Iwo Jima,* 309.
21. Robert Sherrod, *On to Westward: The Battles of Saipan and Iwo Jima* (Baltimore: Nautical and Aviation Publishing Company of America, 1945, 1990), 180.

Chapter 8. Iwo Jima: Would Any of Us Be Left?

1. He also was the first commanding general of the Marines' recently formed overall command level, Fleet Marine Force Pacific (FMFPAC). He had lobbied for creation of the command and was commander of all the Marines in the Pacific, but he wasn't at all thrilled about holding a noncombat slot.
2. The accounts of Jim Ronayne's and Red Qualls's combat and postcombat activities are based on interviews of them by the author.
3. One of the division's regiments, the 3rd Marines, was not landed despite the pleas of the division commander. Smith and Maj. Gen. Harry Schmidt, CG of V Amphibious Corps, believed that the island was too congested to take another regiment. There is a belief that Smith also wanted to save it for the invasion of the home islands.
4. Jim also credits his sports experience and religious background for helping prepare him for his ordeal. "Football is a team sport and if one guy misses a tackle another one makes it," he says. "The Church teaches you that you don't call the shots."
5. At both BC and Dartmouth, Jim was a teammate of another All-American, lineman Jim Landrigan, a SOCS classmate who played professionally after the war; playing a wartime shortened seven-game Ivy League schedule, Dartmouth lost only to Penn and its star tailback, Howie O'Dell. Both Jim and Red had played with and against All-Americans like McFadden on their V-12 teams; Reds' 1943 V-12 team at North Texas beat Southern Methodist and Texas Tech and tied Texas A&M.
6. George W. Garand and Truman Strohbridge, *Western Pacific Operations,* vol. 4 of *History of U.S. Marine Corps Operations in World War II* (Washington, D.C.: Historical Branch, G-3 Division, Headquarters, U.S. Marine Corps, 1971), 589–90.
7. This was one of about twenty-six hundred emergency landings by the B-29s before

the Japanese surrender. With a ten-man crew, the number of American fliers involved were about equal to the Marines' casualties in capturing the island. At the height of the B-29s' assault on Japan in the summer of 1945 an average of twenty made emergency landings each day.

Chapter 9. Okinawa: Battle of Attrition

1. Spruance alternated command of the fleet with Adm. William F. Halsey. When Halsey was in command it was Third Fleet.
2. George Feifer, *Tennozan: The Battle of Okinawa and the Atomic Bomb* (New York: Ticknor and Fields, 1992), 133.
3. Estimates of the toll of this atrocity are as high as two hundred thousand. Some historians say Cho issued the order on instructions from Prince Yasuhiko Asaka, an uncle of Emperor Hirohito.
4. Wheeler, *A Special Valor*, 410–14.
5. Feifer, *Tennozan*, 527–34.
6. Frank and Shaw, *Victory and Occupation*, 884.
7. Murray and Millett, *A War to Be Won*, 515.
8. Bud and the other Marines on Okinawa would encounter the 27th Division again. The 27th weighed in substantially in the Marine Corps history in World War II. It was made famous, or infamous, when Marine Lt. Gen. Holland M. ("Howlin' Mad") Smith, the ground forces commander in the Marianas, relieved its commanding general on Saipan because of his dissatisfaction with its performance.
9. The battalion was formed around cadres from the 2nd Marine Division in the spring of 1944. It was originally named the 2nd Separate Infantry Battalion, but was redesignated as 1st Battalion 29th Marines while on the transports to Saipan, where it was attached to the 2nd Division and suffered more than 50 percent casualties. The regiment's other two battalions were formed up in 1944 at Camp Lejeune, N.C., where they engaged in field exercises and had an altercation with the SOCS before being shipped to the Pacific. See chapter 5.
10. He was told that it was the *West Virginia*, but it probably was the *New Mexico*, which was hit in May for the second time; the first was on 2 April. His battalion's Special Action Report for 12 May laconically mentions it: "BB hit at 1915."
11. Bevan G. Cass, ed., *History of the Sixth Marine Division* (Nashville, Battery Press, 1987), 107.
12. A year later Bud met Nimitz at an event in Washington and it turned out the admiral also remembered the incident. Fortunately, he also thought it was funny.
13. Murray and Millett, *A War to Be Won*, 346, 360.
14. Ibid., 515.
15. Clement, *The SOCS 400*, 262–75. Oral and written histories by Jeptha J. Carrell in ibid., and Marius L. Bressoud Jr., "The Way It Really Was, I Think: A Personal Account of the Okinawa Campaign" (1994), 148–54.
16. Clement, *The SOCS 400*, 280.
17. Karr enlisted in Dallas in 1943 at the age of 17 after getting into an argument with the owner of the A&P food market where he worked. He was sworn in a block away from where President John F. Kennedy would later be assassinated and after boot camp in San Diego was shipped to New Caledonia. He arrived in February 1944 and then

joined the 1st Marine Division on Pavuvu Island in the Russells. He left China on 19 January 1946, his twentieth birthday, and when he got back to San Diego he still wasn't old enough to legally buy a drink in the bars there. Wearing his greens and combat service ribbons, he offered to buy a couple of cases of beer to take out on the sidewalk and drink there but that turned out not to be necessary.

18. Japanese snipers looked for troop leaders. Officers and NCOs who carried pistols soon learned to wear them in shoulder holsters under their dungaree jackets and to hide binoculars hanging from their necks inside their jackets.

19. The rain and mud badly hampered supply for the entire battalion during the last week in May and the official Marine history reports that some men had resorted to drinking from shell-holes due to their extreme thirst. One of Phil's SOCS classmates, Gerald G. McNamee, in Company F, 5th Marines, and his men were isolated and cut off from supply for six days, but their ordeal was eased somewhat when they found a cave full of sake and caught a two-hundred-pound pig, which they roasted.

20. The two are still friends. In 1995 they traveled to Okinawa together for the fiftieth anniversary of the battle.

21. Frank and Shaw, *Victory and Occupation,* 284–86.

22. Needless to say, this didn't help the already frayed relationship between the Army and Marines. The tension between the two services dates back to World War I when the Army was resentful of the publicity and credit the Marines claimed for their brigade, which operated as part of the Army's 2nd Infantry Division. The Army retaliated after World War II by proposing to eliminate the Marine Corps when the Department of Defense was formed.

23. Sledge, *With the Old Breed,* 267–86. Sledge provides a horrendous description of the mud, maggots, corpses, and revolting horror of the stalemate in front of Half Moon Hill and Shuri during the driving rains of the last days of May. It is nerve-wracking just to read; anyone not there can only try to imagine what it was like.

24. Clement, *The SOCS 400,* 367–68.

25. RG 127, World War II, Box 260, National Archives, College Park, Md.

26. Murray and Millett, *A War to Be Won,* 510–22.

Chapter 10. The Atom Bomb and the Invasion of Japan: You Second Lieutenants Are Expendable

1. Sledge, *With the Old Breed,* 322.

2. Those wounded were Samuel A. Dunlap, Sam Menzelos, Aram Puzant Pakradooni, and Sidney Wassenberg. The sixth was Daniel M. Ross.

3. Thomas B. Allen and Norman Polmar, *Code Name Downfall: The Secret Plan to Invade Japan—And Why Truman Dropped the Bomb* (New York: Simon and Schuster, 1995), 295–303.

4. Murray and Millett, *A War to Be Won,* 520.

5. John Ray Skates, *The Invasion of Japan: Alternative to the Bomb* (Columbia: University of South Carolina Press, 1994), 102–4.

6. D. M. Giangreco and Kathryn Moore, *American Heritage* (December 2000): 81–83.

7. Gar Alperovitz, *Atomic Diplomacy: Hiroshima and Potsdam* (Boulder, Colo.: Pluto Press, 1975), 236–73, 285–90.

8. Gar Alperovitz, *The Decision to Use the Atomic Bomb: And the Architecture of an American Myth* (New York: Knopf, 1995), passim, particularly 459–71, 643–68.

9. Murray and Millett, *A War to Be Won,* 520–25.

10. Ibid., 569.

11. Jim Lehrer graphically describes the brutal treatment of captured B-29 crewmen in his novel, *The Special Prisoner* (New York: Random House, 2000).

12. Paul Fussell, *Thank God for the Atom Bomb and Other Essays* (New York: Ballantine Books, 1988), 5–15.

13. Quoted in Skates, *Invasion of Japan,* 254–57.

14. Connor, *The Spearhead,* 145–62.

15. Clement, *The SOCS 400,* 420–25.

16. J. Robert Moskin, *The U.S. Marine Corps Story* (New York: McGraw-Hill, 1982), 407–16.

Epilogue: Fifty Years Later

1. Clement, *The SOCS 400,* 473–75.

2. Ibid., 490–91.

Bibliography

Alexander, Joseph H. *Closing In: Marines in the Seizure of Iwo Jima*. Washington, D.C.: Marine Corps Historical Center, 1994.

Allen, Thomas B., and Norman Polmar. *Code Name Downfall: The Secret Plan to Invade Japan—And Why Truman Dropped the Bomb*. New York: Simon and Schuster, 1995.

Alperovitz, Gar. *Atomic Diplomacy: Hiroshima and Potsdam*. Boulder, Colo.: Pluto Press, 1975.

———. *The Decision to Use the Atomic Bomb: And the Architecture of an American Myth*. New York: Knopf, 1995.

Ambrose, Stephen E. *American Heritage New History of World War II*. Revised and updated. New York: Viking, 1997.

———. *We Band of Brothers: E Company, 506th Regiment, 101st Airborne from Normandy to Hitler's Eagle's Nest*. New York: Simon and Schuster, 1992.

Aurthur, 1st Lt. Robert A., USMCR, 1st Lt. Kenneth Cohlmia, USMCR, and Lt. Col. Robert T. Vance, USMC, eds. *The Third Marine Division*. Nashville: Battery Press, 1988.

Bergerud, Eric. *Touched with Fire: The Land War in the South Pacific*. New York: Penguin Books, 1996.

Berry, Henry, ed. *Semper Fi, Mac: Living Memories of the United States Marines in World War II*. New York: Berkley Books, 1983.

Blum, John Morton. *V Was for Victory*. San Diego: Harcourt Brace, 1976.

Brady, James, with Ron Powers. *Flags of Our Fathers*. New York: Bantam Books, 2000.

Bressoud, Marius L., Jr. "The Way It Really Was, I Think: A Personal Account of the Okinawa Campaign, April 1 to June 21, 1945." 1994.

Cass, Bevan G., ed. *History of the Sixth Marine Division*. Nashville: Battery Press, 1987.

Clement, J. Fred. "The SOCS 400." 1996.

Condit, Kenneth W., Gerald Diamond, and Edwin T. Turnbladh. *Marine Corps Ground Training in World War II*. Washington, D.C., Historical Branch, G-3, H.Q. U.S. Marine Corps, 1956.

Connor, Howard M. *The Spearhead: The World War II History of the 5th Marine Division*. Nashville: Battery Press, 1987.

Feifer, George. *Tennozan: The Battle of Okinawa and the Atomic Bomb*. New York: Ticknor and Fields, 1992.

Fleming, Lt. Col. Charles A., USMC, Capt. Robin L. Austin, USMC, and Capt. Charles A. Braley III, USMC. *Quantico: Cross Roads of the Marine Corps.* Washington, D.C.: Historical and Museums Division, Headquarters U.S. Marine Corps, 1978.

Frank, Benis M., and Henry I. Shaw Jr. *Victory and Occupation,* vol. 5 of *The History of U.S. Marine Corps Operations in World War II.* Washington, D.C.: Historical Branch, G-3 Division, U.S. Marine Corps, 1968.

Fussell, Paul. *Thank God for the Atom Bomb and Other Essays.* New York: Ballantine Books, 1988.

Garand, George W., and Truman Strohbridge. *Western Pacific Operations.* Vol. 4 of *The History of U.S. Marine Corps Operations in World War II.* Washington, D.C.: Historical Branch, G-3 Division, Headquarters U.S. Marine Corps, 1971.

Goodwin, Doris Kearns. *No Ordinary Time: Franklin and Eleanor Roosevelt: The Home Front in World War II.* New York: Simon and Schuster, 1994.

Hoyt, Edwin P. *The Marine Raiders.* New York: Pocket Books, 1989.

Johnston, Richard W. *Follow Me! The Story of the Second Marine Division in World War II.* Nashville: Battery Press, 1987.

Keegan, John. *The Second World War.* New York: Penguin Books, 1989.

Krulak, Victor H. *First to Fight: An Inside View of the U.S. Marine Corps.* Annapolis, Md.: Naval Institute Press, 1984.

Leckie, Robert. *Okinawa: The Last Battle of World War II.* New York: Viking, 1995.

Lehrer, Jim. *The Special Prisoner.* New York: Random House, 2000.

Linderman, Gerald F. *The World Within War.* New York: Free Press, 1997.

Manchester, William. *Goodbye Darkness: A Memoir of the Pacific War.* New York: Dell, 1982.

Mayer, Lt. Col. George N., USMCR, Ret. "The Marine Corps 400." *Marine Corps Gazette,* October 1990, 72–74.

McMillan, George. *The Old Breed: A History of the First Marine Division In World War II.* Washington, D.C.: Infantry Journal Press, 1949.

Moskin, J. Robert. *The U.S. Marine Corps Story.* New York: McGraw-Hill, 1982.

Murray, Williamson, and Allen R. Millett. *A War to Be Won: Fighting the Second World War.* Cambridge, Mass.: The Belknap Press, 2000.

Nalty, Bernard C., and Lt. Col. Ralph F. Moody. *A Brief History of U.S. Marine Corps Officer Procurement, 1775–1969.* Rev. ed. Washington, D.C.: Historical Division, Headquarters U.S. Marine Corps, 1970.

O'Neill, William L. *A Democracy at War: America's Fight at Home and Abroad in World War II.* New York: Free Press, 1993.

Perrett, Geoffrey. *Days of Sadness, Years of Triumph: The American People, 1939–1945.* Madison: University of Wisconsin Press, 1973.

Pratt, Fletcher. *The Marines' War.* New York: William Sloane Associates, 1948.

Proehl, Carl W., ed. *The Fourth Marine Division in World War II.* Nashville: Battery Press, 1988.

Ricks, Thomas E. *Making the Corps.* New York: Scribner, 1997.

Ross, Bill D. *Iwo Jima: Legacy of Valor.* New York: Vintage Books, 1986.

Schneider, James G. *The Navy V-12 Program: Leadership for a Lifetime.* Boston: Houghton Mifflin, 1987.

Sherrod, Robert. *On to Westward: The Battles of Saipan and Iwo Jima.* Baltimore: Nautical and Aviation Publishing Company of America, 1945, 1990.

Skates, John Ray. *The Invasion of Japan: Alternative to the Bomb.* Columbia, S.C.: University of South Carolina Press, 1994.

Sledge, E. B. *With the Old Breed: At Peleliu and Okinawa.* New York: Bantam Books, 1983.

Spector, Ronald H. *Eagle Against the Sun.* New York: Free Press, 1985.

Sulzberger, C. L., and the editors of American Heritage. *The American Heritage World History of World War II.* Boston: American Heritage Publishing, 1987.

Wheeler, Richard. *Iwo.* Annapolis, Md.: Naval Institute Press, 1980.

———. *A Special Valor: The U.S. Marines and the Pacific War.* New York: Harper and Row, 1983.

Index

About the Author

James R. Dickenson spent nearly thirty years as a political reporter, editor, and columnist in Washington, D.C., working for *The Washington Post,* the *Washington Star,* the National Observer, and United Press International. He has covered the presidencies of Lyndon Johnson, Richard Nixon, Gerald Ford, Jimmy Carter, and Ronald Reagan, as well as the Watergate scandal and numerous other stories around the country. He is also the author of *Home on the Range: A Century on the High Plains,* a history of the Western frontier during the nineteenth century. His book was nominated in 1995 for both the National Book Award and the Pulitzer Prize for history.

From 1954 to 1958, Dickenson served as a lieutenant in the U.S. Marine Corps, where he was a platoon leader and a company commander in 2nd Battalion, 1st Marines, 1st Marine Division. He is a graduate of San Diego State University, holds an M.A. degree from the University of Iowa, and has studied for a Ph.D. in American history at Iowa. He is currently the coordinator and moderator for "The Smithsonian Forum on the Media and Society," and he works as a media consultant to the Library of Congress Russian Leadership Program. A native of Kansas, he and his wife, Mollie M. Dickenson, live in Maryland.